D0337619

ZEN ENLIGHTENMENT

ZEN ENLIGHTENMENT
Origins and Meaning

by Heinrich Dumoulin

translated from the German by

John C. Maraldo

New York • WEATHERHILL • *Tokyo*

This book was originally published under the title *Der Erleuchtungsweg des Zen im Buddhismus* (The Zen Way of Enlightenment in Buddhism) by Fischer Taschenbuch Verlag, 1976.

First English Edition, 1979

Published by John Weatherhill, Inc., of New York and Tokyo, with editorial offices at 7–6–13 Roppongi, Minato-ku, Tokyo 106, Japan. Copyright © 1976, 1979 by Fischer Taschenbuch Verlag; all rights reserved. Printed in Korea.

Library of Congress Cataloging in Publication Data: Dumoulin, Heinrich. /Zen enlightenment. / Translation of Der Erleuchtungsweg des Zen im Buddhismus. / Bibliography: p. / Includes index. / 1. Zen Buddhism—History. / I. Title. / BQ9262.3.D.8513 / 294.3′ 927′ 09 / 78-27310 / ISBN 0-8348-0141-8

Contents

Introduction   *ix*

1 The Western View of Zen   *3*
Five Phases in the Introduction of Zen to the West,
3 · D. T. Suzuki: Psychology and Wisdom, 4
Rudolf Otto: "Born of the Gravity of the Numinous," 7 · Beat Zen, Psychotheraphy, Esoterism,
8 · Japanese Zen Meditation and Pluralism, 9
Zen Meditation for Christians, 11

2 Indian Roots   *14*
Shākyamuni, 14 · Zen and Yoga, 18 · Is Zen Nar-
cissistic and Asocial? 22

3 The Birth of Zen in China   *25*
Mahāyāna Foundations, 25 · Relationship with the
Spirit of Taoism, 28 · Taoist and Zenist Medita-
tion, 31

4 Bodhidharma   *35*
The Figure of Bodhidharma, 35 · Bodhidharma as
a Master of Meditation, 37 · Bodhidharma's Role
in the Zen Tradition, 39

5 The Sixth Patriarch   *42*
Preliminary Remarks on the History of Zen in

China, 42 · From the Life of Hui-neng, 43 · The Way of Sudden Enlightenment, 46 · The Doctrine of No Mind, 50

6   The Zen Movement in China   *53*
Zen Activity, 54 · Doctrinal Aspects, 56 · Communal Life in the Monasteries, 58 · Lin-chi and the "Five Houses," 60

7   The Koan in Chinese Zen   *65*
The Origin of the Koan Practice, 65 · The *Hekiganroku* and *Mumonkan* Koan Collections, 68 The Significance of the Koan for the Zen Way, 72 · The Koan Exercise from the Viewpoint of the History of Religions, 74

8   Zen Buddhism in Japan   *77*
The Religious Climate, 77 · The Transplanting of Zen Buddhism, 79 · Zen Schools in Japan, 80 · Ways *(Dō)* and Arts, 82 · The Sacred and the Profane: The Law of Buddha and the Law of the World, 84

9   Dōgen, The Master of Zazen   *88*
Life and Character, 88 · The Promotion of Zazen, 90 · Zazen and Enlightenment, 92 · Zazen as the Focus of a Buddhist Spirituality, 95

10   Dōgen's Religious Metaphysics: The Doctrine of Buddha-Nature   *102*
Buddha-Nature as a Religio-Metaphysical Concept, 102 · Buddha-Nature and Reality, 104 · Metaphysical Realism, 107 · The Being of Buddha-Nature, 111 · The Way of Negation, 115 · Buddha-Nature and Becoming, 119

11   The Zen Experience in Contemporary Accounts   *125*
The Course of Practice in the Exterior, 128

Previous Experience and Preparation, 129 · The
Austerities of Practice, 131 · Devotion, 133
Repentance and Purification, 136

12 Satori: Zen Enlightenment   *139*
Psychic Changes During Practice, 140 · Symptoms
and Preliminary Stages, 143 · Cosmic Consciousness and Nothingness, 144 · A Naturalistic Hue,
146 · Sudden Release, 147 · Accompanying Traits,
148 · The Root of Nothingness, 149

Afterword: The Ten Oxherding Pictures   *154*

Chinese-Japanese Equivalents   *157*

Notes   *159*

Bibliography   *165*

Index   *171*

Introduction

INTEREST IN THE ZEN BUDDHIST WAY of enlightenment, growing steadily in the West since the end of World War II, is evidently more than a short-lived vogue. For many, Zen meditation has become a matter of daily commitment; and it would also appear that our knowledge of the Zen way, with its rich variety and depth, has entered into a new phase. Research in the last two or three decades has brought to light a wealth of material that enables us to learn of Zen more clearly and more extensively, to learn of its historical aspects as well as of its essential, meditative side.

History and essence are tightly interwoven in Zen Buddhism. As a particular way to enlightenment founded, according to traditional accounts, on the direct transmission of mind outside the writings, Zen was launched in China by spiritually gifted men who knew how to pass on their own experience to followers of equal capacity. Zen Buddhists trace their school's way of enlightenment back to Shākyamuni, the founder of the Buddhist religion. Hence, a well-rounded understanding of Zen requires that one look back to the beginnings of Buddhism in India and include in his study the Yoga that had spread throughout the Indian subcontinent, for the practice of Zen owes much to this Yoga. And the soaring metaphysics of the Mahāyāna movement will also require attention.

This spiritual legacy of India took root in China. There, the Mahāyāna Buddhism of Indian origin met with Chinese Taoism, an encounter essential to the formation of the Zen school, the meditation school of Mahāyāna, as we may call it. And there, primarily through the activity of the great masters of the T'ang period (618–906), Zen acquired its distinctly Chinese character. I have attempted in this book to elucidate some of the more obscure points of early Chinese Zen history. Here the figure of the Sixth Patriarch of Chinese Zen, Hui-neng, towers above all else. Quotations from Chinese Zen literature, that is, the collections of koans and sayings of the masters, add color and perspective to the fascinating picture we have of the early Chinese Zen movement. In particular, the *Record of Lin-chi* punctuates the rapid climb of its development. In connection with such typical Chinese masters as these, the characteristically Chinese practice of the koan finds its expression. Koan practice has aroused the interest of today's psychologists especially; but from the perspective of the history of ideas, it remains wholly within the Mahayanist world view.

Transplanted to Japan, Zen became the fountainhead of a high degree of culture and art during the middle ages. This expansion into the secular realm was characteristic of the Zen school. Thus it is misleading to consider Zen asocial, as happens occasionally, because of its followers' unrelenting meditation and concentration on the self. Zen's contributions to culture are not to be seen as a mere byproduct of the activity of its monasteries. For, of all Buddhist schools in Japan, Zen was able to relate "worldliness" with religious endeavor most clearly. Historical research confirms this as an essential trait of Zen that is still evident today.

The number of Japanese Zen masters is considerable, most likely larger than that of Chinese masters if we take the present into account. I was able to include relatively few within the limits of my presentation here. I have given considerable space to Dōgen, for the spiritual fruits that so intrigue people today are most clearly visible in him. Moreover, he is the sole original Buddhist thinker in Japan prior to its encounter with the West. It is not by accident that the most significant Japanese philosophical movement today, the Kyoto school founded by Kitarō Nishida and now led by Keiji Nishitani, has recourse to Dōgen in its endeavor to link Eastern and Western thought. For this reason I have devoted an entire chapter to Dōgen's teaching on Buddha-nature.

The final chapters of this book relate, in translation from the original Japanese, the accounts of contemporary Zen students. These reports illustrate Zen practice in the concrete. Long hours of silent sitting in the lotus posture, which is not without its perils, forms the basis of this practice. The ineffable experience of enlightenment can only be described indirectly in terms of its effects on the practitioner. As a radically subjective experience, it is not amenable to any generally accepted interpretation or judgment concerning its authenticity.

During the many centuries of its history in East Asian countries, the Zen way of enlightenment was always of a ramified and varied nature. Today Zen has come to the West, only to increase its diversity. The meditation movement, which has become a worldwide phenomenon significant for spiritual life in our day, proceeds along a variety of paths. Indeed, it is characterized by a pluralism of method and goal. In the modern Zen movement as well, accommodations have been made to the times and circumstances. Diversification into a number of forms is well under way. Under these circumstances we cannot predict what the future holds in store for Zen. The extent and character of its diversification will to a large degree be determined by the meditation movement as a whole. And undoubtedly this movement has a future, ensured not only by the urgent needs of our times but also by the timeless value of meditation. For man is ever in need of meditation.

It goes without saying that my primary concern in this book has been to give those who have little or no knowledge of Zen an accurate, clear, and reliable account of its origins and meaning. But it is at the same time addressed to those already engaged in Zen practice. How can this be? Are not Zen practitioners warned daily by their masters in the meditation hall that theories are of no use in Zen, that they must only practice, that is, sit and sit and sit? On the other hand, no one can escape responsibility for what he undertakes. And thus it can be of value for the avid practitioner in particular to acquire a balanced view of the history and essence of Zen Buddhism. To be sure, for those who practice and experience Zen, the practice and experience justifies itself. Yet it is not a matter of indifference how the way of Zen and the goals of this way are presented.

This book is based upon lectures I gave while I was a visiting professor at the University of Munich. The original lecture format has been preserved as much as possible to facilitate easy access to the topics under discussion. I have at times taken sides on some of the issues that remain controversial from the point of view of Zen scholarship, without, however, burdening the reader with innumerable footnotes and references. Since it is primarily by way of Japan that Zen has become known in the West, traditional expressions and technical terms are given in Japanese. The reader will find their meaning explained in context, eliminating the need for a separate glossary. Proper names of Chinese Zen masters are, however, given in their Chinese reading; a list of the Japanese equivalents of these names has been added at the end of the book for the convenience of those more familiar with the Japanese pronunciation.

I am left with the pleasant obligation of expressing my thanks to all who helped in the preparation of this book: to the University of Munich School of Philosophy for its invitation to lecture on Zen; to Dr. Hans Brockard, who read the manuscript and offered many pertinent comments; and to my students for their encouraging response. Dr. John C. Maraldo, himself well acquainted with Zen Buddhism, undertook the exacting task of translation into English. He rearranged the order of presentation and made small additions in a few places to facilitate understanding by an American audience. Finally, I owe thanks to John Weatherhill, Inc., for its care in preparing the manuscript for press and undertaking the publication.

HEINRICH DUMOULIN

Tokyo, October 1978

ZEN ENLIGHTENMENT

ONE

The Western View of Zen

THE THEME OF THIS BOOK is Zen Buddhism—more exactly, the "Zen Buddhist way of enlightenment." It is meant to express above all the essential features of Zen: Zen presents us with a way that leads to the awakening of the self and hence to the depths of being human. This way was opened up within the domain of a religion—namely, within Buddhism. Of course it is quite possible to speak of Zen in a more general sense and to view every enlightenment experience in connection with the way of Zen. But as it came to pass in human history, Zen is found in Buddhism. For this reason, any serious study of Zen must make reference to its Buddhist foundations.

With the introduction of Zen to the West in our century we were presented on the one hand with a typical phenomenon of East Asian spirituality. On the other hand, Zen claims a certain universality for itself, and thus is of especial significance for the encounter between East and West. If historians such as Toynbee have counted the ongoing encounter of these two hemispheres among the most important events of our day precisely because of its religious content, surely the reception of Zen in the West deserves our attention. Moreover, current interest in Zen is by no means of a merely academic nature; many people today look to Zen for support in their daily lives.

Five Phases in the Introduction of Zen to the West   We must first look at the Western view of Zen. Since this view is not without its ambiguities, it will help if we first approach this complex theme from various angles. Today, of course, Zen is known generally throughout the West. But the ideas people have about Zen vary considerably. And the evaluations can often be nearly diametrically opposed. There are those who in esoteric rapture attach messianic expectations to Zen, and those who warn of the Asian peril. We can get a better grasp of these widely differing reactions by recalling how Zen was introduced to the West. Five phases or factors are discernible in this process—all occurring in the twentieth century. To be sure, Europe came to know of Asia at the beginning of the modern era (*viz.* the figure symbolizing Asia on the inside of the dome of San Ignacio, a seventeenth-century Roman baroque church), and in the nineteenth century Buddhism came to be intensively studied by Western scholars. But Western Zen itself is entirely a twentieth-century phenomenon, and during the last five decades or so a great deal has happened with and to Zen in the West.

D. T. Suzuki: Psychology and Wisdom   Let us begin not with the very first contacts between the Western world and Zen, but with the decisive phase initiated by the work of D. T. Suzuki (1870–1960), that great interpreter so uniquely successful in bridging East with West. Suzuki was extremely qualified and well equipped for his mission. During his days as a university student he enjoyed close contact with Zen Buddhism, and after graduating he took up practice under the famous Zen master Shaku Sōen, the abbot of the Rinzai monastery in Kamakura. Shaku Sōen had been the Japanese Buddhist representative at the memorable World Congress of Religions in Chicago in 1893. Upon his return to Japan, Sōen sent the young Suzuki, his most gifted disciple, to America to assist in the publishing of Buddhist and other texts from the East Asian heritage. The work at the publishing house gave Suzuki an excellent opportunity both to perfect his English and to learn all he could about Western, especially Anglo-Saxon, civilization. He married an American who was both religious and open to Eastern spirituality, and soon he felt at home in the Western world. But his mind and heart remained devoted to Zen. If Suzuki's achievements in introducing Zen in the West were epoch-making, the key ideas and peculiarities of his understanding of Zen cast those achievements in a particular light. Hence it is worth while to examine the specific characteristics of the Zen interpretations in his works.

Suzuki was a prolific writer: his collected works in Japanese comprise some thirty volumes,[1] and his writings in English, as yet uncollected, would take up at least ten. The works can be considered from various standpoints. Chronologically, the Second World War brought about a decisive turning point. Prior to the outbreak of the Pacific War, Suzuki had completed a series of works that was comprehensive in its own way. This does not mean that he had produced a systematic presentation of Zen Buddhism—during his over ninety years, he did not write one systematic work. But in the first half of his years of literary production, he touched upon practically all the important points of Zen. His three-volume *Essays in Zen Buddhism,* which first appeared in England in 1927–34, together with his trilogy *Introduction to Zen Buddhism, The Training of the Zen Buddhist Monk* (both 1934), and *Manual of Zen Buddhism* (1935), present Zen in its entirety, as Suzuki saw and experienced it and desired to introduce it to Westerners. In transmitting the teachings, Suzuki naturally interprets and adapts them to Western ways of thinking, as he was familiar with those ways. He consciously accentuates certain aspects in Zen literature while cautiously developing thoughts of his own.

The most obvious characteristic of Suzuki's early Zen interpretations is their predominantly psychological bent. His essays make use of the descriptive categories that William James developed in *The Varieties of Religious Experience.* But this influence was not a merely superficial borrowing of terms. Suzuki felt a certain affinity with the ingenious American philosopher-psychologist, who, like himself, esteemed experience above all else and displayed a genuine appreciation of religion. As is well known, the apex of religious experience in Zen is enlightenment—the experience of satori, which Suzuki considered the very quintessence of Zen. Of hardly less importance is the use of koan, methodically ordered in the Rinzai school to lead to the satori experience. Satori and the koan form the center of Suzuki's teachings on Zen and are presented chiefly from the psychological angle in his early works. During the first half of his life, philosophy and metaphysics were of secondary interest for Suzuki. And his appreciation of history was so limited that there arose lively debates between him and the Chinese historian Hu Shih, who openly criticized Suzuki for this deficiency.

In the postwar period, Suzuki's writings reached widespread audiences and took a new turn. The courses he gave at various American universities, especially Columbia, were widely acclaimed, as were his lecture tours throughout America and Europe. Everywhere he went he was recognized as the leading authority on Zen. Many people, moreover, welcomed him as one of the few living sages of the East. During this period, his theme remained Zen Buddhism, but he was less concerned with communicating factual information about Zen than with showing the way to an ultimate, comprehensive, and supreme truth.

In the later writings of Suzuki, a philosophical-metaphysical element clearly comes to the fore. Properly speaking, Suzuki was never a philosopher. However, one of his closest disciples once related to me that his master felt a predilection for philosophy throughout his life. Be that as it may, Suzuki surely counts as one of those true masters of life who, as Meister Eckhart put it, excel a thousand masters who do not but lecture. Each of his stimulating lectures and essays was sure to contain some real insight. A deep religiosity shines through his learned wisdom and never fails to impress us. For a better understanding of Christian mysticism, Suzuki went to Meister Eckhart, whose writings he esteemed highly.[2] And in the last years of his life, Suzuki concerned himself a good deal with the Amida devotees of the Shin school, the so-called Buddhism of faith. Just before his death I had the pleasure of attending his final public lecture, which treated the pious Amida faithful known in Japanese as *myōkōnin*, literally, "wonderfully happy people."

In evaluating Suzuki's contribution to the Western view of Zen, one must keep in mind that the presentation of Zen in his writings and lectures is confined to the Rinzai school—one of the two great schools of Zen transplanted to Japan from China. The second, historically no less important Sōtō school, introduced into Japan by the great medieval master Dōgen and still active today, is hardly mentioned by Suzuki. That is no mean superficial oversight, for it affects the understanding of Zen as such. Certain essential traits of Rinzai Zen, such as the paradox and the suprarational, are to some extent overemphasized in Suzuki, but these are particularly suited to his style of thinking. On the other hand, he has little interest in the meditation in everyday life that is so stressed by the Sōtō school. Hence a certain one-sidedness is undeniably present in the Zen that Suzuki conveyed to the West. Nevertheless, Suzuki's contribution to the scholarly study of Zen was considerable, and we shall have occasion to return to him, for this wise man of Zen counts among the most influential religious figures of our age.

Suzuki's view of Zen gave rise to widely divergent interpretations in the West. Above all, the uprooting of Zen from its native Buddhist soil can be traced to his teachings. His tendency to psychologize and generalize matters could easily lead one to lose sight of the Buddhist roots of Zen. Suzuki's disciples, who heard their revered master say over and over again that Zen was neither a philosophy nor a religion, proceeded to interpret Zen in their own terms, which were usually alien to traditional Buddhism. Japanese Zen Buddhists were often astounded at the transformations Zen was undergoing in the West, and they differentiated between the traditional forms of Japanese Zen and that which they called "Suzuki Zen." Zen in the West unmistakably bore the spirit of Suzuki for a long time.

Rudolf Otto : "Born of the Gravity of the Numinous"   Before we go on tracing the development of the Zen movement in the West as it was inspired by D. T. Suzuki's wide range of activities, we must turn back to a curious occurrence of much interest to the student of the history of religions. The great German scholar Rudolf Otto was deeply impressed when he accidently came across the earliest essays the young Suzuki wrote on Zen for the 1922 issues of *The Eastern Buddhist*. Otto refers to Suzuki's "thought-provoking essays" in an article on the experience of the numinous in zazen ("Das numinose Erlebnis im Zazen"), included in the volume entitled *Das Gefühl des Überweltlichen* [The Sense of the Transworldly]: *Sensus Numinis* (1931).[3]

The first book about Zen in German, *Zen: der lebendige Buddhismus in Japan* (Zen: Living Buddhism in Japan), was published in 1925. It consisted of selected Zen texts in translation, primarily pieces taken from two important Chinese collections of koan, the *Hekiganroku* (The Blue Cliff Records) and the *Mumonkan* (The Gateless Barrier). The book's introduction, translations, and commentary were by the hand of Ōhasama Shūei, a lay Japanese Zen Buddhist and professor from the Rinzai school. The young German scholar August Faust assisted in adapting the language and content to the German reading public. It was auspicious that Rudolf Otto wrote the preface for this first literary presentation of Zen in Germany, for, whereas the translations are obsolete today, Rudolf Otto's preface is still worth reading. This preface, as well as the above-mentioned essay on the experience of the numinous in zazen, signify precisely the point where Zen was discovered in Germany for the first time. Shortly prior to this, Friedrich Heiler had touched upon Zen in his noteworthy study of Buddhist meditation (*Buddhistische Versenkung*, 1918). But since Heiler's interest was directed to the early Buddhist meditation described in the Pāli canon, he considered Zen a degenerate form of the original. Otto changed this negative appraisal when he discovered in Japanese Zen an excellent and unique form of *theologia negativa*. Zen, Otto writes in his essay on the experience of the numinous in zazen, "is by its very nature born of the most profound gravity of the irrational in the numinous itself. At the same time this aspect is so exaggerated that we who come predominantly from the rational side of religion are at first completely unable to note that it is a religion—an uncommonly strong and deep religion—with which we have to do.''[4]

In evaluating Zen, the history of religions will always fall back upon Otto's lucid presentation of the West's first view of Zen. Otto grasped the eminently religious character of Zen and classified it as mysticism, for which the supreme truth is the ineffable ''wholly Other.''

Beat Zen, Psychotheraphy, Esoterism The next three phases in the introduction of Zen to the West are to a large extent contemporaneous, covering the developments of the 1950s and 1960s. Each phase has its particular characteristic to add to the Western view of Zen.

During the 1950s, a decadent form known as ''Beat Zen'' emerged in America. For the youth dissatisfied with the technocratic consumer society of the West, Zen mysticism offered a new life style, one that appealed to young people all the more for its blatant opposition to conventions and rational thought—at least that was as much as this group was able to get out of the paradoxical koan stories they read in Suzuki and the flood of literature on Zen that appeared in those years. Beat Zen was quite popular for a time in California, the Eldorado of the new religions, but quickly faded from the public eye. Few traces of it are visible today, although this ephemeral phenomenon was captured by American literature, especially in the evocative novels of J. D. Salinger. To a lesser extent there arose another form that Ernst Benz termed ''Zen snobbism,'' rather widespread among intellectual circles. It is impossible to tell just who is responsible for all the nonsense identified with Zen in the public eye. The view of Zen in the West still betrays some traces of a faddish character.

Much more serious is another deviation from Zen, namely its incorporation into psychotherapy. Although justified from a medical standpoint, the psychotherapeutic employment of Zen meditation must be regarded as essentially alien to Zen. A Zen severed from its foundations in Buddhism was included among numerous psychic healing techniques, regardless of its religious nature. Insofar as healing is possible with the aid of Zen or other kinds of Asian meditation (often simply called Yoga without differentiation), one can only welcome this addition to medical treatment. Nevertheless, as I have written previously, it still remains true that ''Zen is robbed of its soul if it is made to eke out its existence in the psychological laboratory. Born as it was from the primal religious urge of man, and nourished by religious resources, Zen for many centuries inspired great religious achievements. Therefore psychology cannot speak the final word regarding the value and usefulness of Zen."[5] Yet psychotherapeutical notions are still part of the Western conception of Zen.

In this connection we may say a word about the practice of Zen in esoteric circles, which were attracted to Zen meditation for its supposedly parapsychological effects. These groups occasionally sought support in Suzuki, but without ground. For all his predilection for the paradoxical and supra-rational, Suzuki was a far cry from miracles, parapsychology, and magic. This Japanese scholar was no esoterist, even if he did take into account the esoteric element undeniably present in Zen. In esoteric circles, that element is the focal point of interest; the altered state of consciousness linked with Zen enlightenment is the main concern. Such esoterism fails to recognize that in Zen an altered state of consciousness is no more than an ancillary phenomenon, never to be sought after for its own sake. When altered states and the expansion of consciousness are emphasized, as occurred in America and Europe, Zen falls into the proximity of drugs—an association not heard of in Japan. It is true that in some places psychological techniques were employed as a shortcut to the peak experience of the practitioners. But the authoritative Japanese masters of both the Rinzai and Sōtō schools repudiate such coercive methods, as well as any attempts to bring about an altered state of consciousness through hypnosis. In this respect Zen is unlike some of the methods employed in Yoga and in Theravāda Buddhism.

Although Japanese Zen masters reject hypnosis, they have nothing against a scientific investigation of the alteration in brain waves that occurs during Zen meditation. Recently a number of such experiments have been carried out, and with quite interesting results. Electroencephalograms of people practicing Zen meditation showed the same pattern of alpha waves observed in the state shortly before sleep, experienced as a state of relaxed alertness. Such experiments have been able to confirm the reciprocal psychosomatic effects one might expect in Zen.[6]

Japanese Zen Meditation and Pluralism   As a fourth factor in the reception accorded Zen by the West, we may mention the effective work done by Japanese Zen teachers to spread their way on many fronts. Westerners whose hearts were touched by Zen and sought its authentic form turned to Japan, the land of a living Zen tradition. Japanese Zen Buddhists responded to the call and willingly taught Zen to Americans and Europeans. In some cases the eager disciples traveled to Japan, in others Japanese teachers themselves took up residence in Western countries. The main obstacle to their efforts was the language barrier, but difficulties in communication were eventually solved. Some Japanese Zen monasteries nearly always have Westerners practicing Zen meditation. And there are Zen monks giving Zen courses in the United States, England, France, and Germany.

The Zen that has been transmitted to the West in this way is different by no small account from Suzuki's spirited and sagacious version. Rinzai and Sōtō, the two great Japanese schools, are almost equally represented in this movement. Practices vary according to the school and the line of descent within it. Sōtō stresses the practice of *zazen* (sitting in the lotus posture), whereas Rinzai emphasizes satori and the koan. But pluralism is not confined to the difference of Japanese Zen schools. Individual Japanese Zen Buddhists who give meditation courses in the United States and Germany frequently evince divergent spiritual leanings.

Of course not all teachers are of the same quality. Among Zen groups in Japan, one often hears differing opinions about Zen masters, including those active in the West. Therefore it is not unkind to say that Japanese Zen masters have their weak points and their strong points. Moreover, the Zen that they teach is linked to their Buddhist religion in varying degrees. Even when a Zen course takes place in a Buddhist hall, the degree to which the meditation is guided by the Buddhist religion depends upon the individual teacher. One certainly cannot hold it against a Buddhist monk if he proclaims his deep conviction of the Buddhist faith. He does not thereby violate religious tolerance. I know of Japanese Zen masters who gave much of themselves to guide the Zen practice of believing Christians, without making them any the less sure of their faith. In the case of Japanese Zen teachers, therefore, one cannot speak of a "Buddhist mission to the West" without qualification. The reality is more complex and variegated.

It is possible that even in those courses under the direction of Buddhist monks in the West, Zen is being severed from its roots in Buddhism. One must consider that the transplantion of Zen to the West itself somehow moves in that direction. This observation then leads to the general problem of whether, and in what ways, Zen and Buddhism in the West are undergoing changes in comparison with Zen and Buddhism in their native Asian lands. A final question is raised: are the changes indicative only of a certain modernization and secularization, or do they penetrate the very core of Zen Buddhism?

Zen Meditation for Christians   Our survey of the phases and aspects of the introduction of Zen to the West would be incomplete if we failed to mention the phenomenon of "Christian Zen." As remarkable as it might seem at first sight, the fact that believing Christians have turned to Zen for assistance in their own spiritual way is understandable in the light of their rapidly growing interest in meditation. One can already speak of a Christian Zen movement in America, Germany, and Japan. Courses are offered on such topics as Zen and Christian mysticism, and instruction in "meditation in the style of Zen" is not infrequently given at Christian retreat houses. The Irish Jesuit William Johnston and the English Benedictine Aelred Graham have published books on Christian Zen in the United States and England, and the German Jesuit H. M. Enomiya-Lassalle is the acknowledged pioneer of "Zen Meditation for Christians" in Germany. Similar efforts to utilize Zen meditation are found among Christians in Japan.

Apparently the uprooting of Zen from its Buddhist foundations is at a quite advanced stage here. We cannot overlook the fact that this kind of adaptation poses serious problems that are not easily resolved. In the case of the adaptations of Zen mentioned previously, we were concerned with shifts of emphasis that occasionally also touched the very nature of Zen. Thus one perhaps exaggerated the psychological aspects at the expense of religious connections, but the Buddhist basis was left unviolated. Christian adaptations of Zen, on the other hand, signal an incomparably more radical dissociation from Buddhism. There can be no doubt that the world views of Zen Buddhism and Christianity differ radically, and this is readily admitted by the pioneers of Christian Zen.

In this respect we can raise two questions concerning Christian Zen. First, can the specific practice of Zen meditation be so totally divested of its religious and metaphysical underpinnings that Christians can take up the practice without endangering their faith? And second, can a Zen so radically severed from its Buddhist foundations still properly be called Zen? These questions were clear to me as long as ten years ago when I stressed that any total secularization that ignores the religious element necessarily alienates Zen from its traditional essence. Christianity commends the resurgent turn to transcendence, which one can certainly observe in Zen meditation. The ways do not part until an interpretation of experience is reached, but there they part completely. On the other hand, Father Enomiya-Lassalle has in his publications continually represented the position that the Zen method of meditation can be fruitfully applied by Christians, and that Zen meditation can be of assistance in experiencing God in Christian terms.

But the Christian Zen movement, as it has progressed in recent years, is not a monolithic block of teaching and practice; a multiplicity of endeavors is involved. All of them are convinced of the overall value of Zen meditation and attempt to integrate the specific merits of the Zen way into Christianity. Meditation leaders inspired by Zen follow different ways in certain respects and, more important, betray different degrees of fidelity to their prototype. Some believe that new Zen ways are presently in the coming, but this involves the encounter of Zen not only with Christianity but also with modern mentality.[7] It is still too soon to estimate the effects, but the two points I raised earlier stand as questions not yet fully resolved.

Thus far we have attempted to delineate the Western view of Zen in a few essential strokes in order to highlight some of the problems of vital concern to Zen today. These problems, which will accompany us in our historical investigation, seem to converge finally in the one question of the essential nature of Zen. Through this book we can hope no more than to help elucidate the nature of Zen.

In our look at the adaptations of Zen meditation in the West, we frequently met with a detaching of Zen from its Buddhist foundations. Perhaps what is at stake here is a phenomenon explicable only in terms of the complexity of the twentieth-century world and its converging forces of modernization, secularization, and advancement of technology, under the aegis of Western humanism, be it Christian or not.

Origins and Meaning was chosen as the subtitle of this book in order to stress the importance of understanding Zen in its multifaceted context of Buddhism, Yoga, and Taoism. The origin and history of Zen in Asia are of central concern because we believe it is the history of Zen that reveals its form and its nature. But we shall also have occasion to touch upon East Asian culture, art, and religious education as we follow Zen from its roots in India through its emergence and flowering in China to its consummation in Japan. We shall endeavor to take into account the many sources of Asian religiosity as they have shaped this East Asian way of enlightenment.

Yet the aim of our investigation is not primarily to gain knowledge, as desirable as that may be in itself. For we would also aspire to a genuine spiritual encounter with East Asia, one for which, in this hour of building a unified world, we are held responsible and which, to the extent it is successful, can only enrich us with new and vital values.

TWO

Indian Roots

THE PECULIAR WAY OF ZEN meditation, with its practice of zazen and the koan and its goal of the satori experience of enlightenment, has its origins in China, where the first Zen masters taught and the first Zen schools sprang up. But the Zen way has roots deeply embedded in the native soil of Buddhism in India. The Indian roots are primarily evident in two respects. First of all, Zen is connected to Shākyamuni, the founder of the Buddhist religion. Second, Zen is closely linked to the ancient Indian tradition of Yoga, which goes back even further than Shākyamuni. We shall first treat the Indian founder in order to show how Zen belongs to Buddhism. We shall then consider the Yogic aspects of the Zen way.

Shākyamuni Shākyamuni is venerated by the faithful of all Buddhist schools as the Buddha—that is, the Enlightened One. He was a historical figure who lived in the fifth century B.C. Through him a new category—namely that of the Buddha—entered the history of religions. The experience of enlightenment counts as the central event of his life. Buddhist scriptures report of the event in detail: how the ascetic Gautama, after six or seven years of frustrated attempts to gain an experience through the force of austerities and Yogic practices, was driven anew to sit beneath a pipal tree (a kind of fig tree, usually called the Bodhi tree, or tree of enlightenment) near the Neranjarā River. He resolved not to get up until his goal had been reached. The texts describe how in the course of a night he acquired threefold knowledge: in the first night watch, knowledge of his previous lives; in the second, knowledge of the karmic chain of world occurrences; and in the third, the redeeming knowledge of suffering—its causes, its cessation, and

14

the way to the cessation of suffering. It is also said that he consciously passed through the four *dhyāna* (meditation) stages.

The importance of this account for Zen lies in the actual experience of enlightenment: the great breakthrough in that hour when the eye of enlightenment was opened in Shākyamuni and he became a Buddha. Zen Buddhists reading the ancient accounts of the enlightenment of Shākyamuni will pay special attention to the experiential aspects of the event. The enlightenment occurred as a sudden breakthrough. Gautama's ascetic endeavors during the preceding years are depicted in such detail in order to highlight the suddenness of the experience. The event itself, although drawn out through the night according to the sources, is a genuinely sudden satori experience. Shākyamuni did not gain enlightenment in a gradual ascent of degrees of knowledge, but rather attained it all at once. Hermann Oldenberg, in his classic study of the Buddha, remarked on the affinity of the Buddha's enlightenment with the experiences of sudden transformation and cosmic consciousness reported by William James.[1]

The transformation is expressed in the new self-consciousness of Buddha. When asked by the ascetic Ajīvika Upaka who his master might be, the Buddha replied:

> I have no master, and no one can be compared with me.
> In the world of devas there is no equal to me.
> I am an Arhat [Holy One] to the world.
> I am the One Fully Awakened . . .[2]

Legend put the same words, in a slightly different version, into the mouth of the Buddha child, who immediately after his birth took seven steps in the four celestial directions and then said: "I alone am honored in heaven and on earth."[3] Since these words were set down in the Chinese scriptures as the birth verse of the Buddha (Japanese: *tanjōge*), they are familiar to Japanese Buddhists. Zen Buddhists interpret the verse in terms of the state of enlightenment in which the identity of the self, the universe, and Buddha is experienced. In a report of a contemporary experience, a Zen disciple tells how he felt gripped by this verse as his experience unfolded: "I alone am honored in heaven and on earth." The veneration of the Buddha derives from his enlightenment. Throughout all Buddhism there sounds forth the proclamation: "The Perfected One is the holy, supreme Awakened One."

The Zen school further traces its origins back to a special event in the life of Shākyamuni. Chinese Zen chronicles, referring to an apocry-phal sutra, report of the transmission of mind from Shākyamuni to his disciple Kāśyapa. This very occurrence can serve as a means to en-lightenment in Zen; that is, it is practiced as a koan. The sixth case of the *Mumonkan* reports the event as follows: "Once when the World-Honored One was staying on the Mount of the Vulture, he held up a flower before the assembled ones. All fell silent. Only the venerable Kāśyapa broke into a smile. The Honored One then spoke: 'The Eye of the true Dharma, the wonderful Mind of Nirvana, the true formless Form, the mysterious Gate of the Dharma, which rests not upon words and letters, and a special transmission [which is identical with the first four] outside the scriptures; this I hand over to the great Kāśyapa."[4]

Zen finds the origins of its transmission expressed in this occurrence. The earliest tradition contains only the first three terms, namely, the "Eye of the true Dharma," "the wonderful Mind of Nirvana," and "the true formless Form." The last two terms were added later. The "mysterious Gate of the Dharma" signifies the Zen school, which passes on the spirit in a "special transmission outside the scriptures." What is significant for disciples of Zen is that this special transmission that carries so much weight in the Chinese Zen writings goes back to Shākyamuni himself. (We shall return to this point later.)

Master Wu-men, the collector and commentator of the *Mumonkan*, concludes the case with the following thought: "If everyone in the con-gregation had laughed, how then would the Eye of the true Dharma have been transmitted in a single line? Or if Kāśyapa had not laughed, how then would the Eye of the true Dharma have been passed down at all?" This remark holds the paradox of Zen for us: on the one hand, enlightenment and the Buddha-nature realized in enlightenment are equally accessible to and present in all people; on the other hand, there is need for the special transmission of mind in the Zen school if people are continually to be brought to enlightenment. In the foregoing case, this is expressed by the fact that only Kāśyapa smiled where all of the disciples could have. For this reason the Buddha entrusted the special transmission of mind only to Kāśyapa. In the Zen school, Shākyamuni ranks as the first patriarch, Kāśyapa as the second, and so on down the line of twenty-eight Indian patriarchs, concluding with Bodhidharma, who is at the same time the first Chinese Zen patriarch.

This event from the life of Shākyamuni, even if it is legendary, does not merely tie the founder of the Buddhist religion historically to Zen. It also most impressively conveys the spirit of Zen. A deep silence hovers over the occurrence; not a word is spoken. The Buddha holds up the flower, the disciple smiles. The mind of the master and the mind of the disciple smile. Thus is Zen. Because supreme truth cannot be spoken in words, there has to be a wordless transmission outside the scriptures. It has happened that iconoclasm, rejecting every form of pictorial representation, accompanies this sort of *theologia negativa*. We shall see how it is with Zen. For now the point is that according to the Zen tradition, the Buddha did not speak the supreme truth in words. The Buddha's silence is a sign of his wisdom.

No other school of Mahāyāna Buddhism venerates the historical Buddha Shākyamuni as strongly as Zen has from its very beginnings in China. It is true that in Japan today, in the course of a general religious renewal, practically all Buddhist schools are turning to the sources of Buddhism and hence to Shākyamuni. But the Zen school has always displayed special veneration to the Buddha from the Shākya tribe. In many Japanese Zen temples the image of Shākyamuni is set up as the primary object of worship. The writings of Dōgen (1200–1253) reveal an intimate personal relationship to the Buddha Shākyamuni, who embodies the Buddha-nature in a unique way for this medieval Japanese Zen master. Personal devotion to Shākyamuni is widespread among Japanese Zen Buddhists today. The famous Japanese Zen master Yamada Mumon of the Rinzai school, for example, wrote a book entitled *Return to the Honored Shākya* (Shakuson ni kaere). Like many contemporary Japanese Buddhists, Yamada Mumon Rōshi had gone on a pilgrimage to Buddhist sites in northern India and been deeply impressed. His book relates some of his experiences. At the memorial of the enlightenment of the Buddha in Bodhgaya, the sight of the stupa and the Bodhi tree moved him to tears and occasioned a short poem:

> While I peer
> up at the lofty stupa,
> towering into the red dawn,
> softly my tears fall.[5]

Once at a meeting of Zen Buddhists and Christians, another Japanese master of the Sōtō school held a lecture that I shall never forget on the significance of Shākyamuni for Zen Buddhist spirituality. For him, Shākyamuni is the supreme exemplar, the one who followed the way to its end most perfectly and attained supreme enlightenment. Hence

Shākyamuni is an object of veneration to whom he feels intimately bound. In his case, too, the personal relationship to Shākyamuni far exceeds the respect accorded the founder in the system of teachings.

For hundreds of years East Asian Mahāyāna Buddhism was cut off from its roots in India; but modern means of transportation are bringing it, and hence Zen Buddhism as well, closer to the Indian heritage, as the wave of Japanese Buddhist pilgrims to the shrines in the northern part of India shows. The historical Buddha Shākyamuni has become personally dear to East Asian Buddhists today, and many features in the description of his life have taken on a concrete meaning for them. Among these features are Yogic practices, which comprise much of the Buddha's biography.

Zen and Yoga The relationship of Chinese-Japanese Zen to Indian Yoga is important both historically and intrinsically, and is of particular interest today. We tend to name Yoga and Zen together as paths of Eastern meditation, and it is common that the praise given or the fault found with one is applied without difference to either, i.e., to Eastern meditation in general. The similarities between Zen and Yoga are indeed unmistakable, but these two paths are by no means identical. To make inferences about Zen simply on the basis of phenomena in Yoga is to oversimplify the matter and to pave the way for patently false conclusions. Hence a critical investigation, which recognizes and maintains similarities but avoids identification, is in order.

All of Indian spiritual life is saturated with Yoga. The roots of the word literally mean to yoke or bind together; Yoga thus signifies all the corporeal, psychic, ascetic, and especially meditative efforts harnessed to help the spirit attain freedom. As a psychosomatic technique, Yoga embraces body and mind and brings their reciprocal relationship to bear on the full range of human activity. Yoga contains an enormous number of practices, ranging from entirely natural breath and concentration exercises employed in the posture of meditation to eccentric Fakir arts possible for only a few ascetics. What is practiced as Yoga in India and today in the West is legion.

Yoga has been in India since ancient times, probably going back before the Aryan influx. In Vedic literature it is found in connection and mingled with ancient Indian asceticism. What is important for our investigation is the fact that, in India, Yoga has been associated with widely varying philosophical systems, views of life, and religious movements. From Vedic Yoga an infinitely ramified way leads through

Buddhist Yoga, Jainist Yoga, Tantric Yoga, Vedānta Yoga (to name some of the most important branches) on to the modern forms employed in Ramakrishna community and Sri Aurobindo's integral Yoga. There is hardly an Indian philosophical school or religious community without its Yoga.

The special system of Indian philosophy that bears the Yoga (one of the so-called six orthodox systems, or *darśana*) has its scriptural basis in the *Yoga Sūtra* of Patañjali. It can be taken as representative of Indian Yoga. It is of interest to us because the classical Yoga of Patañjali is closely related to early Buddhism.

The *Yoga Sūtra* of Patañjali, called a "practical manual of ancient techniques" by Mircea Eliade,[6] summarizes the Yogic way in eight "members" *(aṅga)*. The first two members, the restraints *(yama)* and disciplines *(niyama)* concern the moral and ascetic preconditions for the exercises. The two following exercises are related to bodily postures *(āsana)* and control of breathing *(prāṇāyāma)*. The fifth member, the withdrawal of the senses from objects *(pratyāhāra)*, forms the bridge to the inner Yoga of concentration *(dhāranā)*, meditation (dhyāna), and absorption, or trance *(samādhi)*. As Friedrich Heiler demonstrated in his still-relevant study *Buddhistische Versenkung*, the members of this way of meditation are found one and all in the early Buddhist meditation of the Pāli canon. To be sure, historically Buddhism is considerably older than the work of Patañjali (the date of completion of the *Yoga Sūtra* is commonly held to be sometime in the fifth century A.D.), but the sutra represents the systematic, written form of much more ancient Yogic doctrines.

We do not know just how much or what kind of Buddhist Yoga is historically rooted in Shākyamuni himself. Apparently the founder of the Buddhist religion did practice and experience Yoga. According to the ancient biographies, two yogis, presumably adhering to the philosophy of Sāṃkhya, guided Shākyamuni into the ascetic life after he had left his father's house. For six years he applied himself to severe ascetic practices and meditation exercises taught in Yoga, but did not attain his goal on this path. Tradition also reports that the Buddha passed through the four dhyāna stages known to Yoga on the two great occasions of his enlightenment and his death (entrance into nirvana). Nevertheless, it is not historically certain to what extent the Yogic schema of meditation in early Buddhism is anchored in the teachings and life of Shākyamuni. Insofar as the Buddha expressly repudiated bodily castigations and magical or eccentric acts, Zen can find support for its radical simplification of meditation practice in the founder of the Buddhist religion.

With these considerations in mind—especially Shākyamuni's questioning of Yoga and the connection between classical Yoga and early Buddhist meditation—we now turn to our theme of the similarities and dissimilarities of Zen and Yoga. It is well known that D. T. Suzuki repeatedly stressed the difference between Zen and the early Buddhist dhyāna meditation inspired by Yoga. "Zen is not the same as dhyā-na,"[7] he emphasized, "Zen is not a type of dhyāna";[8] or "In the view of Zen, dhyāna does not correspond to the true practice of Zen."[9] Suzuki held this view out of his conviction of the singular uniqueness of Zen. (His works just as often pointed out the Indian roots of Zen.) We shall first expose the unmistakable relationship of Zen and Yoga, while keeping in mind Suzuki's words about the distinction between the two.

The similarity of Zen and Yoga is above all evident in their three basic techniques of meditation: namely in sitting, breathing, and concentrating. Of the many various sitting postures of Yoga (a treatise on Hatha Yoga describes thirty-two different kinds), Zen teaches the lotus posture *(padmāsana)*, considered the most perfect of all postures in Yoga as well. In Buddhism it is the posture of the Buddha, a sacred position from which magical effects pour forth. The regulation of breath (prāṇāyāma) is likewise common to Zen and Yoga, but Zen employs only one of the Yogic methods of breathing: rhythmical breathing in and breathing out (with the latter more drawn out), which the beginning student keeps count of. Coercive breathing techniques, suppression of breathing, etc., are not employed in Zen. The non-thinking of Zen, that is, the clearing out of all conscious impressions, desires, and thoughts, is similar but not identical to the Yogic exercise of concentration. (We shall return to this exercise in another connection later.) It is evident that Zen reduces the psychosomatic techniques of Yoga to a minimum. Zen is of the conviction that this simplification only facilitates the exercises and beneficial effects of meditation. Another mutual trait of Zen and Yoga is their high estimation of spiritual guidance. Just as the guru is indispensable to Yoga, so too the *rōshi,* or master, is essential to Zen. Zen fits into the tradition of Eastern meditation by way of its Yoga-like method.

We now come to the differences between Zen and Yoga. An initial distinction is apparent in Zen's simplification of Yogic technique. Suzuki does not mention this point. In stressing the uniqueness of Zen, he has in mind primarily the typical Chinese prototype whose peculiarity is already evident in the form of its appearance. A Chinese or Japanese Zen monastery is radically different from an Indian Yoga ashram or a Theravāda vihāra in Sri Lanka or Southeast Asia. The Zen monastery exhibits a freer, more open atmosphere, and this is not confined to external appearances only. The Chinese prototype of the Zen way reshaped the Buddhist monastic ideal, accentuating above all the sudden experience of satori and the paradoxical koan exercise. The differences that come to bear here should not be taken lightly. Zen enlightenment, precisely by breaking through the layers of the conscious, rational mind to transobjective being, proves itself a genuine experience of reality. The relation with reality in the Yogic and dhyanistic experiences, on the other hand, is not so evident.

Upon further investigation of the distinction between Yoga and Zen, we come across differing interpretations of the aspired goal. Experiences arrived at in meditation are ineffable, to be sure, but they are interpreted differently according to the practitioner's underlying philosophical views. In comparing the Zen and Yogic interpretations of experience, different views of the self come into play. Since Yoga is attached to various views of life and philosophical systems, the significance of the self will depend upon the particular school. We confine our discussion to classical Yoga.

In Patañjali's classical Yoga, as in the dualistic philosophy of Sāmkhya upon which this Yoga depends, the self *(puruṣa)* is opposed to nature *(prakṛti)*. The puruṣa is indescribable, spiritual, pure and free, but inactive and, for inexplicable reasons, bound to nature or matter (prakṛti). The practice of Yoga effects the liberation of the puruṣa, that is, its release from prakṛti. The liberation attained in this way appears as a state of total isolation *(kaivalya)*. Nothing binds the self any longer to nature; there is no longer any connection to physical or psychic natural processes. Innumerable puruṣa exist in isolation, like monads separate from the world and from each other as it were, each one free and autonomous in itself. This state of existence is achieved through Yoga, or so the experience of liberation attained in samādhi is interpreted by the Yogi.

The Zen experience is interpreted in the context of Mahāyāna philosophy. In the Mahāyāna view, self and universe, microcosm and macrocosm, ultimately coalesce into one. The self is not the same as the individual ego; the experience of the self is a cosmic experience. A well-known passage by Dōgen reads: "To learn the Buddha's Way is to learn one's own self. To learn one's self is to forget one's self. To forget one's self is to be confirmed by all dharmas. To be confirmed by all dharmas is to effect the casting off of one's own body and mind and the bodies and minds of others as well."[10]

This passage about the self in Zen radically differs in mood and in content from the classical Yoga doctrine of the purusa. The self, as experienced by this Zen master, stands in essential relation to all of reality. One learns by forgetting, that is, in a stripping off of all conscious egoity from the self. One learns most intensely by being "confirmed" (literally, "enlightened") by all Dharmas, that is, by the whole of reality. In this experience, all oppositions and distinctions—even that between oneself and others—vanish. In Dōgen's terms, body and mind signify the total person in its corporeal and conscious aspects. The casting off of body and mind *(datsuraku)* is the transcending of ego and liberation from it in enlightenment. But this experience, as Dōgen later emphasizes, cannot be forced by the ego. The ego can only be willing and open to enlightenment by the reality of all beings. The experience of the self, for Zen, is a transcendent one. In the words of Dōgen, it is the Buddha-nature that is experienced.

Is Zen Narcissistic and Asocial? Our deliberations on the similarities and dissimilarities between Zen and Yoga have convinced us that Zen is deeply rooted in Indian spirituality. At the same time they prepared us to recognize what is new in Zen—the topic of what follows. But before we leave the theme of Yoga and Zen, we must deal with some basic misunderstandings that result when the two are too readily identified in the West. I shall mention two of the most important: first, the charge that the Zen way, like Yoga and ultimately like all Eastern forms of meditation, so they say, promotes a narcissistic egocentrism and, second, that it encourages an asocial attitude in its adepts. These charges may be partially justified in the case of classical Yoga and other schools related to it, but they certainly do not apply to Zen, nor to all Yoga schools without reservation.

In answer to the charge of exaggerated egocentrism, we must first of all consider that all meditation implies a way inward. Christian spirituality is known for the importance it attributes to inwardness and interiority. Inner concentration has a place in the meditative way just as does inner recollection. The way inward has been successfully pursued by many mystics in the East and the West. Augustine exhorts us to take this way. It goes without saying that interiority and inwardness should never be absolutized. The nonthinking taught by Zen practice entails stilling the conscious activities of the ego in order to prepare for the experience. This Zen exercise reduces the ego to silence and clears space for what is essential. What thereby occurs is anything but the cult of the ego, narcissism, or egocentrism. Rather, the ego is compelled to make room for an experience that establishes communication with the reality of all existing things. This experience does not result in an isolation of the self; moreover, it is radically different from states of enstasis, trance, or hypnosis.

Thomas Merton warns of the danger of egocentric meditation, the kind that Hui-neng, the advocate of sudden enlightenment, ascribes to the quietistic Northern school of Chinese Zen: ''. . . this clinging and possessive ego-consciousness, seeking to affirm itself in 'liberation,' craftily tries to outwit reality by rejecting the thoughts it 'possesses' and emptying the mirror of the mind, which it also 'possesses.' . . . So the ego-consciousness is able, it believes, to eat its cake and have it. . . . But since this nature is regarded as one's possession, the 'spiritualized' ego thus is able to affirm itself all the more perfectly, and to enjoy its own narcissism under the guide of 'emptiness' and 'contemplation.' ''[11] Egocentric meditation, as Merton goes on to detail, is alien to the genuine Zen way represented by Hui-neng. We shall deal more with the controversy between the Southern school of Hui-neng and the Northern school of Shen-hsiu later.

The charge of asociality is likewise without ground in the case of Zen, and can be answered on two counts. The first follows from the Mahayanist attitude cultivated by Zen. In distinction from Hīnayāna or Theravāda Buddhism, Mahāyāna placed the Bodhisattva ideal characterized by wisdom and compassion in the center of its teachings. In Zen, the Bodhisattva figures as the ideal enlightened one, towering above in wisdom and bowing down with compassion toward all living beings.

The charge of asociality made against Zen, however, does not so much concern its Mahayanist attitude as the practice and experience of Zen meditation. Like the practice and experience of Yoga, it is attacked as fit only to make one asocial. The charge as stated must be dismissed. The Zen way is asocial neither in principle nor in its concrete manifestations. In Japan, experienced Zen masters engage in a wide range of religious and social activities, and encourage their disciples (especially those of advanced training) to develop a sense of social responsibility and to undertake social service. The difference from classical Yoga has practical consequences in this case.

Our investigation of the Indian roots of Zen led us back to the ancient sources of Asian religious culture. We met with the two important phenomena of Shākyamuni, the enlightened founder of the Buddhist religion, and of Yoga. We caught sight of the links between religion and psychosomatic techniques characteristic of the East. When treating of the birth of Zen in China in the next chapter, we shall learn how Zen arose at a point of contact between India and China, the two great Asian civilizations that both play an essential role in the formation of Zen.

THREE

The Birth of Zen in China

THE TRANSPLANTATION OF BUDDHISM from the Indian to the Chinese cultural sphere forms a fascinating chapter in the history of religions. The process occurred over a period of three to four hundred years, in the first centuries A.D., when Indian Buddhist monks bore the teachings of Shākyamuni to the "Central Kingdom" and, with the help of newly converted Chinese, translated the enormous bulk of Buddhist scriptures into that language. This work of gigantic proportions was completed in spite of profound difficulties. One need only recall the extent of the two great Asian civilizations, the differences between Indian and Chinese mentality, the complexity of the Buddhist religion, and the natural resistance offered the ascetic ideal of Buddhist monasticism by a Chinese feudal society centered on the family. But in spite of all, the Chinese accomplished the difficult task of appropriating such a typical Indian religion as Buddhism and imprinting upon it a unique East Asian character.

Zen in particular is a product of the fusion of Indian Buddhism with Chinese culture. Representative of this process of amalgamation and yet possessed of a unique creative energy, the Zen school in China has no counterpart in Indian Buddhism. Its acknowledged founder was Bodhidharma, who is supposed to have transported the peculiar tradition underlying Zen from India to China. We turn first to look at the offspring of Zen from the marriage of the Chinese and the Indian mind.

Mahāyāna Foundations Zen belongs to Mahāyāna Buddhism, and in China as well as Japan is exemplary of Mahāyāna meditation. All branches of Buddhism were originally transplanted to China, and at first Hīnayāna and Mahāyāna were more or less equally represented.

25

But only Mahāyāna was able to establish a basis and spread through-out the country. This is not the place to explain in detail the differences between Hīnayāna and Mahāyāna. In short, Hīnayāna takes the much more strict and narrow stand in all areas, whether they concern monastic discipline, cultic practices, or metaphysical doctrines. The wider view and flexibility of Mahāyāna, it can be claimed, was largely responsible for its success in China. The cosmic view of the Mahāyāna teachings above all appealed to the Chinese, who since antiquity were on intimate terms with a cosmic philosophy. The Mahāyāna doctrine of the cosmos encountered analogous ideas in Chinese universalism—a circumstance that greatly facilitated rendering the basic Mahayanist notions in Chinese ideograms. Mahāyāna, moreover, with its numerous Buddhas and Bodhisattvas, offered a world rich with religious symbolism that (like the myth of the Buddha Amitābha) appealed to the Chinese intelligentsia as well as to the common folk. The most important Indian Mahāyāna schools sank roots deep in the Chinese soil and gradually developed original forms complementing the old. During a period of about a thousand years Chinese Mahāyāna offered the spectacle of a wide-ranging, ramified, and vivacious religion.

The Chinese Zen movement takes its place within this sphere of Chinese Mahāyāna Buddhism. Zen, too, is at home in the spiritual heritage of the great Mahāyāna sutras. In an earlier work, I examined the connection between Zen and four Mahayanist sutras—namely the *Sutras of Perfect Wisdom* (Prajñāpāramitā Sūtra), the *Garland Sutra* (Avataṃsaka Sūtra), the *Vimalikīrti Sūtra,* and the *Laṅkāvatāra Sūtra.*[1] The religious teachings of Zen were inspired by all of these.

We can isolate a few points of particular significance for the Zen way of meditation and enlightenment. First is the negativity that we have already encountered in Shākyamuni's silence and that penetrates all forms of Buddhism, whether of Hīnayāna or of Mahāyāna derivation. In Zen is found the Mahayanist negativity that forms the core of the *Sutras of Perfect Wisdom.* The key terms are "empty" *(śūnya)* and "emptiness" *(śūnyatā),* which apply equally to the metaphysics and to the way of meditation. The phenomenal world and all that appears in it is empty, void of definition, qualities, or characteristics, without substance and essence. Even the empirical and conscious human ego is empty and without essence. For this reason, one is mistaken as long as he clings to appearances and to his own ego. In meditation he faces the task of emptying his mind of all phenomenal forms. This movement of negation is nevertheless a thoroughly positive endeavor; and the experience attained by way of it, though negatively formulated, is something positive. Neither the process nor the end of this emptying should be evaluated as simply negative. It finds its Christian counterpart in the so-called "dim contemplation" of John of the Cross and other mystics. This aspect of the way of enlightenment, then, should be understood in light of a *theologia negativa*.

The cosmic teachings of Mahāyāna are also of fundamental importance for Zen. Buddhist cosmotheism, epitomized in the *Garland Sutra*, considers all things in the universe to be organically interrelated, and senses the essential sacredness of all things—not in opposition to the profane, but in complete grasp of reality. All of reality shines in transcendence; all things reflect the splendor of the universe, even the smallest particle of dust. All this is realizable in the Zen experience. The fact that Zen does not dull one's touch for things by overstressing introspection, but rather sharpens this sense acutely, is proved by the art arisen from Zen. Numerous works express the organic, vital unity of all nature. The Japanese Zen painter Sesshū (1420–1506), for example, immersed in the life of nature, accomplished a sense of the changing four seasons in a few strokes of the brush, found among his famous ink drawings.

A cosmic element is also at work in the koan, although this exercise is designed primarily to overcome all distinctions, including that between the sacred and the profane. "Vast emptiness—nothing sacred," Bodhidharma is said to have answered when the Chinese emperor asked what the supreme and sacred truth was. One of the cases in the *Mumonkan* gives the answer "A dried shit-stick" to the question "What is the Buddha?"[2] Here the sense for the reality of all things is at its peak. The point is to realize this reality.

The *Vimalikīrti Sūtra* expresses the typical manner of Zen more concretely than any other Mahāyāna sutra. This sutra tells of the Bodhisattva of Wisdom (Mañjuśrī), who is especially emulated in Zen. After several other Bodhisattvas had expressed themselves in well-chosen words about overcoming all oppositions in an all-embracing unity, the Bodhisattva of wisdom turned to the lay disciple Vimalikīrti, to hear his answer to the essence of reality. But, as the sutra has it, Vimalikīrti said not a word, and was showered with praise. His answer of silence revealed supreme enlightenment, bound to no office and no monastic order. Vimalikīrti, the lay disciple and housekeeper, proclaimed his perfect enlightenment without saying a word.

Many other Zen-like sayings are found in the Chinese Mahāyāna sutras. D. T. Suzuki investigated especially the *Laṅkāvatāra Sūtra*,[3] which pays a good deal of attention to psychic processes, in this connection. The *Laṅkāvatāra Sūtra* is directed to the inner experience that no words can communicate. Grotesque gestures, grimaces, or shouts, as the sutra relates, often take the place of verbal sayings in Buddha lands. Such means of expression became commonplace in Zen. This sutra contains a wealth of psychological remarks. Of special significance for for Zen is the description of inner turning *(parāvṛtti)* at the very root of the mind; here is a hint of the suddenness of Zen enlightenment that opens new and higher perspectives. In its psychological outlook the *Laṅkāvatāra Sūtra* may be regarded a close relative of Zen.

The Mahāyāna sutras that we have considered the basis of Zen all stem from India. Hence significant elements of Zen are already found in Indian Buddhism. Indeed, the entire philosophical content of the Zen teachings is rooted in the Indian Mahāyāna sutras. But the particular points in Indian sources singled out by Chinese Mahāyāna must also be taken into account. Chinese Buddhism as a whole owes the wealth of its variety to such accentuations, and Zen in particular received the marks of its character from them.

There has been a tendency to find Zen so radically different from other Buddhist schools, especially during the Zen boom in America, that a distinction was drawn between Zen and Buddhism in general. It goes without saying that this sort of distinction is nonsense. Zen in its entirety belongs to Chinese Mahāyāna Buddhism. It counts as one of the classical Buddhist schools in China, each of which can claim a certain autonomy. Zen itself professes to be that particular lineage of immediate transmission which, bound to no holy scriptures, hands down to progeny the original way to Buddha-enlightenment. It is, in brief, the meditation school of Mahāyāna Buddhism.

It must of course be added that Zen, more than any other lineage of Chinese Buddhism, was the receptor of a strong influx from the indigenous Taoism. Chinese Zen combines the spirit of Mahāyāna Buddhism with the down-to-earth appeal of Taoism. There is evidence of a close connection between the metaphysical content of each teaching, and a similarity in their practice of meditation is observable.

Relationship with the Spirit of Taoism   The Taoist streak in Zen is by and large identical with the sinification of Mahāyāna Buddhism in the Central Kingdom. The Taoism indigenous to China aided the transplantation of Mahāyāna into Chinese culture in a significant fashion. It was able to do this by virtue of the religious content of the Buddhism. Whereas Confucianism, the other great Chinese religious tradition, bears no resemblance to Buddhism, Taoism exhibits many essential traits of Mahāyāna thought, such as negativity and cosmic perspective. Lao-tzu's book of wisdom, the *Tao-te ching* (The Way and Power Classic, c. third century B.C), proclaims the inexpressible character of the Tao in its opening verses:

> The Tao [Way] that cannot be told of
> Is not the eternal Tao.
> The name that can be named
> Is not the eternal name.[4]

The Tao is "empty" and "deep," "silent" and "complete"; it is the mother of the universe:

> There was something nebulous yet complete,
> Born before Heaven and earth.
> Silent, empty,
> Self-sufficient and unchanging,
> Revolving without cease and without fail,
> It acts as the mother of the world.
> I do not know its name,
> And address it as "Tao."[5]

The Tao transcends Being and Non-being:

> All things in the world come into being
>   from being,
> Being comes into being from non-being.[6]

The Tao is the unfathomable source, "Yet within it is an image. . . . Yet within it is a substance. . . . Yet within it is an essence. This essence is quite genuine and within it is something that can be tested."[7] The primal source is present in all the cosmos:

> The great Tao flows everywhere:
> It can go left; it can go right.
> The myriad things owe their existence to it,
> And it does not reject them.[8]

Man cannot fathom the ever-present meaning of the Tao, but he can reach its roots by way of silent meditation.

> The teeming things
> All return to their roots.
> Returning to one's roots is called stillness.
> This is what is meant by returning to one's destiny.
> Returning to one's destiny belongs with the eternal.
> To know the eternal is enlightenment.[9]

The experience of the Tao is the goal set for man.

Chuang-tzu, the second great proponent of Taoism, proclaims the inexpressible character of the Tao: "In the great beginning, there was nonbeing. It had neither being nor name."[10] "If words were sufficient, in a day's time we might exhaust it; since they are not sufficient, we may speak all day and only exhaust the subject of things. The Tao is the extreme to which things conduct us. Neither speech nor silence is sufficient to convey the notion of it. Neither by speech nor by silence can our thoughts about it have their highest expression."[11] The Tao, without beginning and without end, Chuang Tzu writes in another passage, is the great principle that penetrates all things: "It is everywhere."[12]

Mahāyāna Buddhists could just as well have referred to the cosmic Buddha, the ineffable primal source of the universe, as to the Tao. And this they did in China, the home of the Taoism they considered so close to their Buddhism. The connection between Mahayanist and Taoist thought took on vast proportions.

Zen Buddhism has a number of expressions for the absolute ground of reality. "Buddhahood," "Buddha-nature," "Buddha-mind," "Cosmic Body of the Buddha," and similar expressions directly mentioning the Buddha are without a doubt the prevalent ones. But "Nature" and "Mind" by themselves can also indicate absolute reality. The Chinese Tao, or Way, fits into the latter kind of expression. One treatise, until recently held to be a genuine writing of Bodhidharma, is entitled "Two Entrances to the Tao." Chinese Zen literature conceives the enlightenment of the Buddha as an "awakening to the Tao." A twelfth-century Chinese Zen master tells his disciples that "the Shākya of old, sitting at the foot of the mountain of enlightenment, raised his head to look at the morning star and awakened suddenly to the Tao."

Hui-k'o, the patriarch successor to Bodhidharma, was "a seeker of the Tao" as Zen chronicles record it. In early Chinese Zen literature there is a hymn ascribed to the third patriarch that betrays a very strong influence from Taoism. Entitled the "Treatise on Believing Mind" or the "Treatise on Faith in the Mind" according to the translation, it is a singular eulogy to the Tao, as its very first verse shows:

> The Perfect Way is only difficult for those
>   who pick and choose;
> Do not like, do not dislike;
>   all will then be clear.[13]

The entire hymn is filled with Taoist motifs and can be considered an example of Buddhist infusion into the Chinese language. It clearly anticipates the intimate relationship between Taoism and Zen.

We shall come across other Taoist motifs in later Chinese Zen masters when treating the flowering of Chinese Zen in the T'ang period (618–906). For now suffice it to quote one text that gives clear testimony to Taoism's direct influence on Zen literature. Master Huang-po, a disciple of Ma-tsu in the ninth century and teacher of the famous Lin-chi (Rinzai in Japanese), is reported to have said in a sermon: "Fearing that nobody would understand, they [the Buddhas] selected the name 'Way' [Tao]. You must not allow this name to lead you into forming a mental concept of a road. So it is said, 'When the fish is caught, we pay no more attention to the trap.' When body and mind achieve spontaneity, the Way is reached and Mind is understood."[14] The comparison with the fish and the trap is taken from Chuang-tzu, whose humanity, spontaneity, and humor made a lasting impression on the Zen masters. In the same sermon Huang-po expressly remarks that the Way is equivalent to the Mahāyāna Mind.

Taoist and Zenist Meditation   In evaluating the Taoist influence on Zen, we must consider not only the philosophical teachings but also the meditation that played a significant role in the sphere of Taoist folk religion. A distinction was drawn in ancient times between Taoism as a teaching and the cult of Taoism, in which the practice of meditation enjoyed considerable popularity. Breathing techniques were mentioned as early as the sixth century B.C.

Chuang-tzu, in a remarkable text on meditation, treats of "sitting

and forgetting everything." In Book VI of his writings, he records
the following conversation between the master Confucius (Kung-tzu)
and Yen-hui:

> Another day Yen Hui saw Confucius again and said: "I have made
> some progress."
> "What do you mean?" asked Confucius.
> Yen Hui said: "I forget everything while sitting down."
> Confucius' face turned pale. He said: "What do you mean by
> sitting down and forgetting everything?"
> "I cast aside my limbs," replied Yen Hui, "discard my intelli-
> gence, detach from both body and mind, and become one with
> Great Universal [Tao]. This is called sitting down and forget-
> ting everything."[15]

In addition to "sitting and forgetting everything," Chuang-tzu also
mentions the "fasting of the mind"; but the expression "zazen"
(sitting in meditation) is not used. The methodical efforts required in
meditation seem to be more removed from Chuang-tzu's philosophy of
"non-doing" *(wu-wei)* and spontaneity.

A writing of the second century A.D., the *Chou I Ts'an T'ung Ch'i* of
Wei Po-yang, contains detailed instructions on meditation. This
treatise is probably the earliest source of the description of meditation
called the Inner or Golden Elixir, which was distinguished by Taoists
of later centuries from exterior elixirs promising immortality and
eternal youth.[16]

Later centuries amply testify to the mutual influences of Buddhist
and Taoist meditation on one another. Tao-sheng (c. 360–434), the
earliest proponent of sudden enlightenment in Chinese Buddhism,
received much impetus from Taoism.[17] He applied Chuang-tzu's
analogy of the fish trap that should be forgotten as soon as the fish is
caught to the sudden enlightenment he taught. And the Chinese Zen
master Ha Shan (1546–1623) wrote a commentary on Lao-tzu's *Tao-
te ching,* saying the work could only be understood "if one has a personal experience" of the Way.

Taoist meditation is full of elements that remind one of Zen. For
purposes of comparison, much material is provided by a Taoist book
called *The Circles of Light: The Experience of the Golden Blossoms,* translated
into German and annotated by the Japanese scholar Mokusen Miyuki.
Since, however, this Taoist text derives from a period when Zen was

already in full bloom in China, it is impossible to tell for certain whether the similarities stem from Zen or from Taoism.[18] The Taoist meditation does not imply any genuinely Buddhist doctrines; rather what is attained is a Tao experience. "The In and Out of breathing in meditation is itself the experience of Tao—Yin and Yang breaking through into the microcosm—that which Lao-tzu signified as Emptiness."[19] It is an experience of the ineffable primal source, but, as Miyuki points out, it is intimately related to the Self: "In the exercise of 'sitting' described in the doctrine of the Inner Elixir, all of one's psychic energy is turned inward and concentrated on the innermost core of one's personality, the Self. This is symbolically expressed as a homecoming to the pure Yin of absolute stillness and passivity, which gives rise to the creative power of pure Yang and hence to a new cycle of the micromacrocosm."[20]

The Circles of Light contains numerous suggestions for performing Taoist meditation, as do Chinese Zen texts for Zen meditation. Techniques of sitting and breathing, reducing the activities of the senses, and concentrating inward are considered indispensable conditions for meditation in both Taoism and Zen. The extensive sections of this Taoist work giving instructions on the practice of meditation could just as well be contained in a Chinese Zen manual.

The author of *The Circles of Light* was evidently aware of the similarity of many of his instructions and descriptions to those in Zen Buddhism. Hence he devotes one section to the differences between his teaching and Zen. His remarks nevertheless apply more to other forms of Buddhist meditation than to Zen. He warns, for example, against "entanglements and distinctions" as the realm governed by the evil five aggregates. In warning against other things, a naturalistic tendency is clearly discernible in the Taoist author. "One should make it clear to himself," he writes, "that the mind plays no leading part in the exercises, and should forget the teachings and live in the expanse of the living [absolute], where *ch'i* [vital power] is harmonized and the mind compensated. In this way one will be able to enter the state of stillness. And consequently one will experience in stillness the moment of concordance [*chi*] and the Open [*ch'iao*]."[21]

Although the Zen disciple could take this advice without qualms, a specifically Taoist coloring is still apparent in the formulation. The difference is quite clear where the efficacy of the Tao is said to reveal itself to the Taoist "step by step." This places Taoist meditation in the tradition of the gradual attainment of enlightenment, as opposed to the Zen way of a sudden realization. In general, Taoist meditation can be characterized as tending more toward passivity, quietism, and naturalism, whereas authentic Zen accomplishes the breakthrough to the depths by way of a dynamic and spontaneous power of the mind.

The Taoist impact on Buddhism is an important factor in the origin of Zen in China. Profound similarities between the Buddhist and Taoist views of life brought about a convergence of fundamental ideas and motifs. The fact that doctrines and expressions often conformed in the two religions, as our examples have indicated, speaks for some mutual dependence, although few corroborating details are known, at least in the case of Zen.

It is definite, however, that Zen owes its typical Chinese character to its proximity to Taoism. The original Zen masters belong to the same family as the Taoist sages. Zen art partakes of the refreshing flavor of Chinese soil in its naturalness and down-to-earth character. In Chinese Zen literature, as in the monasteries, one finds oneself in a thoroughly Chinese world; the Indian roots of this unique religious atmosphere remain concealed. The Chinese considered Zen so much their own that, of the rich assortment of Buddhist schools in China, only Zen and the Amida faith were carried on into modernity. Modern Chinese Buddhism consists almost entirely of Amida veneration along with Zen, and the two schools are commonly found together in the same monasteries and places of worship. If Amidism is the more popular, it is clear that Zen takes the leadership spiritually.

From our investigation of the Mahāyāna doctrines and Taoist elements combined in Zen Buddhism, we may conclude that Zen definitely has an identity of its own. Western Zen scholars occasionally went so far as to take for Zen's very foundation the Taoist elements that surround and permeate it like an atmosphere. The more correct view, however, seems to be that Zen is based on Buddhism, that it is the Chinese meditation school of Mahāyāna that is saturated with Taoism. It is evident that Zen was born of the marriage of the Indian and the Chinese spirit. Inspired by the Tao, Buddhadom began a new life on Chinese soil, embodied by the Indian Bodhidharma and his patriarch successors.

FOUR

Bodhidharma

WE NOW COME TO THE HISTORY of Zen in China. The meditation movement in Chinese Buddhism, which began shortly after the arrival of the Buddha religion in that country, is important for the prehistory of Zen in many respects. Mention must be made above all of the two prominent Chinese Buddhist monks Seng-chao (384–416) and Tao-sheng (c. 360–434).[1] Seng-chao was the first Chinese to present the central doctrine of Zenist metaphysics. His treatise on "Wisdom Not Being Knowledge" masterfully clothes the quintessence of Mahāyāna philosophy in Chinese garb. Tao-sheng's teaching on the suddenness of the meditative experience anticipated another essential part of the Zen way. We shall return to Tao-sheng later in this chapter.

We can assume that meditation had held the interest of Chinese Buddhists ever since Buddhism was introduced to China. But only those elements that came to bear within the known schools of Chinese Buddhism afford any certainty. We shall omit the historical details of Buddhist meditation in China and turn immediately to the origins of the Zen school connected with the name of the Indian Bodhidharma.

The Figure of Bodhidharma The legendary founder of Zen, Bodhidharma, is veiled in obscurity.[2] Although rather definite dates are given for his birth and death at the end of the fifth and the beginning of the sixth centuries, we have no historically certain knowledge of the twenty-eighth Indian and first Chinese Zen patriarch, as he is known in the tradition. Every one of the writings attributed to him has proved to be spurious, despite efforts by Japanese historians in the first half of this century to salvage his authorship. We can only conjecture how and why the legend of Bodhidharma originated.

The main features of the legend can be traced back to the eighth century, but it was not fully developed within the Chinese Zen school until the tenth and eleventh centuries. At that time Zen was in full bloom in China, and apparently a need was felt to highlight the beginnings of the movement. Hence a founder was invented—or, what is more likely, some historical figure who had been a Buddha-monk was elevated to mythical proportions and called the founder. I personally tend to assume that there was a historical person at the beginning of the Zen movement in China and have sought to give foundation to this view in many of my writings. However, the historical arguments for this supposition are not entirely convincing.

The name Bodhidharma is first mentioned in a description of forty-five temples in the capital city of Lo-yang, contained in the *Lo-yang Ch'ieh-chi*, written about 547, not long after the legendary death of Bodhidharma. But according to this writing, a Shramana Bodhidharma came from Persia. Miraculous tales are told of this Shramana, but no mention is made of his having practiced or taught a way of meditation. More pertinent is the testimony of the Chinese historian Tao-hsüan (d. 667) given some century and a half later. Tao-hsüan devotes part of his generally reliable work *Hsü-kao-seng-chuan* to a brief biography of the "Dharma Master" Bodhidharma. Here the profound wisdom of Bodhidharma is extolled, as is his enthusiasm for the teachings of Mahāyāna and for meditation, but the miraculous and grotesque stories of the later legends are missing. Tao-hsüan's biography makes it at least probable that a Mahayanist meditation master by the name of Bodhidharma actually existed. But to try to extract the historical core of the Bodhidharma legends is a hopeless undertaking.

Legends report that Bodhidharma, an offspring of the Brahmin class of southern India, perhaps even of royal blood, came to South China during the reign of the emperor Wu-ti (502–50). After meeting the emperor, he crossed the wide Yangtze River on a reed and propagated a new version of the Mahāyāna doctrines and a new way of meditation in North China. The central part of the legends is the story of his sojourn in the Shao-lin-ssu monastery, where for nine years he sat facing the wall and passed down the seal of the Buddha-mind to his disciple Hui-k'o. The legends also report miraculous deeds after the death of Bodhidharma.

The legends depict the founder of the Zen school as a powerful personality. People in China, Korea, and Japan have commemorated him and placed him among their heroes. The legless Daruma doll (one version has it that Bodhidharma's legs withered away during his nine-year meditation) is a popular toy in East Asia. Zen artists have painted his portrait and done ink drawings of him. Anyone who looks at these works is captivated by the large, piercing eyes of the patriarch.

In the Zen school, the question of why Bodhidharma came from the West (that is, made the journey from India to China) is regarded as the question of the very nature of Zen enlightenment. This question is a favorite koan and has evoked innumerable responses. The koan, of course, is not concerned with the historical or legendary person Bodhidharma, or the reason for his journey. The point is, rather, one of ultimate truth, embodied in Bodhidharma but not bound to him; it can occasion the breakthrough from rational thought to enlightenment. One case in the koan collection *Mumonkan* reads:

> Chao-chou was once asked by a monk: "What is the meaning of the first patriarch's coming from the West?"
> Chao-chou answered: "The tree of life in the front garden."[3]

Another Zen master responded to this same question: "Hand me that support over there!" And still another answered: "No meaning"— echoing for us the familiar *mu* (not) of negativity of the Zen school.

Because Bodhidharma is such a central figure in the Zen tradition, however things may stand with the historicity of his person, he cannot be simply removed from the scene when we consider the historical beginnings of Zen in China. This would be to distort the picture. In the formation of the Bodhidharma legend, the point for the representatives of the Chinese Zen school was doubtless to safeguard the traditional lineage, which ranked Bodhidharma as the first Chinese and twenty-eighth Indian patriarch, and hence to connect Zen with the founder Shākyamuni. For all its liberality, Zen is very conscious of tradition. The transmission of the patriarchate and the seal of the Buddha-mind from master to disciple plays a prominent role. The figure of Bodhidharma found in Zen today must be seen in light of the later developments, but to the extent that it is an authentic expression of Zen itself, it helps illuminate the entire course of Zen history. This becomes even clearer when we have a closer look at the new way of meditation opened, according to Zen tradition, by Bodhidharma.

Bodhidharma as a Master of Meditation   In an ancient text ascribed to Bodhidharma, his way of meditation is characterized by the Chinese word *pi-kuan*, literally wall-gazing or wall-contemplation. Except for the word pi-kuan, the same passage is found in a Mahāyāna sutra; it reads: "When one, abandoning the false and embracing the true, in simplicity of thought abides in pi-kuan, one finds that there is neither selfhood nor otherness, that ordinary men [*pṛthagjana*] and the saints [*ārya*] are of one essence."[4] The sutra speaks of the "vision of enlightenment [*chüeh-kuan*]" at this point—an expression that also occurs in Zen literature. Whatever the case may be, with the insertion of the word pi-kuan into this text (most likely taken from the sutra), the expression pi-kuan and the whole text indicated a manner of meditation that later generations typified as "Bodhidharma Zen." Bodhidharma himself was called the "wall-gazing Brahmin."

Adherents of Zen interpreted pi-kuan, the wall-gazing attributed to Bodhidharma, in the light of Zen meditation. They understood this expression as referring less to Bodhidharma's sitting facing a wall than to the characteristic qualities of enlightenment—namely, steepness and suddenness. From its beginnings, the Zen way shows itself to be a way of sudden enlightenment. Of course, in Chinese Buddhism there is nothing new about striving for sudden enlightenment. As opposed to the Indian teaching of a gradual, step-wise enlightenment, Chinese Buddhists from early times advocated a way of sudden enlightenment—something that they felt corresponded better to Chinese mentality. Here we come across an important finding in the prehistory of Zen, something that must be seen in connection with the introduction of Buddhism to China and its adaption to Chinese mentality.

Along with the teachings of Hīnayāna and Mahāyāna Buddhism, there spread throughout China different techniques of Buddhist meditation, including both the Hīnayāna forms of early Buddhism and various Mahayanist forms. The Sanskrit term for meditation (dhyāna) was translated—that is, semantically transcribed—into Chinese by the two Chinese ideograms that read *ch'an-na*; later this was abbreviated to the one ideogram *ch'an*, which in Japanese reads *zen*. At first dhyāna, ch'an, or zen was the collective name for all manner of Buddhist meditation that the Chinese avidly acquired together with related Yogic practices. Long familiar with meditation from Taoism, the Chinese could well understand the emphasis placed on experience in Buddhist meditation. They, too, strove for the realization of transcendent reality by way of meditative experience.

In the course of the sinification of Buddhism, there came a turn to the meditative way of sudden enlightenment, which can be regarded as a decisive step toward Bodhidharma Zen. Tao-sheng, a prominent Chinese Buddhist of the school of the great translator Kumārajīva (d. 413), declared that the doctrine of a step-wise ascent to enlightenment might well be harmonious with the Indian thinking, which distinguished various stages in everything, but was less appropriate for Chinese Buddhists, who could grasp enlightenment in a sudden experience. Moreover, he said, the sutras themselves gave indications of a nongraduated way of sudden enlightenment.

Tao-sheng's teaching was taken as an innovation. The early history of Chinese Buddhism reports heated arguments, continuing to the end of the fifth century, between the advocates of the way of sudden enlightenment and the proponents of a graduated ascent. These disputations were concerned not so much with differences of technique in meditation as with opposing interpretations of the Buddha's teachings, and they had profound metaphysical consequences. We shall return to this theme in connection with the disputations within the Zen movement over the suddenness or gradualness of enlightenment. Together with its metaphysical implications, the sudden experience is the note that distinguishes the Chinese way of enlightenment from Indian mysticism.

Despite scholarly efforts to establish a connection between Tao-sheng, together with his disciples, and Bodhidharma, nothing certain is known. If we nevertheless speak of Tao-sheng's school as a precursor of Zen Buddhism, we do so not in the sense of a lineage within a tradition of teachings, but rather because both grew out of and operated within the same spiritual climate. We know that Buddhist dhyāna masters of all schools journeyed throughout China during the fifth and sixth centuries, recruiting disciples for their particular ways of meditation. Against this background Bodhidharma, the master of pi-kuan, appears as one dhyāna master among many. Yet his way to enlightenment was destined to surpass all other ways of Buddhist meditation, and to acquire a unique place in history and worldwide significance today.

Bodhidharma's Role in the Zen Tradition   Zen chronicles report mainly three episodes in the life of Bodhidharma. The three, all of which presuppose a fully developed form of Zen meditation, include Bodhidharma's conversation with the emperor Wu-ti shortly after the master's arrival in China, the admission of his disciple and patriarch-successor Hui-k'o, and the last conversation with his disciples directly before his death. These koan-like episodes, which belong to later legends, reveal as much the very core of Zen as the significance of Bodhidharma in the Zen tradition.

Zen chronicles of the Sung period (960–1279) give various accounts of the conversation said to have taken place between Emperor Wu-ti and Bodhidharma at their first encounter. A succinct version of this meeting also became the object of a koan exercise. The chronicle account underscores the difference between Zen and the then current brand of Chinese Mahāyāna Buddhism. Emperor Wu-ti, a zealous Buddhist himself and not a little proud of his achievements for the sake of Buddhism throughout the land, asks Bodhidharma:

"What merit have I gained by having innumerable temples built, sutras written down, and monks initiated, ever since I ascended to the throne?"

The Master answered: "No merit whatever."

The Emperor replied: "Why no merit whatever?"

The Master said: "All these are impure motives for merit; they bear the puny fruit of rebirth as a human being or a deva. They chase a figure like a shadow, but have no reality."

The Emperor said: "What then is true merit?"

He answered: "It is pure knowing, wonderful and perfect. Its essence is emptiness. One cannot gain such merit by worldly means."

Thereupon the Emperor asked: "What is the sacred truth's first principle?"

The Master replied: "Vast emptiness, nothing sacred."

The Emperor said: "Who is it that now stands before me?"

The Master replied: "I don't know."[5]

This dialogue is truly filled with the spirit of Zen. Bodhidharma remains aloof from the merit-seeking institutional Buddhism of that time. He will have nothing to do with a verbalized principle of truth. Reality is vast and empty. There are no opposites. "Not" is the last word.

The story of Hui-ko's admission as a disciple of Bodhidharma is told over and over again in the Zen chronicles. A famous Zen painting depicts Bodhidharma as he sat upright facing the wall and turned to look at the disciple. After waiting patiently in the snow and being refused several times, the disciple resorted to cutting off his arm and presenting it to the master. (According to Tao-hsüan, Hui-k'o's arm was chopped off by robbers.)

Bodhidharma's departing conversation with his disciples is likewise practiced as a koan. The best-known version of this episode is the following:

> Nine years had passed and he [Bodhidharma] now wished to return westward to India. He called his disciples and said: "The time has now come. Why does not each of you say what you have attained?"
>
> The disciple Tao-fu replied: "As I see it, [the truth] neither adheres to words or letters nor is it separate from them. Yet it functions as the Way."
>
> The Master said: "You have attained my skin."
>
> Then a nun, Tsung-chih, spoke: "As I understand it, [the truth] is like the auspicious glimpse of the Buddha land of Akṣobhya; it is seen once, but not a second time."
>
> The master replied: "You have attained my flesh."
>
> Tao-yü said: "The four great elements are originally empty; the five *skandhas* [aggregates] have no existence. According to my belief, there is no Dharma to be grasped."
>
> To him the Master replied: "You have attained my bones."
>
> Finally there was Hui-k'o. He bowed respectfully and stood silent. The Master said: "You have attained my marrow."[6]

Bodhidharma, the legendary founder of Zen in China, stands at the head of a long line of figures significant as bearers of the Zen tradition and distinguished for the unusual capabilities arising from their enlightenment. Although Mahāyāna terminology classifies them as Bodhisattvas, they are not so much objects of worship as part of a hero cult mixing religious awe with popular admiration. Any suggestion of sacredness is diminished; but the authority of the Zen patriarchs and acknowledged masters remains extensive and has both personal and magical overtones. It is astounding that even in anti-authoritarian times like the present, people of all ages willingly accept the authority of the mystically gifted and enlightened, the gurus and rōshis. This willingness stems primarily from their acceptance of irrational powers in man, such as those inspired by the figure of the first Chinese Zen patriarch, Bodhidharma, the symbol of the perfected rōshi.

FIVE

The Sixth Patriarch

Preliminary Remarks on the History of Zen in China   It is not our intention to portray the history of Zen in full. The historical elements are of interest to us only insofar as they help clarify the essence of the Zen Buddhist way of enlightenment. We spoke of the legendary figure of the founder Bodhidharma because his story is indispensable for an understanding of Zen. After Bodhidharma, according to tradition, came four Chinese Zen patriarchs about whom we know very little. When it comes to the Sixth Partiarch, Hui-neng, however, the case is different; all later Zen schools and lineages derive from him. His was born in 638 and probably died in 713. Although we have some historical material covering the end of the seventh and beginning of the eighth century, the biography of Hui-neng is not clearly ascertainable, primarily due to the particular historical circumstances that arose after his death.

As the Zen chronicles on the Zen movement of this time have it, the fifth patriarch, Hung-jen (601–74), attracted a large number of disciples to the seat of his monastery on the East Mountain. The names of eleven of them are known to history. Among these disciples, Shen-hsiu (606?–706) is outstanding. According to the Zen manuscripts from the first half of the eighth century discovered in Tun-huang, Shen-hsiu inherited the Dharma seal of succession from his master. In fact, his name is found in several lists of the patriarchs deriving from this time. The writings portray him as a famous master favored at the imperial court and beloved among the people. His school of Zen was called the Laṅkāvatāra school (Bodhidharma is supposed to have passed on the *Laṅkāvatāra Sūtra* to Hui-k'o, the second patriarch, and all during the early period of Zen in China this Mahāyāna sutra continued to be highly respected). Later the Laṅkāvatāra school of Zen, which spread throughout North China, came to be known as the Northern school.

The Zen manuscripts of Tun-huang also name Hui-neng among the disciples of the fifth patriarch. But beyond the mention of his name, nothing is written there. How did he come to be recognized as sixth patriarch? Briefly, it was a result of a vigorous dispute between the Southern and the Northern schools of Chinese Zen that came to a head in the generation after Shen-hsiu and Hui-neng, and ended with the total victory of the Southern school. The advocate of the Zen school of the South was Shen-hui (d. 762), an otherwise little-known follower of Hui-neng who chose this master as a leader twenty years after Hui-neng's death and defended Hui-neng's claim to the Zen patriarchate. The writings of Shen-hui and his disciples give detailed reports of the debate from the stance of the victorious Southern school and portray the life, teachings, and way of meditation of Hui-neng. The Northern school soon disappeared, and Hui-neng was recognized and venerated as the sixth patriarch of Zen not only within Shen-hui's school but eventually throughout Zen. The Sixth Patriarch (this designation having become a title with him) has been a towering figure in the history of Zen ever since the end of the eighth century.

From the Life of Hui-neng The figure of Hui-neng is depicted in a wealth of Zen literature. The fact that these writings are not historically reliable does not at all mean that every biographical sketch of Hui-neng and every word ascribed to him are simply fictitious half-truths. In many cases the reports could be as authentic as unauthentic. It is just that with the present status of source materials we are not able to distinguish what is genuine from what is not. However, we may register some doubt, especially wherever the Northern school of Shen-hsiu is polemically criticized or even harshly reviled, as well as wherever praise is heaped upon the school of Shen-hui. Doubtful, too, are contradictory passages in the various versions of the biography, and the extremely dramatic or miraculous events. Nevertheless, in the following we shall not preclude all historically dubious elements, for the particular teachings of Hui-neng are best seen in contrast to the opposing school of Shen-hsiu.

From the second half of the eighth century on, several Zen writings treat of Hui-neng, his person, and his teachings. Of special note is the *Sutra of the Sixth Patriarch* (the full title is the *Sutra Spoken by the Sixth Patriarch from the High Seat of the Gem of the Law*). This is the only piece of

Zen literature that bears the honorific title "Sutra." Significant parts of it were probably composed by Shen-hui's school toward the end of the eighth century. The oldest manuscript, discovered among the Tun-huang documents, was written down sometime between 830 and 860. The contents of the sutra include detailed biographical data and speeches of the Sixth Patriarch; it is possible that authentic speeches of Hui-neng form the basis of the latter. Be that as it may, we shall refrain from any further historiographical criticism and simply report the main points from the tradition of the Sixth Patriarch. The events in his life seem to accentuate the basic core of his way to enlightenment.

The center of Hui-neng's life was his encounter with the fifth patriarch, Hung-jen, which, according to Zen tradition, led to the bestowal of the patriarchate on him. In the chronicle, Hui-neng was twenty-four when he arrived at Wang-mei, the monastery of Hung-jen. Filled with religious fervor, he had already experienced sudden enlightenment upon hearing a passage from the *Diamond Sutra* (one of the *Sutras of Perfect Wisdom*). Master Hung-jen set the uneducated boy to pounding rice in the barn. Then one day, the *Sutra of the Sixth Patriarch* tells us, the master had his disciples compose a poem to indicate the degree of their enlightenment. At that time Shen-hsiu occupied the first seat among the many disciples, but in spite of his learned knowledge of the sutras, he had no deep experience. With a great deal of effort he finally produced a verse and that night wrote it on a wall in the temple hall:

> The body is the Bodhi tree [enlightenment],
> The mind is like a clear mirror standing.
> Take care to wipe it all the time,
> Allow no grain of dust to cling.[1]

The next morning Master Hung-jen praised the verse in the presence of all the disciples, but told Shen-hsiu to compose another verse, for his poem showed no sign of enlightenment. Hui-neng, who could not read, had Shen-hsiu's attempt read to him, then composed one himself and told a temple boy to write it on the wall:

> The Bodhi is not like a tree,
> The clear mirror is nowhere standing.
> Fundamentally not one thing exists;
> Where, then, is a grain of dust to cling?

All the disciples marveled at the poem. But the master erased it and stated that Hui-neng, too, was far from enlightenment. The following night, however, he called Hui-neng to his side in order to endow him with the robe and alms bowl, the insignia of the patriarchate, and thus entrust the line of succession to him. Upon the master's command, Hui-neng crossed the Yangtze River the same night and fled south to escape Shen-hsiu's envy and the persecution of the other disciples.

A case in the *Mumonkan* tells of Hui-neng's flight and pursuit by the other disciples. In this version it is not Shen-hsiu who is the leader of the group of disciples, but a monk named Ming, who comes upon Hui-neng in the Ta-yü Mountains. The koan recites the incident as follows:

When the [Sixth] Patriarch saw Ming approaching, he threw the robe and alms bowl on a rock and said: "This robe symbolizes faith. Should one fight over it violently? I leave it to you. Take it and leave!"

Ming tried to lift it up, but it was as immovable as a mountain. Shuddering, he stopped and was overcome with fear and trembling. Then he said: "I came to request the teaching, not for the robe. I beg you, reveal and show it to me."

The Patriarch said: "Do not think, 'This is good'; do not think, 'This is bad.' At this moment what is the original face of Monk Ming?"

At once Ming was greatly enlightened. His body was bathed in sweat. Tears flowed from his eyes. Bowing deeply he asked: "Beside this secret word and secret meaning is there anything else, with even deeper meaning?"

The Patriarch said: "What I have just clarified for you is not secret. If you look back at your face in its light, the secret is in you."

Ming said: "When I was in Wang-mei together with the other disciples, I had indeed not yet seen my own face. Now you have opened the way for me. It is like drinking water and perceiving cold and warmth yourself. Now you are my master!"

The Patriarch said: "If that is the case, then both of us, you and I, equally have Wang-mei [Hung-jen] for our master. Take care!"[2]

This koan depicts Hui-neng's character in thoroughly human terms—he is upright, modest, gentle, and kind. Zen masters summarize these humane traits in the basic Buddhist virtue of compassion. Hui-neng does not defend the robe and bowl with force. He does not claim the title of master for himself, but rather points to the fifth patriarch as their master in common, and hence to the transmission of mind in Zen.

The *Mumonkan* collection relates another incident in the life of Hui-neng in the form of a koan; the same event is reported in other Zen literature as well. Hui-neng visits a monastery in southern China where the Dharma master Yin-tsung lectures on the *Nirvāṇa Sūtra*. At the entrance, the temple flag flaps in the wind. This is the setting of the following koan:

> Once the temple flag was blowing in the wind. Two monks were arguing about it.
> One said: "The flag is moving."
> The other said: "The wind is moving."
> Thus they argued back and forth, reaching no agreement. Then the Patriarch said: "It is not the wind that's moving; it is not the flag that's moving—it's your mind that's moving."
> The two monks were awe-stricken [with enlightenment].[3]

Master Wu-men, the collector of the koan, comments on this case: "It is not the wind that moves, it is not the flag that moves, it is not the mind that moves. Where is the Patriarch caught sight of?" This means: Where is the ultimate and the profound, the essential core, the true mind of the Patriarch? Wu-men's total negation reveals the mind of Zen. He points to a transcendental reality that lies beyond assertion and negation and cannot be expressed in words.

Upon his return to southern China, Hui-neng lived in the seclusion of his homeland mountains and forests for sixteen years. Later he made his abode primarily at the monastery Pao-lin in Ts'ao-chi, Canton. The temple Ta-fan, which is the site of the *Sutra Spoken by the Sixth Patriarch from the High Seat of the Gem of the Law*, has not been identified with certainty.

According to the Zen chronicle *Ching-te ch'uan-teng lu,* Hui-neng, seated in the lotus posture, passed away on August 28, 713, at Kuo-en Temple in Hsin-chou.

The Way of Sudden Enlightenment The phase of Chinese Zen history initiated by Hui-neng is characterized by the opposition between his way of sudden awakening and Shen-hsiu's school of gradual enlightenment. In Zen literature the contrasting schools are known simply as the "Southern Zen of Suddenness" and the "Northern Zen of Gradualness." Hui-neng is celebrated as a new founder for the phase started by way of his work, which likewise has been considered revolutionary. Externally, his investiture with the patriarchate represents something novel and guarantees the authenticity of his Zen way. The Zen tradition regards this as a crowning event; but the inner transformation indicated in the reports is incomparably more significant. The novelty is pregnantly expressed by the enlightenment verse with which Hui-neng vanquished his rival from the battlefield. The two *gāthā*, or verses, are treated as programmatic manifestoes of the two opposing schools or—better—the two divergent ways of meditation, and Hui-neng is celebrated as the founder of the Zen way of sudden awakening because of his verse.

It is uncertain how far this is justified. We know too little about Buddhist meditation in the previous centuries to be able to evaluate Hui-neng's original achievement. It is possible that Tao-sheng, mentioned earlier, had already anticipated the essence of the sudden way of enlightenment. The case would be highly probable if there were evidence of a close spiritual relationship between Tao-sheng and his fellow disciple under Kumārajīva, the ingenious Seng-chao, who died while still very young. For as early as the turn of the fourth century, Seng-chao set out Hui-neng's basic idea, namely that *prajñā* (wisdom) is non-knowing. The *Sutra of the Sixth Patriarch* proclaims Hui-neng to be the originator of a new Zen way of sudden awakening and contrasts the uniqueness of this way with Shen-hsiu's gradual meditation that had been the usual practice until that time. But since we know of Shen-hsiu's way of meditation only from the writings of the Southern school, we cannot tell for sure how much this picture actually corresponds to the teachings of the master of Northern school.

The Zen tradition is fond of elucidating the difference between the two manners of meditation by way of the two enlightenment verses. Both poems compare the mind with a mirror—a simile that goes back to the most ancient Chinese sources. In the third or fourth century B.C. the Taoist Chuang-tzu wrote that "the perfected one uses his mind like a mirror."[4] Meditation has to do with the mirror-mind, but the activity of the mirror-mind is variously interpreted, according to the particular viewpoint. Shen-hsiu's verse depicts the mirror-mind as something passive; it is standing and must be continuously wiped clean, that no grain of dust may cling to it. The dust represents the obscurities and passions *(kleśa)* aroused by the desires, images, and thoughts of the human psyche. Hence the meditator must take pains to appease the activities of his psyche in order to attain a completely quiet mind. This type of meditation proceeds from the view that an originally pure mind, like a spotless mirror, is defiled by obscurities and passions in this life and must be restored to its original purity through meditative effort. "Meditation means purifying one's own mind," a disciple of Shen-shiu explained.

If, accordingly, the goal of meditation is one's own state of mind, then there can be no question of a true liberation to something transcendent. D. T. Suzuki sees the limitations and dangers of this manner of meditation when he writes: "In the dust-wiping type of meditation . . . it is not easy to go further than the tranquillization of the mind; it is so apt to stop short at the stage of quiet contemplation. . . . At best it ends in ecstasy, self-absorption, a temporary suspension of consciousness."[5]

Hui-neng takes up the metaphor of the mirror-mind, but his radical negations overthrow all categories. "Fundamentally not one thing exists." These words point to liberation and transcendence. For the nothingness of Hui-neng, like the emptiness (śūnyatā) of the *Wisdom Sutras* and the philosophy of Nāgārjuna, signifies not nihilism but a supreme affirmation of the ultimate reality that lies beyond all categories and concepts. The enlightenment intimated in Hui-neng's verse is attainable only by breaking through rational, dualistic thinking; no finite object is grasped, but rather prajñā, or transcendental wisdom, is at work in a non-objective way. The latter is the true, free, dynamic mirror-play of the mind. Its advocate Hui-neng bears the honorary title of the Zen Master of the Great Mirror (Chinese: *ta-chien;* Japanese: *daikan*).

In the *Sutra of the Sixth Patriarch* the opposition between these two manners of meditation is clarified by two Chinese ideograms: *k'an-ching* (Japanese: *kanjō*) and *chien-hsing* (Japanese: *kenshō*), meaning "paying attention to purity" and "seeing into one's true nature" respectively. Paying attention is an ego-directed effort, whereas a dynamic seeing into the nature of the self unfolds the mind to transcendence. Accordingly, the two manners of meditation display fundamentally different attitudes toward the kleśa and toward practice. In the quietistic type of meditation, the obscurities are continually wiped clean; but for the mind awakened to seeing into its true nature, the obscurities prove to be no hindrance. Since they arise from discriminating thinking, one can see through them into reality as soon as dualistic thinking is overcome.

Another important difference lies in the relationship between practice and enlightenment. In the teaching of Hui-neng, practice and enlightenment are not causally connected, but, rather, identical. Dhyāna and prajñā are one and the same. Meditation is not an indispensable means to attain enlightenment, but a spiritual discipline that contributes to the process of revealing one's enlightenment. This is a touchy point requiring some clarification. Hui-neng's Zen allows for a good deal of freedom concerning practice; no specific exercises are prescribed as necessary.

This has led some to claim that Hui-neng rejected practice in general. But such an interpretation is unwarranted. The passages in the *Sutra of the Sixth Patriarch* appealed to by this interpretation warn against a false way of meditating, consisting of motionless sitting. "This kind of practice," Hui-neng stresses, "is the same as insentiency and the cause of an obstruction to the Tao."[6] It serves to "obscure true reality." Hui-neng warns against the subtle obligation to be pure, for in paying attention to purity, the meditator inhibits his original nature. Over and over again he emphasizes that external practice is to no avail if one's inner nature is not activated. It is therefore more correct to view Hui-neng as the defender of the true practice, as opposed to false, quietistic exercises. It is symptomatic that, according to the tradition, he died seated in the lotus posture. We may assume that, like many other great Zen masters, Hui-neng spent many hours of his life meditating in this posture.

The contrasting names "Sudden school" and "Gradual school" derive from the divergent views of meditation practice. Shen-hsiu's school of Gradualness also accounts for an experience that is perceived suddenly, at once; but (at least in the reports of Hui-neng's school) it teaches a way of gradual ascent as the practice progresses. Enlightenment is "acquired" by way of practice. This "acquiring," which implies some sort of causation, is unknown to Hui-neng. For him enlightenment comes suddenly, "in no way acquired," "in no way caused." The *Sutra of the Sixth Patriarch* explains: "What is meant by 'gradual' and 'sudden'? The Dharma itself is the same, but in seeing it there is a slow way and a fast way. Seen slowly, it is the gradual; seen fast, it is the sudden [teaching]. Dharma is without sudden or gradual, but some people are keen and others dull; hence the names 'sudden' and 'gradual.' "[7]

The sutra also calls the teaching of suddenness simply the Mahāyāna doctrine, for it alone does justice to the Mahāyāna metaphysics of the enlightened state of one's original nature.

The Doctrine of No Mind   It remains for us to give an account of the metaphysics underlying the doctrine of sudden enlightenment. The partially legendary story of Hui-neng's life tells us that the Sixth Patriarch was familiar with the *Diamond Sutra,* one of the *Sutras of Perfect Wisdom.* In paying due respect to the underlying metaphysics of the sudden way of enlightenment, we must proceed from these sutras. Developed by Nāgārjuna in the school of the Middle Way *(mādhyamika),* their philosophy intends something positive in all its negations. The insight into the nature of the self that is awakened in sudden enlightenment is an insight into emptiness, into nothingness.

Enlightened seeing is non-seeing, knowing is non-thinking (Chinese: *wu-nien;* Japanese: *munen*), the mind is no mind (Chinese: *wu-hsin;* Japanese: *mushin*). Such expressions are not to be understood in psychological terms. When D. T. Suzuki's *The Zen Doctrine of No Mind* makes use of the notion of the unconscious to clarify non-thinking and no mind, at the same time it makes clear the difference from his early, psychologically oriented works. Suzuki writes: "It is evident that in Zen Buddhism the unconscious is not a psychological term either in a narrower or in a broader sense."[8] Rather the negating expressions of the sutras must be understood metaphysically, in terms of the philosophy of the Middle Way.

A whole series of expressions, in part negatively and in part positively formulated, equally signify ultimate reality: non-seeing, non-thinking, non-clinging, non-form, no mind, nature, self, mind, form, suchness, sameness; also Dharma, Buddha, and the names associated with these. Hui-neng is fond of the expressions "nature," "self nature," or "essential nature." He speaks of a "seeing into one's nature and becoming Buddha." But this supreme *positivum* is identical with "non-thinking" and "no mind." The *Sutra of the Sixth Patriarch* reads: ". . . in this teaching of mine, from ancient time to the present, all have set up no-thought as the main doctrine, non-form as the substance, and non-abiding as the basis. Non-form is to be separated from form even when associated with form. No-thought is not to think even when involved in thought. No-abiding is the original nature of man."[9]

As understood by the Southern school of Hui-neng, enlightenment has to do with an experience of ultimate reality, hence with an experience of Transcendence and Being. This metaphysical view contrasts with the Northern school's way of enlightenment, which, in the interpretation of its opponent, strives for a state of psychic purity, i.e., a higher stage of consciousness. Hui-neng's way of enlightenment, on the other hand, is characterized by its objectlessness, its breakthrough to a new dimension of Being, and its experience of transcendence.

Thomas Merton, dealing extensively with Hui-neng, also calls wu-nien, or the non-thinking of Hui-neng, the "ultimate mind," identical with the "transcendental unconscious." "Its destiny is to manifest in itself the light of Being by which it subsists. . . . It becomes one," Merton goes on to say, "with God's own light, and St. John's expression, the 'light which enlightens every man coming into this world' (John 1:9) seems to correspond pretty closely to the idea of *prajñā* and of Hui-Neng's 'Unconscious.' "[10]

Prajñā enlightenment encompasses all things, including the kleśa, or obscurities. Merton describes this kind of enlightenment in a remarkable passage making reference at first to the divergent view of the Northern school: "As Hui Neng saw, it really makes no difference whatever if external objects are present in the 'mirror' of consciousness. There is no need to exclude or suppress them. Enlightenment does not consist in being without them. True emptiness in the realization of the underlying *prajñā*-wisdom of the Unconscious is attained when the light of *prajñā* . . . breaks through our empirical consciousness and floods with its intelligibility not only our whole being but all the things that we see and know around us. We are thus transformed in the *prajñā* light, we 'become' that light, which in fact we 'are.' "[11]

Merton's daring language should not surprise us; it is the language of mysticism. He interprets Hui-neng's sudden enlightenment as a comprehensive experience of Being. This is an essentially religious experience. That which Hui-neng calls nature or mind or even non-thinking and no mind—that ultimate absolute reality is God for the Christian. Hence Merton can say at the conclusion of this paragraph that in enlightenment we know all things "in a vastly different way, as we now know ourselves not in ourselves, not in our own mind, but in *prajñā*, or, as a Christian would say, in God."[12]

Merton's theological reading of Zen enlightenment allows him to compare it with the *todo-y-nada* intuition of John of the Cross: "The infinite emptiness is then infinite totality and fullness."[13] Merton does not hesitate to see a "Trinitarian relationship" and a "Trinitarian structure" in this pure experience of Being. Here Merton refers to

Suzuki's study *The Zen Doctrine of No Mind*, which emphasizes that the "self-nature which is self-being [is] self-seeing, that there [is] no Being besides Seeing which is Acting, that these three terms Being, Seeing, and Acting [are] synonymous and interchangeable."[14]

Hui-neng can be regarded as the second founder of Chinese Zen.[15] His way of suddenness lays the foundation for what is specifically Chinese Zen. The Chinese imprinted on Buddhism the peculiar character of their land, stressing concreteness and dynamism in meditation. In East Asia, meditation in the lotus posture was practiced with more zeal and devotion than in the southern Asian countries. The Zen masters did not aspire for an ascending intuition of eternal truths, as did the Indian seekers of wisdom. Rather they experienced reality in sudden collision, as it were. The practical Chinese, if he succeeded in breaking through, became Buddha by seeing into his true nature.

SIX

The Zen Movement in China

THE ZEN CHRONICLE KNOWN AS *Keitoku Dentōroku* depicts the beginning of the Zen movement in China thus: "West of the river the great 'Solitary One' [i.e., Ma-tsu] is the Master; south of the lake 'Stonehead' [i.e., Shih-t'ou] is the Master. People gather there in crowds. He who has not seen the two great masters is regarded as an ignoramus."[1] The land west of the Yangtze River is today's Kiangsi Province; south of the lake lies Hunan Province. This area is the setting of the Chinese Zen movement during the T'ang period. The two great Zen masters are Ma-tsu Tao-i (709–88) and Shih-t'ou Hsi-ch'ien (700–790), both living in the third generation after Hui-neng. Of their respective masters Nan-yüeh Huai-jang (677–774) and Ch'ing-yüan Hsing-ssu (660–740), we know all too little. Because of this, and the fact that the accounts of Hui-neng are not entirely historically certain, "in one sense Chinese Zen can be said to have really started with Ma-tsu and his contemporary Shih-t'ou."[2] This beginning took place during the middle of the eighth century, i.e., during the T'ang period, a time of cultural flowering in China. This Golden Age of Zen lasted some 150 years, until the decline of the T'ang dynasty. The tenth century saw set forms and patterns taking hold of Zen.

A large number of significant masters taught during the peak of Chinese Zen; they cannot be classified according to school or teachings, but only by generation and lineage. All these Chinese Zen masters trace back to Ma-tsu and Shih-t'ou, and through them to Hui-neng. (The lineage of Shen-hui, the disciple of Hui-neng mentioned earlier, soon died out, as did also the genuine Zen element in this lineage, which was absorbed by the Kegon school.) It is hardly possible to give a systematic presentation of the historical course of the first phase of the

Zen movement in China, which sprang up spontaneously. All the Zen masters of the time named in later chronicles, sayings, treatises, and koan collections appear in Suzuki's works with astounding diversity, and Suzuki is adept at gleaning continually new insights from them. Wilhelm Gundert's German translation of the greater half of *The Blue Cliff Records* gives a masterful account of the spiritual aura of the movement. And nearly all books on Zen, usually relying on Suzuki, tell of the early flowering of Zen in China.

Zen Activity Zen literature characterizes the epoch as "the time of Zen activity [*Zenki no jidai*],"[3] a phrase that celebrates a talent and strong capacity for dynamic action. The masters of that time, spiritually powerful and original figures, led their disciples to the liberating experience in ever-new ways. All of them practiced Hui-neng's Zen of sudden enlightenment.

These early Zen masters did not let themselves be channeled into fixed patterns. To be sure, they practiced meditation, indeed with great fervor, as Hui-neng had. But they retained a free attitude of mind. The official Zen history of the Sung period accords a good deal of importance to a conversation said to have occurred between Ma-tsu and his master Nan-yüeh, but more likely belonging to the uncertain part of the tradition:

> Ma-tsu Tao-i, according to the chronicle, was then residing in the monastery constantly absorbed in meditation. His master, aware of his ability for the Dharma, went to him and asked: "Virtuous one, for what purpose are you sitting in meditation?"
>
> Ma-tsu answered: "I wish to become a Buddha."
>
> Thereupon the master picked up a tile and started rubbing it on a stone in front of the hermitage.
>
> Ma-tsu asked: "What are you doing, Master?"
>
> "I am polishing this tile to make a mirror," Huai-jang replied.
>
> "How can you make a mirror by rubbing a tile?" exclaimed Ma-tsu.
>
> "How can one become a Buddha by sitting in meditation?" countered the master.[4]

This dialogue contains a clear allusion to the manner of meditation of Shen-hsiu's Northern school, which was criticized by the Southern school for directing all attention to the purification of the mind during the practice of meditation. But no amount of purifying or polishing can make a Buddha of anyone if the Buddha-nature is not there right from the beginning. The purpose of meditation can only be to induce a spiritual state in which the liberating experience spontaneously springs forth. No genuine Zen master ever denied the profound benefit of meditating in the lotus posture for such a state of quietude, emptiness, and alertness. Yet even a beneficial practice can hinder the meditator if he clings to it.

Zen particularly regards rational inquiry and academic scholarship as a hindrance along the way of enlightenment. The life story we told earlier of Hui-neng makes the Sixth Patriarch completely illiterate. Although this part of the story is contradicted by other reports giving testimony to his intimate knowledge of the sutras, this illiteracy is taken as a criterion for the authenticity of his way of Zen. Early Zen history relates anecdotes about burning sutras and wooden Buddha images. One famous episode recited as a case in the *Mumonkan* is from the life of Te-shan (780–865), who is named along with his master, Lung-t'an (of the third generation in the lineage of Shih-t'ou). Devoted to the sutras, the young Te-shan advanced in learning; burning with fervor for the true doctrines of the Buddha, he undertook a journey to the south. There Hui-neng's way of Zen, that "special transmission outside the scriptures," was widespread, and Te-shan felt compelled to expose this false teaching and crush it. "On his way," the koan says, "he addressed an old woman in the district of Liu to buy some refreshment from her. The old woman said: 'Virtuous one, what are those writings you are carrying in your knapsack?' Te-shan replied: 'The *Commentaries on the Diamond Sutra*.' Thereupon the woman said: 'In the Sutra it is written: "The mind of the past is ungraspable, the mind of the present is ungraspable, the mind of the future is ungraspable." Virtuous one, which mind do you wish to refresh?' This question left Te-shan speechless. Nevertheless he did not give up, but inquired of the old woman: 'Does a master of the [Zen] school live near here?' The old woman replied: 'About five miles away lives Master Lung-t'an.' Te-shan arrived at Lung-t'an's completely deflated."[5]

Darkness settled on the two of them as they talked about the doctrine. Before leaving, the master lit a lantern and handed it to the disciple. Just as he was about to take it, the master blew it out. "At this instant Te-shan was suddenly enlightened." The following day he made a bonfire of his commentaries on the sutras, and said: " 'Even if one fathoms every obscure saying, it is like a single hair cast into a vast

space. Even if one grasps the axis of the world, it is like a tiny drop
poured into the sea.' He spoke thus and burned his commentary.
Thereupon he bowed and left.''⁶

This episode is one of many examples of the original and fascinating
manner of the early Zen masters. However, one should not generalize
from this case that burning sutras or Buddha images was a common
practice in Zen Buddhism at that time. We have no reason to believe
that Zen disciples favored iconoclasm in principle. The individual
instances of such an attitude known to us rather indicate an unconven-
tionally free mind in Zen followers. The Zen movement evolved within
the Buddhist religion and became the representative form of Chinese
Buddhism in succeeding centuries.

As we noted earlier, in this first phase Zen masters did not differ
from one another in terms of doctrine or school. Hence, personal
idiosyncrasies were all the more strongly developed. Later historical
accounts sharply delineated these idiosyncratic traits and often named
the style of a particular master according to them. In Ma-tsu's school,
it even came to physical blows, as when the master grabbed the nose of
his disciple and twisted it energetically. Zen annals are replete with the
unusual deeds and words of the masters. Many of them were figures of
extraordinary strength, mentally acute, witty, and, as their power to
attract disciples might indicate, of charming personality. They remind
us of those ''great unique figures of ancient China''—Lao-tzu, Chuang-
tzu and Lieh-tzu.⁷ Like them, the Zen masters of the T'ang period inspired many succeeding generations.

It is noticeable that the Zen disciples of this early period usually
experienced enlightenment in an encounter with their master. An
exchange of words was the primary means of direction. To be sure,
the crisp atmosphere of the monastery, long hours of meditation, and
above all an attitude of mental alertness prepared them for the experience. Later this same atmosphere was carried over by the practice of
koans, but in the early phase everything proceeded naturally and spontaneously. The presence of master together with disciples played an
important role in this type of meditation. No trace of an unsound egocentricity or cramped introspection is to be found. Rather it seems that
the ''Zen activity'' brought forth unconscious and unnamed powers
in the individual.

Doctrinal Aspects As far as doctrine is concerned, the Zen masters of
the T'ang period rely heavily on Hui-neng. All their basic motives are

found in the *Sutra of the Sixth Patriarch* and in the discourses of his disciple Shen-hui. Nature is empty (śūnya), the mind is identical with Buddha, wisdom (prajñā) sees emptiness, and in seeing emptiness, Buddha-nature is revealed. We shall point out two aspects here which can lead to a better understanding of the early masters.

First, the Zen masters encourage above all the overcoming of dualities. Enlightenment is an experience of oneness. In practice, this aspect is expressed in the skirmishes of question and answer during the exchange with the master, when the mind awakens to unity. Even the talks of the Zen masters, who ordinarily do not philosophize, stress the aspect of unity. The following verses are handed down as a discourse of Ma-tsu:

> Outside mind there is no Buddha,
> Outside Buddha there is no mind.
> Do not cling to good,
> Do not reject evil!
> Purity and defilement—
> If you depend on neither,
> You will grasp the empty nature of sin.
> In every moment it is ungraspable,
> For no self-nature is there.
> Hence the three worlds are only mind.
> The universe and all things
> Bear the seal of the One Dharma.[8]

This text depicts the universal oneness of reality and must be understood in this sense. The verse on good and evil is not a repudiation of morality. The point is that the mind on the way to enlightenment must transcend such pairs of opposites that characterize dualistic thinking. In the same sense, Hui-neng says that self-nature knows neither good nor evil. This idea recurs in several variations in later Chinese Zen texts. Likewise, purity and defilement have no connotations of moral value in this context. Rather, such statements point in the direction of the Mahayanist axiom of the identity of nirvana and *saṃsāra* (phenomenal world).

The verse on the identity of the mind and the three worlds (i.e., the realms of desire, form, and formlessness) derives from the idealistic philosophy of the Yogācārya school, sometimes considered an intermediate step between Hīnayāna and Mahāyāna. It is not clear whether the notion of mind in some of the Zen texts is meant in the sense of this school or whether it is to be understood as an ontological-metaphysical concept.

The second aspect I would call attention to is the Taoist streak in the teachings of the early Zen masters. As we have seen, Taoism had an influence on Buddhism in China from the time it reached that country. During the period of the Six Dynasties (581–618) and the following T'ang period, the teachings of the Taoist sages Lao-tzu, Chuang-tzu, and Lieh-tzu enjoyed a rise in popularity. A Taoist tint in the Zen masters of this time is unmistakable. The following quotation is taken from the collection of sayings of the renowned master Nan-ch'üan P'u-yüan (748–834), one of Ma-tsu's immediate disciples: "During the cycle [kalpa] of the Void there are no names. Since the appearance of Buddha in the world there are names. On the basis of these names men grasp the external characteristics [of things]. . . . The Great Tao includes everything without [distinction between] the holy and the profane. Whatever has a name is subject to limitations. Therefore the Elder of Kiangsi [Ma-tsu] said: 'This is not mind, this is not Buddha, this is not a thing.' "9

Absolute reality is signified by Tao, the ancient Chinese word for the Way, here as in so many other Zen texts. The Tao is emptiness, the primal ground, the all-embracing, the nameless prior to all distinctions. Nan-ch'üan's words echo a text in Chuang-tzu: "In the Tao, opposites are sublated in unity. Having their existence in their separateness, in arising they come to pass away. All things that are beyond arising and passing away, return to sublation in unity."10

Discriminating thought cannot lead to wisdom. Buddhist philosophy speaks of "discriminating" knowledge (Sanskrit: *vikalpa;* Japanese: *fumbetsu*) and "non-discriminating" knowledge (Sanskrit: *nirvikalpa;* Japanese: *mufumbetsu*). Discriminating knowledge is entangled in the world of desires; non-discriminating knowledge is liberating. (In Japanese, the words for dividing or separating, i.e., *wakeru,* and understanding, i.e., *wakaru,* both derive from the same verbal stem. *Wakaru,* as opposed to the intuitive grasp of *satoru,* is activated by understanding of words, concepts, linguistic structures, etc. It is proper to language, explaining and understanding things through division and separation, i.e., *wakeru.* Hence conceptual understanding, or *wakaru,* is inadequate.)

Communal Life in the Monasteries   A picture of the Zen movement in China must include at least one brush stroke about the form of the communal life of the monks. The Zen chronicles usually depict the masters surrounded by a large group of disciples, with whom they lead a life in common. Even the unreliable historical accounts of the fourth and fifth patriarchs mention this aspect. It appears that by that time the Zen Buddhists had already made at least a partial transition from the unsteady life of the wandering beggar-monk to life in cloistered settlements, with all the changes it demanded—especially strict regulation of the communal life and regular work. The number of monks grew; it is said that at the beginning of the seventh century the fourth patriarch, Tao-hsin (580–651), led more than 500 disciples on the way of enlightenment. Such facts lead us to believe that the Zenist monasteries were independent estates. On the other hand, we know of Zen masters who, together with their disciples, took advantage of the hospitality of other Buddhist schools, either by fitting into the community itself or by residing in a part of the monastery.

The decisive change was brought about by Pai-chang (749–814), who had been the most outstanding of Ma-tsu's followers. When he founded a new monastery he drew up a set of new and appropriate rules for the communal life. It seems he sensed that conditions prevailing up to that time could not persist. On the one hand, the number of Zen disciples continually grew; on the other, the rigid Hinayanist regulations were hardly harmonious with the liberal streak in the Chinese Zen followers. Up to that time, the Hīnayāna Vinaya rules were the widespread practice, since Mahāyāna had initiated some reforms but no adequate set of monastic rules.

Pai-chang's rules show he knew how to combine monastic discipline with spontaneity and naturalness. They take sociological needs into account. "A day without work—a day without eating" was the principle of this master, and by it all who lived in the monastery were obliged to take part in productive work. Meditation, worship, and work were the three interwoven parts of the monk's life, according to the rules of Pai-chang. He himself set an example: even at an advanced age he stood his ground in working in the fields and garden. Once when his disciples took his tools away, the chronicles tell us, true to his principle, he refused to take nourishment. The Zen monks were highly respected in China for their orderly communal life and willingness to work.

Pai-chang's organization of Zen monasticism bears the stamp of his enlightened character. His master Ma-tsu called him the "Great Pearl" —it was a name that stuck and entered history. He was an energetic and successful director of his disciples, exhorting them "to cling to

nothing, to crave for nothing." Both in his treatise on sudden enlightenment and in the records of his conversations with disciples, he proves himself a reliable interpreter of Hui-neng's way of sudden enlightenment.
Like the Sixth Patriarch, he rejects all discriminating thought: "When
you forget the good and the non-good, the worldly life and the religious life and all other Dharmas, and permit no thoughts relating to
them to arise, and when you abandon body and mind—then there
is complete freedom. When the mind is like wood or stone, there is
nothing to discriminate."[11]

As this brief text indicates, Pai-chang's manner of teaching does not
differ from that of other Zen masters contemporaneous with him. It
is important to notice the social and ethical character of Chinese Zen
implied in this context. For a strong communal religious life like Pai-
chang's gives rise to ethical values. Even the Confucianists—those renowned advocates of social ethics in East Asia—had much praise for the
communal life in the monasteries of Pai-chang and his school.

A look at the historical chart tells us that Pai-chang lived in the middle of the Chinese Zen movement. From him the line of descent leads
to his disciple Huang-po (d. 850) and from him to Lin-chi (d. 867),
who founded the largest and most influential school of Zen in China.

Lin-chi and the "Five Houses"   Toward the end of the T'ang period there
emerged several lineages in the Chinese Zen movement that, during
the succeeding period of the Five Dynasties (907–60), coalesced into
the so-called "Five Houses." These five schools, named after the master
at the head of their line of descent, did not at first differ from one another in matters of doctrine or practice. All the lineages belonged to
Hui-neng's school of enlightenment, although the Five Houses did
develop peculiarities of their own.

In the House of Wei-yang (Japanese: Ikyō), for example, which
was named after the two masters Wei-shan (771–853) and Yang-shan
(814–90), one practiced meditation with the aid of "circular figures"
—a method that was not generally recognized in Zen. Yün-men's
(d. 949) peculiarity was his preference for short, one-word answers,
which gave his house its name, "The Barrier of a Single Word." The
House of Fa-yen (885–958), though adhering like the other houses to
the methods of the early T'ang masters, tended toward metaphysical
speculation, as seen in Fa-yen's explanations of the essential oneness
of the six attributes of beings of the *Garland Sutra:* totality and distinc-

tion, identity and difference, becoming and passing away. This tendency is also apparent in the dialectic of the "Five Ranks" in the House of Ts'ao-tung. Hence the Zen of the "Five Houses" does contain certain aspects that distinguish it from Hui-neng's way of enlightenment.

Finally we come to the Lin-chi (Japanese: Rinzai) school, which to this day has not broken its line of transmission. The final part of this chapter is devoted to its founder, Lin-chi (d. 867), in many respects the greatest of the Chinese Zen masters.

Lin-chi I-hsüan lived in the last generation of the Zen masters of the T'ang period. Both the course of his life and his style of teaching recapitulated the original manner of the early Zen masters. As a young man he devoted all his energy to the study of the Buddhist scriptures. His biography makes special mention of his interest in the Vinaya discipline. But although the great systems of Mahāyāna thought were the center of his studies, philosophical knowledge was not able to satisfy him. His fervent longing for an experiential realization of truth led him to the south, where Zen masters continued the immediate transmission of mind outside the scriptures.

Lin-chi lived under Master Huang-po three entire years without once speaking to the master of his ardent desire. Finally, prompted by the foremost monk, he took courage and went to the master with his question about the essence of the Buddha-Law—only to be sent away with blows. Twice again he approached the master, was struck, and sent away. When he was ready to leave the monastery, however, feeling disturbed and dejected, the head monk requested that he at least bid farewell to the master, who then sent him to Ta-yü, also of Ma-tsu's school, where he was sure to receive the right guidance. When Lin-chi told Ta-yü what had happened to him, the reply was that Huang-po had treated him with consummate kindness. Thereupon Lin-chi was suddenly awakened; a light broke through him, and he said: "There's nothing special about Huang-Po's Buddha-Law." When Ta-yü struck him for this mocking comment, he countered with three blows to Ta-yü's ribs.

The story ends with Lin-chi returning to Master Huang-po. The master noticed immediately that his disciple had changed radically, but made only the remark that Ta-yü would have to come and pay for his premature prattle with blows. "No need to wait for him to come," replied Lin-chi, "here you are!" and dealt the master a vigorous blow. Thereupon Huang-po gave out a laugh, and Lin-chi shouted "Ho!" He had experienced the Great Enlightenment and become the Dharma successor to Huang-po.

Lin-chi's style of teaching Zen was particularly strict and harsh. His name is associated with the shout of *ho!* which, as the chronicles tell us, Ma-tsu had first let out with such force that his disciple Pai-chang was left deaf for days. The Chinese character for *ho* is read *katsu* in Japanese; and to this day Japanese Zen masters of the Rinzai school shout *katsu,* while the Chinese roar *ho!* Such shouts are intended to shock and awaken. The chronicles are fond of placing Te-shan and Lin-chi, contemporaneous Zen masters of two lines of descent, side by side—the former for his stick and the latter for his shout—together the consummation of the style of Zen activity as developed by the spontaneous masters of the T'ang period. Many episodes from Lin-chi's life are still practiced as koan.

But if Lin-chi stands in the tradition of the creative masters of early periods, his personality towers high in the "Zen forest"—as the Zen communities were called—of his time. Twenty-two discourses preserved in the *Rinzai-roku* collection give evidence of his incomparably profound understanding of the Zen way. In the view of one living Japanese Zen historian, this collection "gives an account of a man and his teaching whose vitality and power of conviction is unexcelled in Zen literature" (Seizan Yanagida). Lin-chi's dialectical formulas guide one to grasp truth by means of the right comportment toward reality. One example is removing the person but letting the surroundings be, then removing the surroundings but leaving the person, removing both the person and his surroundings, and finally leaving both the person and his surroundings. These four steps indicate the progression from discrimination (between subject and object) through negation to non-discriminating affirmation. In other formulas Lin-chi treats of the host and the guest, the questioned and the questioner, or the view and the deed. We would, however, miss the point if we were to regard such formulas as some sort of dialectical acrobatics. For Lin-chi's constant intention is to overcome all oppositions and multiplicities that hinder seeing into the unity of all things. These formulas are shaped by Buddhist categories of thought.

Lin-chi did not at all discard the wealth of learning he had acquired as a youth when he turned to Zen, but rather integrated it into a transformed spiritual existence. Once at a Buddhist-Christian conference on the religious quest for a true view of the human being, one Zen Buddhist from the Rinzai school spoke of the founder Lin-chi's view of man. In taking the *Rinzai-roku* as his basis, he placed Lin-chi among the Buddhist thinkers of his time. "The discourses of Lin-chi make ample use of Buddhist doctrines; his teachings incorporate a philosophy which transcends philosophy, a philosophy which survived criticism, an illogical logic." The primary influence was from the Hua-yen, or Kegon, school of thought and from the doctrine of "mind only." The speaker, Eshin Nishimura, conceived of Lin-chi's transformation as the step from the mind to the human being in totality. Whereas traditional Mahayanist philosophy took the mind for its foundation and principle, the enlightened Lin-chi saw the human being in his concrete existence as the center: "There is the true man of no rank in the mass of naked flesh, who goes in and out from your facial gates [sense organs]."[12]

The true human being without rank and title is one freed from all fetters. Lin-chi has various expressions for this true, free human self. He also simply calls it "this man" or "the man free his life long," "the well-grounded man who suffers no diversion," "this man learning the Way," "this disciple who hears the Dharma," or even "this disciple without supports." The human being is a "this," here and now, someone concretely existing—not a general concept or an essential nature, and not an isolated and absolutized individual. This becomes clear in his relation to the Buddha-nature, with which he is ultimately identical. In Lin-chi's view, the sacred is not some hidden pearl in a person; rather the entire concrete human being is transparent, revealing the Buddha-nature. This "true human being without rank" infinitely transcends the human being, as Pascal remarked. For the practitioner of Zen, the point is to encounter or come upon the true human being in transcendence. In this way he will be enlightened and liberated.

The German writer Karlfried Graf Dürckheim spoke of this transcendence as follows: "It can occur to us in these experiences that the supernatural or supermundane is not to be sought outside the human being, but that the core of the human being is something that transcends his natural state of personality as conditioned by the world. . . . Today the time has come . . . to recognize that the center of the living, suffering, searching, loving—in short, real human being is something 'unconditioned, superhuman, overpowering' that transcends the ego's capacity for understanding and the horizon of its world view. . . . Yet the unconditioned that lays hold of us in our interior during experiences of being, that transcends the order of the ego and often enough upturns it, is of metaphysical character. But just this is our own proper, most profound essence."[13]

Lin-chi experienced the freedom of enlightenment to an extraordinary degree. His seemingly immoderate demands to remove all barriers to the way of enlightenment can only be understood in this light. "If you encounter the Buddha, kill him; if you encounter the Patriarch, kill him!"[14] In the discussion following the talk on Lin-chi's view of man, the Zen Buddhists emphasized the transcendent character of the enlightenment experience. The "true human being without rank," they reaffirmed, is grounded in the transcendent, the absolute. In the case of the early Zen masters, this transcendence is experienced, not reflectively known. The Zen chronicles tell us that Lin-chi sought the Tao.

The Zen movement of the T'ang period marks a peak in the history of Zen. The Zen disciples of following generations looked to it for the highest possible realization of the Zen ideal. This exemplary character cannot be expressed in words; it is embodied by the Zen masters themselves. We have named only a few, not even all the prominent ones, to give a taste of what went on in Zen at that time. Its strong spiritual current was active long afterward and continues to inspire one today. The Japanese masters of the present day who evoke the admiration of Western people are the heritage of the Chinese of the T'ang period.

SEVEN

The Koan in Chinese Zen

DURING THE LATTER HALF of the T'ang period, innovative Zen masters who led their disciples to enlightenment without much concern about method were active in China. It was not until a later period that the guidance of the masters evolved into a method leading to enlightenment, and that was the method of the koan. We shall now attempt to elucidate what the koan and the point of its practice are.

The practice of koans in Zen is one of the most remarkable phenomena in the history of religions. In spite of a wealth of literature on Zen Buddhism and specifically on the koan, it remains veiled in obscurity. We owe the best monograph on the subject in a Western language to Ruth Fuller Sasaki, an American Buddhist who was married to a Japanese Zen master. In the foreword to *The Zen Koan,* published by her and the Japanese Rinzai master Isshū Miura, she writes: "The koan is not a conundrum to be solved by a nimble wit. It is not a verbal psychiatric device for shocking the disintegrated ego of a student into some kind of stability. Nor, in my opinion, is it ever a paradoxical statement except to those who view it from outside. When the koan is resolved it is realized to be a simple and clear statement made from the state of consciousness which it has helped to awaken."[1]

The Origin of the Koan Practice　In inquiring after the historical origins of the koan, we soon notice that the preliminaries for this practice are familiar to us from the preceding history of Chinese Zen. The terse Zen masters of the T'ang period would often respond to their disciples' questions with quick, direct answers that were applicable to other situations as well and hence were passed down to further generations of followers. Nan-yüan Hui-yüng (d. 930) was the first we know to apply the words of earlier masters in the manner of the koan to the instruction and examination of his disciples. From the beginning, *mondō* (exchanges between master and disciple) were the favorite source of material for the koan. Besides these mondō, pointed expressions of the masters, anecdotes from the daily life of the Zen monastery and occasionally even verses from the sutras were used as koans. One of them was given the disciple, who was to solve it by concentrating and devoting all his attention to it until—as the Zen saying goes—his bite gave way, meaning that he gave up rational thinking and made headway into the suprarational realm of enlightenment.

But let us first consider the historical origins of the koan. The conversations, expressions, and episodes from the life of the early Zen masters provided ample material for the koans. Later masters and interpreters supplemented this fund with additional problems. The first collection of koans set down in writing is the sayings of Fen-yang Shan-chao (947–1024), actually comprising three groups of 100 koans each: the first, a collection of koans of the Elders, to which Fen-yang added a commentary in verse; then a collection of koans and answers he himself made up; finally another collection of old koans, this time with Fen-yang's own answers. The practice of koans became widespread in the Rinzai school that flourished in the Sung period in China and filled the countryside with monasteries led by proficient masters. The Rinzai monasteries of this time acted as a source of inspiration to Chinese spiritual life and greatly enriched Chinese culture. The influence of Zen is clearly evident in the emergent Neo-Confucianism of the time.

In the eighth generation after Lin-chi, the Rinzai school split into two branches, both of which were transplanted to Japan and continue to this day. The branch deriving from Yang-ch'i (992–1049) is largely responsible for the development of koan practice. Two great masters were active in this branch in the twelfth century: Yüan-wu K'o-ch'in (1063–1135) and Ta-hui Tsung-kao (1089–1163), whose names are indelibly entered into the history of the koan.

Yüan-wu K'o-ch'in, himself enlightened on the occasion of a koan-like conversation with his master, considered the practice of koans the best means to come to a realization of truth all his life. Only by way of the koan, he believed, could the spirit of the Sixth Patriarch be preserved in its purity. Credit is due him especially for the *Hekiganroku*, whose hundred cases (and the songs written to them by Hsüeh-tou

Ch'ung-hsien, 980–1052) he amply commentated in lectures to his disciples. A large following held him in the highest esteem.

Among Yüan-wu's many disciples, Ta-hui Tsung-kao was prominent. The story of his enlightenment is recorded in the annals as follows:

> One day when Yüan-wu had taken the high seat in the lecture hall, he said: "A monk asked Yün-men: 'From whence come all the buddhas?' Yün-men answered: 'The East Mountain walks over the water.' But if I were asked, I would not answer that way. 'From whence come all the buddhas?' A fragrant breeze comes of itself from the south, and in the palace pavilion a refreshing coolness stirs."[2]

Upon hearing these words, Ta-hui suddenly awakened to enlightenment. He became the Dharma successor to his master Yüan-wu.

Ta-hui attracted many disciples and led them with the help of the koan. When the Sung dynasty was overthrown in North China, he fled to the south and stayed with his former master Yüan-wu for a while. It is possible that he came to know there a master of the Ts'ao-tung school, Hung-chih Cheng-chüeh (1091–1157), who was visiting Yüan-wu at the time. Later Ta-hui had his own hermitage. He was called by imperial degree to direct a temple near the capital. There, the chronicle tells us, he was at the height of his activity and gathered some 1,700 disciples. But history knows him primarily for the passionate battle he waged against the sort of meditation practiced by the Ts'ao-tung (Japanese: Sōtō) house. Unlike his master Yüan-wu, a tolerant man who maintained good relations with the Ts'ao-tung school and even adapted some elements of its teaching to his own, Ta-hui was of a vigorous, aggressive nature. He kindled the opposition to the Ts'ao-tung school to a blazing controversy, accused his opponents of quietism, and called their sort of meditation the "false Zen of silent illumination." His own school came to be known controversially as the "Zen of gazing upon the word," that is, the koan.

We have here a variation of the confrontation between styles of meditation as it first arose in the Southern and Northern schools of Chinese Zen, and continued to flare up time and again. The issue derived from different positions on mysticism. The silent kind of meditation directed toward intuition, and not inappropriately called the "Zen of silent illumination," led in the extreme to quietism, familiar in the Occident as well as in East Asia. Opposed to it was a dynamic meditation, highly accentuated in the practice of koans. Its goal was a sudden experience of transcendent being evoked either by some adventitious perception or by nothing in particular.

As in the controversy between the Southern and Northern schools of Chinese Zen, it is not easy to specify the exact position of the opponent in the confrontation between koan Zen and the "Zen of silent illumination." Even according to Hung-chih, the representative of silent meditation, enlightenment is a knowledge that does not touch things, an illumination that does not make an object of reality. Hence he too advocated object-less meditation. He did not, incidentally, reject the practice of koans, but rather himself created new cases on occasion and composed verses to the models of the Elders. The controversy did not prevent the koan from becoming a general practice in Zen, with variations, of course, that we shall speak of later.

The Hekiganroku and Mumonkan Koan Collections The literal meaning of the Chinese *kung-an* (Japanese: *kōan*) is "public notice" or "public announcement." Some words of a master or an episode from his life are presented to the disciple as an example for practice and attaining enlightenment. Although the core layer of the koan cases consists of brief reports from the master's life, directives and comments are added by the meditation leader who presents the koan for practice. Short poems revealing the enlightened understanding of the Elders were especially popular. All this material is contained in a wealth of Zen literature, scattered throughout the numerous chronicles, collections of sayings, and treatises. The number of koan cases is estimated at 1,700, but if all the new compositions are counted, there are probably many more.

Some of the koan collections in Zen literature are prominent and contain much valuable material in a form that speaks to the practitioner. The *Hekiganroku* (Chinese: *Pi-yen-lu*) and the *Mumonkan* (Chinese: *Wu-men-kuan*) of the Sung period in China are the two most important. It will be worth our while to have a look at these two works of literary significance.

The hundred cases of the *Hekiganroku* paint a vivid picture of the world of the koan and the Zen movement in China. The *Hekiganroku* is an exacting work of literature. The structure of even a single case makes demands on the practitioner who wishes to appropriate all the material. Each piece consists of a directive, a core case, comment on the case, an explanation of the case, a song forming a second highlight, comments on the song, and an explanation of it. Hsüeh-tou collected the cases and composed the songs, and Yüan-wu furnished all the commentary. Hence each piece is a comprehensive and rather complex whole that can be mastered only with considerable effort.

One case should suffice to convince us of the superb literary and spiritual quality of the *Hekiganroku*. The very first koan treats of the encounter between Bodhidharma and the Chinese emperor Wu-ti, right after the Patriarch arrived in the golden Central Kingdom. This powerful opening suggests many of the leitmotifs of Zen. The two most important parts, the presentation of the case and the verse, based on Wilhelm Gundert's translation, read as follows:

Wu-ti asked the great master Bodhidharma: "What is the supreme meaning of the Sacred Truth?"

Bodhidharma said: "Vast emptiness, nothing sacred."

The Emperor asked again: "Who is standing before us?"

Bodhidharma replied: "I don't know." The Emperor was not content. Bodhidharma then crossed the river and went to Wei.

Later, the Emperor appealed to the noble Bau-dschi and inquired of him. The noble Bau-dschi said: "But surely Your Majesty knows, does he not, who that is?"

The Emperor replied: "I don't know."

Thereupon the noble Bau-dschi said: "That is the great hero Avalokiteśvara, who passes on the seal of the Buddha-mind." This caused the Emperor regret, and finally he dispatched a messenger to recall Bodhidharma.

But the noble Bau-dschi advised: "Better to tell no one, Your Majesty, that you wished to send a messenger to bring him back! The whole country could chase after him, and he would not turn around. . . ."[3]

To this Hsüeh-tou composed the poem:

Sacred Truth—Vast Emptiness!
How shall we know where it strikes?
Who is the man standing before us?
Who replies, I do not know.
Thus he escapes secretly across the river.

How are thorns not to grow around him?
Even if the whole country chases him,
  he does not come again,
And should centuries pine for him,
  it is to no avail.
Cease your longing!
A pure wind goes round the earth—
  where would it ever end?[4]

"Vast emptiness—nothing sacred." Bodhidharma's reply to the question of the supreme meaning of sacred truth forms the core of this koan. Gundert comments that "there are no barriers in this emptiness. In it there is no notion of sacred or profane. In it the individual and particular is superseded, no longer distinguishable. There even one word is too many."[5] Bodhidharma's reply, "I don't know," to the next question is not an evasion. No one can give a truer answer to the question of who he really is. (In fact, the question "Who am I?" is an original koan, practiced by a good number of truth-seekers.) In the last part of the case, where Bodhidharma vanishes, Gundert sees his figure as growing to invisible and supratemporal proportions. Bodhidharma does not return. He "can appear . . . only when people cease regarding the Patriarch as a historical phenomenon they might chase after."[6]

The *Mumonkan* collection, also known as the *Collection of Forty-eight Koans,* was compiled about one century later. As a piece of literature it is simpler and less demanding than the *Hekiganroku.* Intended more for practical use, it has filled its purpose a hundredfold. Japanese Zen masters esteem and prefer the koans of the *Mumonkan* precisely for their simplicity and succinctness. Since the Meiji era (1868–1912), some twenty or more works of explanation have appeared, and new commentaries on the *Mumonkan* are continually being published. Wu-men Hui-k'ai (1184–1260), the compiler of the forty-eight koans, was a prominent master of the Yang-chi branch of the Rinzai school and a leading representative of Zen during the last years of the Southern Sung dynasty. He collected cases comprising the entire Zen tradition, from its Indian antecedents to the masters of the Lin-chi and Ts'ao-tung schools, and added succinct, critical remarks well suited to prod the nagging doubts of the practitioner. The concluding verses, likewise from the pen of Wu-men himself, may not stand up to the highly poetic and profound verses of Hsüeh-tou. But, everything considered, the *Mumonkan's* koans are an excellent aid to progress along the way to enlightenment.

The first koan in the *Mumonkan* collection is not only the most famous of all, but also the most practiced as well. In the Zen tradition it is known as the *wu* or *mu* koan of Chao-chou.

A monk asked Chao-chou: "Does a dog also have Buddha-nature, or not?"

Chao-chou replied: "Mu."

The single ideogram, or word, *mu*, Master Wu-men explains, "is the one barrier to the gate of the Zen school. . . . Devote all your strength to this 'Mu.' If you do not let up, it will be like Dharma light ignited." There follows a verse by the master:

Dog—Buddha-nature:
The valid command is perfectly manifest.
Whoever remains between Being and Non-being
Loses his body and his life.

Everything is at stake. The practitioner must transcend both Being and Non-being. The mu (not) that is the solution lies beyond affirmation or negation. Immediate experience makes contact with the absolute.

Chao-chou (778–897), perhaps the most inventive of all Zen masters, was a disciple of Nan-ch'üan, hence in the lineage of Ma-tsu, and is a character in many koans of the *Mumonkan*. A bizarre story is told (Case 14) of how his master Nan-ch'üan once killed a cat that was the object of an argument among the monks. Hearing of his master's actions, Chao-chou put his sandals on his head—a gesture which Suzuki used any number of times to demonstrate the obvious irrationality of Zen. Another koan (Case 37) has Chao-chou answer the question of the meaning of Bodhidharma's coming from the West with: "the tree of life in front of the garden." Particularly characteristic of Chao-chou's understanding of Zen are the koans in which he shows the way, the Tao, to be the everyday. Thus a newcomer to the monastery asks to be shown the way, and Chao-chou replies: "Have you finished eating your rice gruel? . . . Then go wash your bowl!" Thereupon the monk gained enlightenment. Wu-men's corresponding verse is:

> Since it is all too clear,
> It takes time to grasp it.
> When you understand that it's foolish
>   to look for fire with fire,
> The meal is already cooked.[7]

The Significance of the Koan for the Zen Way   Of what significance is the koan for the Zen way? How is it practiced? What effects does this practice have on the practitioner? Answers to these questions will vary with one's position on the matter. We have quoted Ruth Fuller Sasaki, who attempted with some success to present koans as systematic and reasonable. D. T. Suzuki, on the other hand, toyed with the paradoxical character of koans and marveled at their extreme irrationality all his life. It is likely that both views contain a kernel of truth. There is method to the irrationality, but reason alone is bound to fall short of the koan.

Mental concentration is the first effect of exerted koan practice. In fact, a very high degree of concentration hardly possible otherwise can be attained. The practitioner, concentrating on the koan literally day and night, enters a hyperalert state in which he is aware of one thing only: the koan. This concentration gives rise to a search—at first for the solution to the koan. Utilizing all his intellectual powers, as he naturally would, the practitioner exerts himself with all his might, but to no avail. The illogical nature of the koan resists logical solution. He then enters into a state of helplessness and runs up against the same wall again and again, like someone locked in a small room. He searches for a way out, and yet the door is open—not where his intellect is aimed, however, for the wall does not give in. To see the opening, a one-hundred-and-eighty-degree turnabout is necessary, in the direction of another, novel dimension. D. T. Suzuki's early essays give a psychological description of this process in terms of accumulation, saturation, and explosion. Such terms present a picture of psychic violence in the koan exercise. As a matter of fact, the number of accounts, both contemporary and old, that describe an explosive occurrence in the mind as a result of an intense struggle with the koan is not few. Still, Zen masters also make a far milder comparison with the baby chick that pecks at the eggshell until it breaks out.

We know with any certainty little about the actual form the practice of koans took in early times. It seems that the practice of koans was always connected with a master's individual instruction of a disciple.

All of Zen literature testifies to a very close relationship between master and disciple. What the guru is in India, the "old master" (Japanese: *rōshi*) is for the Zen Buddhism of East Asia. Sure progression along the way of enlightenment is unthinkable without him. It is the koan exercise that best defines the master's role. In former times, the disciple chose his koan himself; today the master usually determines which koan is to be practiced. But in any case, the master supervises the exercise. This occurs primarily during the formal interview (Japanese: *dokusan*), in which the disciple reports to his master on the progress of his practice, on his experiences, or even on disturbances, especially the visions, fantasies, or hallucinations known as *makyō* ("devil's realm")—be they terrifying or exhilarating, they must be unconditionally dismissed. During the practice sessions (Japanese: *sesshin*), each disciple has, if possible, a daily interview with the master for instruction, encouragement, and correction. Such practice sessions resemble in their own way the periods of intensive instruction which, according to the Pāli canon, Shākyamuni gave his disciples each year during the monsoon season. In Zen monasteries, disciples spend the practice session almost uninterrupted in meditation, which includes both zazen and the koan exercise.

The approach to the koan varies with school and master. The content of the koan might, for example, be analyzed and its parts viewed separately, or else it might be grasped as a whole and appropriated to one's inner self. Zen masters are completely at liberty to treat the koan in different manners at different times. During the practice sessions they devote most of their *teishō*, or daily lectures, to the cases in the koan collections, and comment on the expressions and contents at length. There they also find occasion to clarify Buddhist doctrines, but they never fail to exhort the disciples to practice without cease, for that alone can bring about the point of all the exercises—inner realization.

The koans themselves contain suggestions for summarizing their content in one clue word (Japanese: *jakugo*). This treatment is also popular among Zen masters. One condenses the entire koan into a word and then concentrates on it. He carries this word around with him and constantly turns it over in his mind. Zen literature compares this process to a ball of fire that one tosses about in his mouth, wanting to spit it out but unable to do so. The word might be continually repeated, murmured, or exclaimed vigorously. Chao-chou's mu koan is often practiced in this manner today. This is a vast simplification of the koan, practically reducing it to its function of inducing concentration.

Whether the full sense of the koan's content is realized in this fashion is doubtful. In any case, there is a clear resemblance here to another religious exercise: the constant repetition of the name of the Buddha Amida, the so-called *nembutsu*. Throughout his life D. T. Suzuki explicitly pointed out this similarity.

The Koan Exercise from the Viewpoint of the History of Religions   The koan is a Chinese invention and displays typical characteristics of Chinese mentality: above all, a practicality bearing on concrete life. Whereas the Indian seeks after the essence in things and beyond them, the Chinese always keeps in contact with reality in his everyday life. Any situation can become a koan for him, since it manifests the problem of being. The verbal exchanges, clue words, and episodes we have noted are entirely consonant with the early Chinese masters' concrete manner of teaching. Later generations, no longer as creative and inventive, consciously used them as a method to give proper guidance to the growing number of disciples. This was not a process of degeneration, but rather a systematic application of the Elders' spontaneous, natural manner of teaching. The koan method may indicate a decrease in creativity, but it also points to the zeal and sense of responsibility later generations had for continuing the way of sudden enlightenment.

The koan method built into the Zen way of enlightenment is, from the viewpoint of the history of religions, absolutely unique. No exercise of essentially the same nature appears in any other mysticism, neither in the Orient nor in the Occident. Other aspects of the Zen way touch upon the Indian roots, but there is no concentration exercise similar to koans in Indian spirituality. The koan exercise represents the final stage in the development of method in the Zen way of enlightenment.

In this context, Martin Buber's remarks on Chassidism and Zen Buddhism are of great interest. Buber was aware of the distinct character of the Zen way, and called the koan "a genre absolutely peculiar to Zen."[8] But at the same time, he was deeply impressed by the resemblance he saw between Zen and Chassidism. Both contained for him "legendary anecdotes" combined with a completely unique master-disciple relationship. In fact, some Chassidic tales might be taken for episodes in the koan literature. A disciple of Baalschem, for example, when asked what his deceased teacher considered most important, replies: "Whatever he was just doing."[9] Or another disciple, asked what had been of upmost significance for his teacher, Rabbi Mosche von Kobryn, answers: "At all times, whatever he happened to be doing"[10] A Zen disciple might well have made the same reply.

The master-disciple relationship in Zen particularly captured Buber's attention. "The relation between teacher and student," he wrote, "is central to both Zen and Chassidism. Just as there is apparently no other people for whom the corporal bond between generations is as significant as in China or Israel, there is no other religious movement that I know of which links its intuition of the spirit with the concept of spiritual propagation, to the degree that Zen and Chassidism did. In both of these, human truth is venerated, paradoxically, not in the form of a possession but in the form of a movement. . . ."[11] Buber saw something very profound here. It is not easy to find examples of a master-disciple relationship as immediate and dynamic as those in Zen and Chassidism.

Nevertheless, Gershom Scholem, that great specialist in Judaic mysticism, is right when he classifies the Zen koans and the Chassidic legends as two different categories.[12] The Chassidic legends, he stresses, contain an inherent meaningfulness not attributable to the koan stories. Where the koans are handed down in their pure form (as in the koan collections), they serve as a means to break through the conscious mind. As Master Wu-men says in his preface to the *Mumonkan*, they are like "bricks to batter at the gate," aids with which "the ancient masters . . . led the learners according to their capacity."

What is most striking in viewing Chassidism together with Zen is the similarity of finding truth in an encounter with concrete reality. Buber's discovery that absolute truth can be experienced in the concrete I-Thou encounters of everyday life is confirmed by Zen, especially by the koan exercise. In the case of the Zen disciple, there is of course no I-Thou encounter, but rather an awakening to a profound experience of being by way of an encounter with concrete reality. Buber cites a number of examples in Zen that for him exhibit an intimate contact with concrete things: the story of Buddha holding up the flower and Kāśyapa smiling and grasping the meaning; of the master who was asked about transcendence and showed the disciple his wooden staff, "as if to oppose generalities with the concrete," Buber explains; or the story of the teacher who raises his finger, or who shouts katsu, or who deals the disciple a blow. It is always a case of concrete things leading to understanding. Buber sums up: "Through the activity of one's entire spiritual-corporeal being one makes intimate contact with concrete reality; in intimate contact with concrete reality one is able to grasp truth; and the grasp of truth leads in turn to the highest concentration of action."[13]

This passage shows a deep understanding of the Zen way. The activity of the integral body-mind leads the Zen disciple through zazen meditation and koan exercise to the enlightened experience of Being, which lets him see everyday things as they are. He lives in the here and now, and takes joy in things, just as the Chassidist in Buber's interpretation finds delight in the world.

Before concluding these considerations, I would like to repeat that the koan, as a literary genre and an exercise on the way to enlightenment, is of a particular character unique to the Zen way. At the same time, we were able to surmise the possibility of understanding the koan in a broader sense. It comes as no surprise, then, that advocates of Christian Zen look for Christian koans. H. M. Enomiya-Lassalle is convinced of the benefit of the koan for meditation and feels that for Christians certain problems arising from the Christian faith are suitable koan exercises, insofar as they are not rationally soluble. They can help one break through to higher states of consciousness. The Irish Jesuit William Johnston, who likewise lives in Japan, finds the Christian koan epitomized in the Bible. Many enigmatic passages in the Scriptures can become koans in his view. Johnston cites the beginning of the first letter to the Corinthians, then passages from the Gospels such as "Let the dead bury the dead," "Who loves his life shall lose it," or "I am the grapevine, you are the grapes." Indeed the entire Bible is a koan in Johnston's view, and he finds confirmation in a Buddhist monk who told his Christian friend that Christians too would gain enlightenment if they knew how to read their own Holy Scriptures."[14]

If the koan is a singular and unique product of Zen Buddhism, its dynamic elements are nevertheless universally human and touch upon human existence. Hence koans can be said to be important for religious people regardless of their faith. Intuition of a koan, eminently existential in its concreteness, can be a decisive step on the way of self-realization and enlightenment.

EIGHT

Zen Buddhism in Japan

The Religious Climate Buddhism has deeply influenced the religious climate of Japan. But Buddhism adapted to Japan and received the particular imprint of that country to no less a degree. From the time of the introduction of the Buddhist religion, the Japanese people were impressed with its wealth of new religious themes, above all with the prospect of final salvation it promised. In addition, Japan was vastly enriched, culturally and artistically, by Buddhism, which from the beginning sank deep roots into the soil and readily intermingled with Shintō, the indigenous religion. And along with the teachings of Buddhism came Buddhist meditation.

Zen Buddhism did not appear until a later phase, after a considerable number of Buddhist schools had been introduced from China and Korea. The transplanting of the Zen school along organizational lines occurred during the Kamakura period (1185–1336), religiously the most vigorous era in Japanese history. In the three reform schools of Zen, the Amida faith, and Nichiren, Buddhism reached a new peak, perhaps not as powerful in exterior institutions as in the Heian period (794–1185), but excelling in a genuine interiority arising from the depths of the people. During this epoch beset with wars and misery, religious spirituality stands in sharp contrast with the worsening social and political conditions that aroused a general feeling of decline. This religious sentiment found a spontaneous expression in Buddhism. Buddhist theology took up the ancient apocalyptic prophecy of the three ages of the Buddha Law: the genuine fulfillment of the Dharma, the conventional observation of the Dharma, and the degenerate final Dharma *(mappō)*. It was believed that this final period of decline had begun.

The great epic of those days, the *Heike monogatari* (The Tale of the

Heike), paints a dramatic picture of the history of the noble Taira clan, its rise to power under the domineering figure of Kiyomori, and its speedy defeat by the Minamoto clan. The opening verses of the tale clearly betray a Buddhist tone:

> The sound of the bell of the Gion temple echoes
>   the impermanence of all things.
> The hue of the flowers of the Sāla trees declares
>   that they who flourish must be brought low.
> Yea, the proud ones are but for a moment,
>   like an evening dream in springtime.
> The mighty are destroyed at the last,
>   they are but as the dust before the wind.[1]

According to one of the sutras, the bell or bells in this passage were said to have hung in the Hall of Impermanence in the Jetavana-vihāra, the first monastery erected for the Buddha, by the wealthy disciple Sudatta. Jetavana, the name of a grove where the Buddha preached, became Gion in Japanese translation. Gion became the name of a district of Kyoto, that unfortunate old capital of peace so often set aflame in the centuries of struggle. In the last part of the *Heike monogatari*, a Buddhist temple bell, this time of Jakkō-in, convent of repose and light, sounds once more and awakens the hope of the enlightened peace of nirvana in one's heart. Between the two bell tolls of impermanence and nirvana, human life takes place—the *Heike monogatari* becomes the playground of all human passions, full of struggle and intrigue, blood and tears, burning houses, lovers, and the dying, upon whose bodies fall the blossoms of the plum and the cherry. In Buddhist terms this is the world of saṃsāra, setting the Japanese people in motion.

It was this religious climate, permeated by Buddhist sentiment, that was dominant during the Kamakura period when Zen was introduced to Japan and began to spread. The outspoken religious motives of Buddhism came to full fruition in this atmosphere. The opening verses to the *Heike monogatari* lead us back to the origins of Buddhism. The conclusion to the first verse (*shogyō mujō*—"the impermanence of all things") is part of the Japanese translation of the Buddha's Four Noble Truths, and the second verse mentions Sāla, or teak trees, because it was in a grove of such trees near Kushinagara that Shākyamuni entered the peace of nirvana. These ancient Buddhist themes are entirely familiar to Japanese Buddhism, including Zen.

Japanese Zen masters make ample use of the theme of impermanence to lead their disciples to the non-attachment they deem absolutely necessary on the path of enlightenment.

Japanese Zen Buddhism partakes of the Buddhist path of salvation within Japanese history and surrounded by this religious climate. In their existential plight, the Japanese people of the Kamakura period expected liberation of the Buddha religion. They strived to grasp salvation in meditation. All branches of Japanese Buddhism employ absorption (Sanskrit: samādhi; Japanese: *zammai*), which in a broad sense signifies all experiential realization of truth. Zen has a prominent place in Japanese Buddhism because of its pronounced emphasis on meditation and enlightenment.

The Transplanting of Zen Buddhism   Zen Buddhism was introduced to Japan from China through the Rinzai and Sōtō schools, which flourished during the Sung period. History reckons Eisai (1141–1215), the first to transmit the Rinzai tradition to Japan, as the founder of Japanese Zen. Dōgen (1200–1253) transplanted the line of transmission of his Chinese Zen master Ju-ching. He rejected any formation of sects within Buddhism and wanted nothing to do with a Zen sect. The Zen that he taught his disciples was in his view nothing other than the line of enlightenment proceeding from Shākyamuni, the founder of Buddhism. Later, however, the Zen school of Dōgen was organized as the Sōtō sect and became quite widespread.

Besides these two pioneers, many other Japanese Buddhist monks journeyed to China and exposed themselves to the mysteries of Zen. Hardly less numerous were the Chinese masters who went to Japan in the following decades and were paid the highest respect in the Japanese Zen monasteries. For several generations a vast network of contacts existed between Japanese and Chinese Zen Buddhism.

The first prominent centers of Zen life and culture were the so-called Five Mountains *(Gozan)*, the five great monasteries of the Rinzai school situated in Kyoto and Kamakura, the two capitals of the times. These centers, founded as places of religious practice in emulation of the Five Mountains in China, disseminated art and culture throughout the land.

In Zen, that which is most Chinese in Chinese Buddhism was transmitted to Japan. The Japanese had been in continual contact with the Asian mainland since their early history and had always held China in great esteem. The accounts of the period under treatment here testify to an unbounded willingness and fervor in their reception of Zen. Contrary to the Buddhist schools of a more Indian tint introduced earlier to Japan, Zen made an impact on the Japanese precisely because of its Chinese character. The practical religion of Zen, born in China and directed to concrete life, fulfilled the wishes of the Japanese.

The transplanting took place during the Sung period, after Zen had reached its peak in China, but at a time when monasteries (particularly those of the Rinzai school) were culturally influential and attracted the Chinese mentality epitomized in the Neo-Confucianism of the Chu Hsi school. We know that practically all the leading Neo-Confucianists of that time established connections with Zen. It comes as no surprise, then, that from the Great Land of Sung (as the Japanese chronicles call it), Zen and Neo-Confucianism were transported to Japan on the same ships, often by the same people. The Five Mountains of the Rinzai school in Kyoto and Kamakura were simultaneously centers of Confucian scholarship. Many Zen monasteries in Japan had *tera-koya* (temple schools) attached to them where Chinese schooling, especially Confucianism, was given. Many of the highly educated Zen monks were equally learned in Buddhism and Confucianism. As D. T. Suzuki put it, they were "Buddhist Confucianists," or perhaps Confucian Buddhists.

Zen Schools in Japan   Rinzai and Sōtō were long the only Zen schools and remained the representative form of Japanese Zen even after the little-known Ōbaku sect was introduced from China in the seventeenth century. As far as teaching is concerned, there is little difference between the two. Both embody authentic Zen (in their outlook on life as well), and follow in the lineage of the Sixth Patriarch, Hui-neng. If one looks for points of difference in content, he will find only variations in styles, which are indeed clearly distinguishable.

However, one cannot simplify the matter so crudely as to say that in Rinzai the koan is practiced, whereas Sōtō is devoted exclusively to meditation in the lotus posture, or zazen. The koan is practiced in Sōtō Zen as well, not merely in exceptional cases, but with some masters regularly and vigorously. Likewise, in Rinzai monasteries practice without meditation in the lotus posture is absolutely unthinkable. Ruth Fuller Sasaki, the American Buddhist who was ordained in the Rinzai school and directed a hermitage within the Daitoku-ji monastery in Kyoto until her death, wrote that "supported by faith in this teaching, these early Zen masters forged ahead with indomitable courage to gain this realization for themselves through the method Shākyamuni had used and advocated, that is, meditation." She emphatically concludes that "meditation certainly remained the basic practice. Though methods of meditation were developed in Zen that differed from those in other Buddhist sects, whether of Indian or Chinese origin, we have no evidence that meditation itself was ever abandoned or neglected. . . ."[2] By this she means that Zen meditation in the lotus posture was practiced in all Zen monasteries of Japan.

In the style of practice, of course, differences between Rinzai and Sōtō, or even within the same school, are not few. One can rightly speak of a plurality of styles that continues to increase in the wake of the creative endeavors of masters and disciples. Frequently the differences concern only subtleties in the treatment of the koan or the sitting meditation valued by the practitioners. Naturally, the most palpable distinctions exist in the realm of organization—by sect and lineage, head temple and branch temple.

Because of its influence on the noble and samurai ruling classes, Rinzai Zen outflanked all other Buddhist schools in Japan toward the end of the Kamakura period and during the following Muromachi period (1336–1568). In comparison with the mighty Rinzai school, Sōtō Zen, with its center in the Eihei-ji monastery, had a rather modest existence, but it also developed into a powerful sect with numerous adherents during the course of the centuries. Today both Rinzai and Sōtō are significant establishments in Japan, comprising universities and schools of all sorts, social work and printing presses, as well as their monastery centers and temples in the cities and the country.

The ethical dimension of Japanese Zen—that is, its Confucian element—grew out of its historical links with China and is evident in many writings of Japanese Zen masters. Even after the Tokugawa regime enforced a strict separation of Buddhism and Confucianism at the turn of the seventeenth century, Zen monks retained their Confucianist ethic and educated their disciples in this attitude. Two Zen masters distinguished for their ethic, as different from one another as they were in other respects, were Suzuki Shōsan (1579–1653) of the Sōtō school and Hakuin Ekaku (1685–1768) of Rinzai.

We could well devote an entire chapter to Hakuin, the greatest Japanese Rinzai master.[3] This eminent figure was unusually many-sided and possessed a brilliant personality. During his long life he had many inner experiences of astounding intensity. But he also engaged in outward activities as a director of numerous disciples and an educator of the populace. His drawings and calligraphy show that he was a highly gifted artist. Furthermore, his name is closely linked to the koan exercise.

We have attempted to clarify the nature of this remarkable meditative practice in portraying the rise of the koan in Chinese Zen, without, however, depicting the individual forms of the exercise. In the context of the history of Zen in China, koan-like peculiarities in the comportment of Chinese Zen masters often came to light. The Zen master Hakuin perfected the koan exercise in Japan and, we may say, in general. He is the source of the famous koan so often practiced to our day: "If someone claps his hands, a sound arises. Listen to the sound of the single hand!"

In Hakuin's view, the koan is particularly suited to awaken the Great Doubt *(taigi)* in the practitioner. Hakuin himself experienced this state of mind and characterized it with much psychological subtlety. He knew how to push his disciples to the extremes of nagging doubt—so important to him because of the conviction based on his experience that the greater the doubt, the more intense the experience of enlightenment.

Ways (Dō) and Arts   Throughout the entire history of East Asia, China and Japan have been closely allied in spirit and culture. We would do well to regard this fact in as many contexts as possible. To this very day in Japan there has existed an immense respect and deeply rooted reverence for the Chinese. Nevertheless, the Japanese have always retained a degree of independence, which is also manifest in their reception of Zen. Zen in Japan bears the particular imprint of that country. This we can observe in the Japanese "ways" and arts inspired by Zen.

A large number of arts and skills are called "way" *(dō)* in Japan. There is a way of flowers *(kadō)*, a way of tea *(sadō)*, a way of the sword *(kendō)*, of archery *(kyūdō)*, of self-defense *(jūdō)*, a way of poetry *(kadō)*, and of calligraphy *(shodō)*. The wealth of Zen-inspired arts likewise includes ink drawing and the style of gardening that gave rise to so many magnificent temple gardens in Japan. How closely the ways and arts are connected to Zen meditation depends upon the individual case, but all the above arts are inspired by the spirit of Zen. That does not mean that every masterful work or artistic accomplishment arises directly from a state of enlightenment, nor that these arts provide a sure access to religious experience. But we do know that such great Japanese artists as Sesshū and Bashō (1644–94) were far advanced along the Zen way and had attained some realization. Quite a few Zen masters, the most prominent being Hakuin, made a name for themselves in art. Anyone who has witnessed a Zen master in a state of inner concentration form a circle or a Chinese ideogram with a single stroke of the brush will not doubt the intimate relation between Zen and art. The same state of mind is expressed in artistic creation as in meditation. To be sure, the religious experience of satori is something different from artistic activity. Not every religiously advanced person possesses the skills necessary for the creation of art works, and inner experience is not the only measure of artistic perfection. But Zen does provide a spiritual atmosphere in which ways and arts can be developed. The sources of art genuinely inspired by Zen are deep.

The effect of the spirit of Zen on ways and arts exhibits something characteristic of Japanese Zen—namely, its proximity to nature and everyday things. The particularly Japanese feeling for nature finds expression in the Zen arts more than anywhere else. Visitors to modern Japan and Japanese who today travel widely throughout their own country find this sense of nature portrayed in the Zen gardens of the ancient capital, Kyoto, in a way visible to everyone. And the art historian can appreciate it more deeply in the works of Sesshū and Bashō, who epitomized Zen art in their drawings and poetry.

Sesshū's ink drawings *(sumie)* give an incomparably delicate yet forceful picture of the life and activity of nature. As depicted in his masterwork of the four seasons, nature is continually changing. This is an artistic portrayal of the Zen philosophy of becoming. Realism and symbolism are inextricably interwoven.

Bashō's poems bring world acclaim to Japanese literature. Lyrical poetry is of course tied to a language, never adequately conveyed in foreign tongues. The Japanese haiku, consisting of three lines of five, seven, and five syllables respectively, has a brevity and wealth of connotation totally resistant to translation. The spirit of Zen permeates Bashō's haiku. Here the fusion with nature is complete; nature lives its own interior life in these haiku and touches the depths of the reader. The most famous haiku of Bashō, in Donald Keene's translation, reads:

> The ancient pond—
> A frog leaps in,
> The sound of water.[4]

Other haiku immersed in the spirit of Zen are:

Such stillness
The cries of the cicadas
Sink into the rocks.

Why am I aging so
this autumn?
A bird flying into the clouds.

On a journey, ill—
and my dreams, on withered fields
are wandering still.[5]

Since the transformation of nature indicates impermanence and fore-shadows death, a nameless melancholy underlies Japanese poetry about nature. Life and death are bound together in Zen as in nature. Turning to the things of everyday life, sadness is dispelled. The natural and reverential simplicity of dealing with everyday things finds its consummation in the way of tea. Here a solemnity befitting all reality is given to a common, everyday occurrence. "Everyday things are the Tao" and "Every day is a good day" are expressions of the basic wisdom of Zen, superbly illustrated in the cult of tea. The conduct exhibited in the tea ceremony, when the precious yet everyday drink is enjoyed in common, is exemplary for all daily activities. All things are to be treated with the same caring yet simple reverence. Such an attitude toward things springs from the spirit of Zen and nourishes its realization.

The Zen ways and arts draw a bridge from real artistic creation (in painting, architecture, poetry) to artistic skills like flower arrangement and gardening, and ultimately to all of everyday life. Zen thus becomes a formative source of life. The religious is found in the everyday, the sacred in the profane; indeed the everyday is religious, the profane is sacred. On the one hand, the history of Japanese Zen clearly shows the process of secularization; on the other, Zen retains a religious core through the centuries. Let us conclude our persual with an attempt to clarify this matter further.

The Sacred and the Profane: The Law of Buddha and the Law of the World
In the ways and arts inspired by Zen a spiritual dimension, attributable primarily to Zen meditation, is clearly discernible, though of course not to the same degree in all arts. On the other hand, a process of increasing secularization begins with the first phase of these cultural

developments and continues through the centuries of Japanese history. Three names representative of Zen art and the tendency toward secularization can be mentioned here: Musō Kokushi (1275–1351), Ikkyū (1394–1481), and Kobori Enshū (1579–1647).

Musō Kokushi, whose monastic name was Soseki, is regarded as the leading figure in Zen at the beginning of the Muromachi period. He was as important for the religious movement of the time as for the creative activity in the arts inspired by Zen. His writings breathe the spirit of Shākyamuni and teach a Zen way based upon an existential insight into impermanence and directed toward an experience of transcendent Being. An art thoroughly imbued with spirituality was preserved for later generations in the gardens attributed to him. As the abbot of the Tenryū-ji monastery and, for a time, of Nanzen-ji, he lived and worked for the monastic community, but he also considered the things of the world important and devoted considerable attention to them.

About one century later there lived in Kyoto the Zen monk Ikkyū. He was the center of the Zen movement in the latter half of the Muromachi period. Filled with Buddhist religiosity and gripped by a sense of the impermanence of all things, he set about helping his fellow men achieve liberating insight. Still, he remained bound up with worldly things. His humorous folk songs show an understanding of the cares of the world and human weaknesses, but a trace of critical rationalism can also be heard.

If the religious and the worldly are balanced in Ikkyū, the profane definitely predominates in Kobori Enshū, the third representative Zen artist, who was active and influential early in the Edo period (1603–1868). The tearoom and gardens of the Katsura Rikyū, the famous Edo-period imperial villa in Kyoto, are connected with his name. Just as Zen painting reached its consummate form in Sesshū and haiku in Bashō, Zen-inspired architecture and gardening were perfected in the secular Katsura villa, unexcelled in the beauty of its simplicity. We know little about Kobori Enshū's roots in religion, but his relation to Zen Buddhism is proved clearly enough by the fact that he finally became a monk, spent the last years of his life in a monastery, and was buried in the Daitoku-ji cemetery. Yet it was in secular ways and arts that his religiosity found expression.

The Zen arts, like the Zen way, originated in China, but in their Japanese form display something characteristic of Zen Buddhism in Japan—namely, the unity of religion and the secular, of the sacred and the profane. It is worth noting that the Zen movement of both the

Rinzai and Sōtō schools at first attracted the aristocracy in Japan, but eventually both turned to the common people and bore much fruit among them. This direction can be traced back to the early periods of Japanese Buddhism, when such significant figures as Dōgen and Ikkyū proclaimed their love for the people. This movement came to fruition during the Edo period, when many Zen masters preached in a manner that spoke to the people and wrote in an easily understood Japanese. The discourses and treatises of that time frequently thematized the unity of religion and life, and the Zen masters formulated the principle of the identity of the Buddha Law and the law of the world. Secular life, it was held, is not opposed to the practice of the Buddha religion; both arise from the same source and are basically the same: the Law of Buddha is identical with the law of the world. Although this was not actually a novel view, it was newly and emphatically articulated in Japanese Buddhism. It helped the masters to construct a social ethic for lay people that did justice to life in society, and especially to work. Monks as well as laymen were to actively promote the common good. Under no circumstances were monks to look down upon secular people. Such views do not rescind the classical Zen doctrine of practice and enlightenment; rather, consequences for practical life and a sound morality for the people are drawn from the basic religious insights of Zen.

By equating the Buddha Law with the law of the world, Zen fulfills a basic requirement of all spirituality: the need for a unity between religion and life, God and world, sacred and profane. Interior conduct in Zen is not cut off from the world, as shown by its love for nature, artistic creativity, everyday activity, and social ethic—all of them expressions of an attitude fundamentally open to the world, eliciting joy and delighting people. Here Zen is in the neighborhood of many forms of mysticism. Just as Martin Buber saw "the gap between God and the world closed" in Chassidism,[6] so too are the sacred and the profane, the Law of Buddha and the law of the world inseparably bound together. Joy in the world and openness toward it find their full justification, despite the Buddhist sense of impermanence and sorrow. The experience of an ultimate unity between God and the world evokes delight in man, though the interpretation of this experience will vary widely with the particular religion or weltanschauung.

In our venture into the history of Japanese religions we encountered many novel elements in the development of Zen Buddhism. The breadth of Zen in Japan is indeed astounding. We were able to mention only a few historical facts, but did not overlook the cultural and artistic phenomena associated with Zen. Moreover, it seemed important to touch upon the generally neglected attempts of Zen to reach the ordinary people and their life in Japanese society.

NINE

Dōgen, The Master of Zazen

THE PROCESS OF SECULARIZATION that appeared in connection with the cultural developments of the Zen way was, however, only one component in the history of Japanese Zen. Other tendencies arose that, while rooted in the religious foundation of Zen Buddhism, were in part diametrically opposed to secularization. It is preeminently Dōgen, perhaps the greatest figure of all in Japanese Buddhism, who represented the religious efforts of Zen in Japan. Dōgen is highly revered not only within the Sōtō school of Zen that derives from him, but in all Japanese Buddhist schools and, over and above the confines of Buddhism, by the Japanese people in general. If his particular significance ultimately arises from his religious character, his accomplishment was twofold. First of all, Dōgen is the recognized master of zazen, and, as such, one of the best guides to the way of enlightenment. Furthermore, the endeavors of his thinking gave a new integration to the core of Buddhist teaching. His works serve as a source of inspiration for the only original philosophical school of Japan, the so-called Kyoto school of Kitarō Nishida (1870–1945). Because of his unique place in the history of Japanese religions, we shall treat of Dōgen's life and work more fully, particularly with respect to the two aspects of his accomplishment. We begin by honoring him as the master of zazen.

Life and Character Early in his childhood and later in his youth, Dōgen had two bitterly painful, yet salutary, experiences that were to be decisive for his spiritual way of life. As a child of only two years, he lost his father, and with the death of his mother five years later, an indelible impression of the impermanence of all earthly things sank deep into his heart. An offspring of nobility, he had a brilliant career open to him. But at the age of twelve he left the house of the uncle who had fostered him and entered the monastic life, though during the feudal age this step by itself did not necessarily mean a lifelong renunciation of the world. On Mount Hiei, the center of the powerful Tendai sect and a locus of Buddhist scholarship, he put his efforts into studying the scriptures. But—and this is the second decisive experience—mere knowledge could not satisfy him; his search was for more, for the very heart of truth.

Like other now famous contemporaries of his, Dōgen eventually left Mount Hiei. After several futile peregrinations, he once more came into contact with Zen, this time at the Kennin-ji monastery of Kyoto, where Eisai had implanted Zen after returning from China. There Dōgen perceived the hiatus that lay between theory and teaching on the one hand, and practice and experience on the other. He realized that only practice and experience would bring him the goals he aspired to, and in pursuit of the sources, he crossed the sea to China in 1223 and went directly to the Zen monastery on Mount Tien-ts'ung. There he practiced earnestly, but did not at first find complete satisfaction. Again he took to wandering, until he went back to Mount Tien-ts'ung. By that time the abbot had died and a new master, Ju-ching (1163–1268), led a large congregation on the way to enlightenment. Dōgen had already had minor experiences and soon attained the Great Enlightenment. The experiences and knowledge he gained in China remained decisive his entire life.

Returning to Japan in 1227, he first took up residence again at Kennin-ji, but no longer found the original spirit of serious practice and strict discipline present there. Thus on the outskirts of Kyoto he founded a new center for practice as he understood it. Later, after several preparatory attempts, a new monastery called Kōshōhōrin-ji, or Kōshō-ji for short, was established for the increasing number of his disciples. There Dōgen stayed eleven years, guiding many able people. From the viewpoint of the influence he exerted, these years were the highlight of his life. But in 1243, while still in his prime, Dōgen retreated to the solitude of the mountains in Echizen Province, where a lay disciple had bequeathed him a plot of land. The monastery established there was called Eihei-ji, the Temple of Eternal Peace. To this day it remains the center of the Sōtō school of Zen that traces back to Dōgen.

The strength of Dōgen's character is best disclosed in his works, but in the course of his life the essential traits are already visible. First of all, there is his strong resolve and tremendous willpower to attain his goals without the least hesitation. Each stage of his life indicates a step forward: becoming a Buddhist monk, studying on Mount Hiei; journeying to China, practicing and attaining enlightenment under Master Ju-ching; then developing and spreading the Zen movement in Japan. In fulfilling his vocation, he took a tremendous workload upon himself. In addition to establishing two centers for the practice of Zen and guiding numerous disciples, he produced one of the most comprehensive literary works in Japanese Zen, unexcelled in quality. His main work, the ninety-five-chapter *Shōbōgenzō*, is the most significant of its kind in Japanese Zen literature.

In Japanese Buddhism, Dōgen is preeminent for the pure integrity of his character. In a critical study of Japanese Buddhism, the scholar Shōkō Watanabe names magic, formalism, political involvement, and disregard of the monastic rule as its principal faults in the course of its history. Watanabe sees Dōgen as the outstanding exception, one of the few eminent Japanese Buddhists who observed the monastic rule all their lives.[1] In spite of his relationship with people of high standing, he scrupulously avoided any connections with the imperial court. Although toward the end of his life he accepted an invitation by the military government to go to Kamakura for a time, he refused its offer to erect a monastery for him there. He likewise rejected the gift of a fief in Echizen Province and is said to have thrown out of the monastery the monk-disciple Gemmyō, who brought him the deeds to the feudal estate. Although later, after twice refusing the luxurious purple robe sent as an imperial gift, he finally agreed to accept it, he did not wear it even once during his lifetime.

Dōgen was a perpetual questioner and seeker. For him nothing in this constantly fluctuating life was ultimate. Even the experience of enlightenment did not mean a final, static condition to him. As he taught and lived, the enlightened one must be one who practices. This point brings us to the heart of practice, as Dōgen conceived it.

The Promotion of Zazen Dōgen's first work, written in the classical Chinese style, bears the title *The Universal Promotion of the Principles of Zazen* (Fukanzazengi). Upon his return from China, he was concerned with familiarizing the people of Japan with the practice of zazen as he had learned it on the mainland. In China he had realized that the practice of zazen was the quintessence of the Buddhist way of enlightenment.

"Why do people no longer practice?"—this was the question that plagued Dōgen in face of the indifference of his fellow Japanese monks. He arose to confront his contemporaries with the exhortation: "You should therefore cease from practice based on intellectual understanding, pursuing words, and following after speech, and learn the backward step that turns your light inwardly to illuminate your self. Body and mind of themselves will drop away, and your original face will be manifest. If you want to attain suchness, you should practice suchness without delay."[2]

Thereupon he gives precise instructions: One should sit on two cushions, placed one on top of the other, in a quiet room, in the full or half lotus position, the left hand placed on the right, thumb tips touching. "Thus sit upright in correct bodily posture, neither inclining to the left nor to the right, neither leaning forward nor backward." All one's efforts should be directed at overcoming the inner unrest that arises from discursive thinking: "Cast aside all involvements and cease all affairs. Do not think good or bad. Do not administer pros and cons. Cease all the movements of the conscious mind, the gauging of all thoughts and views. Have no designs on becoming a Buddha. This has nothing whatever to do with sitting or lying down."[3]

Dōgen concludes his description of zazen meditation with the notable words: "This . . . is the essential art of zazen. . . . It is simply the Dharma-gate of repose and bliss. . . ." Yet this last characterization should not blind us to the fact that the practice of zazen requires a great deal of effort and that this state of inner harmony and blissful repose can only be attained by way of persistant practice.

For this reason Dōgen never tires of exhorting the disciple to constant, vigorous practice. To illustrate the effort required, he is fond of alluding to the prototypes of early times, to Shākyamuni who, according to the Zen tradition, sat upright in meditation for six years before he awakened in enlightenment; to Bodhidharma's gazing at the wall for nine years; to the early Chinese Zen masters; and not least to his own experience in the monastery on Mount Tien-ts'ung. There, under the strict guidance of Master Ju-ching, one literally sat day and night. Dōgen devoted himself entirely to the practice and physically experienced its rigors, which he describes as follows: "When I was in China in the assembly under Ju-ching, I . . . practiced zazen day and night. Many monks gave up when it was very cold or very hot, fearing that they would get sick. But at these times I thought to myself: 'Even if I get sick and die, I must just practice zazen. If I do not train while I am healthy, what use is this body of mine?'"[4] Dōgen thought of the privilege he enjoyed by being able to practice under a Zen master in the great Sung China, and reflected: "If I practice but die before gaining enlightenment, I am sure that my next life will be that of a Buddhist follower."[5]

As Dōgen illustrated to his disciples, the thought of death only spurred the practitioners on to even greater efforts. When these genuine Zen disciples fell ill, they practiced zazen all the harder.

The exhortation to practice zazen and its promotion runs through Dōgen's writings like a leitmotif. His conviction of the importance and exigency of practice was deep, and his realization of its efficacy and wealth of value was profound. The dignity of that practice derives in Dōgen's view from its relation to Buddha-nature, with which it is fundamentally identical. The equation of practice with enlightenment is a crucial point in Dōgen's teaching. It has been misinterpreted as a quietistic devaluation of the satori experience, but is actually thoroughly consistent with the tradition of the Sixth Patriarch. Let us see how this master conceived the relation between the practice of zazen and enlightenment.

Zazen and Enlightenment   First of all, it should be kept in mind that Dōgen had a very strong experience of sudden satori. The occasion was when a disciple sitting next to him in Ju-ching's Zen hall in China kept dozing off and was scolded and struck by the master, who shouted (in the Japanese reading): *"Shinjin datsuraku!"* The four Chinese ideograms for this phrase mean "body and mind are cast off," or in the imperative form as spoken by the master: "In practicing Zen, body and mind must be cast off; you cannot attain it by sleeping!" The state in which body and mind have been cast off—i.e., in which the ego has completely disappeared from consciousness—is a most exact characterization of the enlightened mind. Upon hearing these words, Dōgen awoke to the Great Enlightenment. After this experience, he had a conversation with his master, preserved in the Zen chronicles and very much in the style of the mondō between the ancient Chinese masters and disciples.

The experience of satori remained for Dōgen throughout his life the "casting off of body and mind." He makes use of this expression over and over again in this precise sense. The word "satori" also appears in his writings, but more frequently he speaks of "attaining the Way" *(tokudō)* or "the Dharma" *(tokuhō)*. In the *Shōbōgenzō* chapter entitled "Bendōwa" (Discourse on Negotiating the Way), Dōgen answers the first question about the reason for zazen with the words: "Because it is the right entrance to the Buddha Dharma."[6] He goes on to elucidate the significance of zazen for "attaining the Way" and "the Dharma," and for achieving realization.

Dōgen characterizes the experience of enlightenment in terms of the light of Buddha reality perceived in zazen: it is a conscious and luminous experience. According to Dōgen's metaphysics of the universal unity of world, Self, and Buddha, reality is "one bright pearl" (the title of a chapter in the *Shōbōgenzō*); in it shines the light of the Buddha and the Self. At the moment when "body and mind are cast off," reality shines forth. Hence, upon reflection, satori appears as an experience of being. Dōgen is fond of illustrating the psychological process of the sudden breakthrough to enlightenment with the image of "taking one step beyond the top of a hundred-foot pole." This phrase is taken from the forty-sixth case of the *Mumonkan*, and it elucidates how normal consciousness is released and transcended. Dōgen therefore has knowledge of the sudden experience of satori, but does not wish it to be conceived separately from the practice of zazen.

Although, according to Dōgen, zazen is not a mere means to attain enlightenment (we shall return to this point later), it does have a mediatory function with regard to the sudden experience of satori. Zazen is the preeminent, if not the only, means to the way of enlightenment. Dōgen accentuates this point in ever new turns of phrase, hardly differing in content. The following text from the *Zuimonki*, a collection of the master's lectures compiled by his disciple and Dharma-successor, Ejō, renders Dōgen's view in all its subtlety: "Dōgen instructed: 'The most important point in the study of the Way is zazen. Many in China gained enlightenment solely through the strength of zazen. . . . The Way of the Buddha and Patriarchs is zazen alone.' "[7]

When asked by Ejō whether it was not more beneficial to combine zazen with the study of the scriptures and the practice of koans, Dōgen answered: "Although a slight understanding seems to emerge from examining the koans, it causes the Way of the Buddhas and the Patriarchs to become even more distant. If you devote your time to doing zazen without wanting to know anything and without seeking enlightenment, this is itself the Patriarchal Way. Although the old Masters urged both the reading of the scriptures and the practice of zazen, they clearly emphasized zazen. Some gained enlightenment through the koan, but the merit that brought enlightenment came from the zazen. Truly the merit is in the zazen."[8]

Zazen is the preferable way, first of all because it is the universal way of all Buddhas and patriarchs. Zazen has an advantage over the koan in that it contains no intellectual elements to hinder the breakthrough to enlightenment. Yet Dōgen does not completely reject the practice of koans. His writings display an intimate knowledge of the koan exercise. He frequently cites koan cases of the Chinese masters of old, and koan-like expressions often appear in his own explications. Not only the koan, but other ascetic exercises as well can help toward enlightenment. The only point is an unflinching resolve to achieve the goal. Dōgen assures the serious practitioner of success. Whoever lets go of world and ego and gives up everything will be enlightened: "If the desire to search for the Way becomes as intense as this, whether you concentrate on doing zazen alone, investigate a koan by an old master, interview a Zen teacher, or practice with sincere devotion, you will succeed, no matter how high you must shoot or no matter how deep you must plumb."[9]

Dōgen's zazen is no mere technique. The physical posture alone is not sufficient. The one practicing Zen must devote himself to the way with conscious resolve and give up all clinging to the self or the body. Dōgen instructs: "Even though you study deeply the sayings of the old Masters and practice zazen, remaining as immobile as stone or iron, you will never gain the Way of the Buddhas and the Patriarchs, even if you try for endless eons, unless you can free yourself from attachment to the body."[10] Another time he said with equal intensity: "Even though you study a thousand sutras and ten thousand śāstras and sit so hard that you break through the zazen seat, you cannot gain the Way of the Buddhas and the Patriarchs without this determination [to cast off body and mind]."[11]

Dōgen was familiar with the famed conversation between Nan-yüeh and Ma-tsu that concludes that one cannot make a mirror by polishing a tile; no one will become a Buddha by sitting in meditation. In Dōgen's understanding, Nan-yüeh was not trying to proscribe zazen itself, but warning Ma-tsu against striving for Buddhahood and enlightenment.[12] In any case, Dōgen's zazen is not a gradual purification of the mind in the manner of wiping a mirror. As he often enough emphasizes, there is no causal connection between practice and enlightenment. Practice is not the cause that brings about enlightenment. Various things can occasion the experience of awakening to enlightenment, if the mind is ready. To be sure, nothing is more valuable for the preparation of the mind than zazen. For one's unconditional determination is borne out by zazen; there the letting-go of world and ego becomes concrete. In true sitting, "body and mind are cast off." And this is the very quintessence of being enlightened.

Enlightenment has a twofold signification in Dōgen's writings. It is first the vent of sudden awakening here and now that can occur in the Zen hall, or "upon hearing the sound of bamboo when struck by a tile or on seeing blossoms in bloom,"[13] or under the most ordinary circumstances of everyday life. Second, it is the enlightenment that is present always and everywhere that constitutes the essence of reality and is given many names by Dōgen. Zazen is related to both aspects. As a casting off of body and mind, it is in the closest proximity to the experience of satori. In the enlightened view of reality, the essential oneness of practice and enlightenment becomes evident. In the "Bendōwa" Dōgen says: "In the Buddha Dharma, practice and realization are identical. Because one's present practice is practice in realization, one's initial negotiation of the Way in itself is the whole of original realization. . . . As it is already realization in practice, realization is endless; as it is practice in realization, practice is beginningless."[14]

The inner relation of practice and enlightenment spoken of here is founded in the one, self-identical Buddha-nature. This view shows the experience of satori as a shining forth of Buddha-nature. It follows that the experience of enlightenment does not constitute the terminus of a way. Practice must be continued, because it is practice in enlightenment. And enlightenment must continually be confirmed in practice. The enlightenment of the practitioner and the practice of the enlightened one are rooted in the same ground and are absolutely necessary for the confirmation of Buddha-nature.

When zazen is understood in the comprehensive meaning that it has in Dōgen, the scandal of "sitting only" (shikan taza) that has become the watchword of Dōgen's teaching is dissolved. As spoken by Dōgen, this phrase, which looks like a huge exaggeration and intolerable intolerance, does not indicate that an exterior method is absolutized. Such an absolutizing is hardly compatible with the magnanimity of the master or with his attention to the essentials of the matter. For Dōgen, zazen comprises the fullness of the Buddha-Way; it is, as he so often says, the practice of the Buddha par excellence.

Zazen as the Focus of a Buddhist Spirituality Zazen, the integrative practice of the way of enlightenment, is made the focus of a Buddhist spirituality by Dōgen. "Spirituality" here signifies not some mysterious dimension, but the leading of a mentally awakened life. In this sense, this term seems to convey Dōgen's mental bearing quite well. Like all genuinely Buddhist spirituality, Dōgen's is based on the experience of impermanence, which arose from his determination to detach himself radically from the world and the ego. This resolve is concretized in zazen, developed in everyday life, and completed in the attitude of compassion toward all living beings.

Dōgen's spirituality weaves through all his writings; even in his philosophical discussions it comes to the fore over and over again. The discourses collected in the *Zuimonki* are a prime example of how his thoroughly religious view of life is carried over into all possible situations. To begin with, we quote a brief text that summarizes some of the most important points. Dōgen once instructed his monks as follows: "Now, as men who have left your homes, if you are to enter the Buddha's house and become priests, you must learn thoroughly what you are supposed to do. To learn these things and to maintain the regulations mean to cast aside attachments to the Self and to conform to the teachings of the Zen Masters. The essential requisite is to abandon avarice. To do this, you must first free yourselves from egoism. To be free from egoism is to have a deep understanding of transiency. . . . You may say that you understand but still cannot give up certain things; and practice zazen while holding on to various attachments. If you take this attitude, you sink into delusion. . . . Without arguing about who is clever and who inept, who is wise and who foolish, just do zazen. You will then naturally improve."[15]

This text places the release from the ego in connection with the sense of transiency. In Dōgen's view these two points are intimately related. When Dōgen never ceases to exhort the disciples to give up all egoistic attachment, he knows that this is possible only if they are deeply aware of the impermanence and ephemerality of all things on earth. The experience of impermanence is basic for this reason. Hence all one's efforts are directed toward casting aside world and ego. This becomes concrete in the actual poverty that Dōgen himself practiced exemplarily and unconditionally demanded of his monks.

The ideal of poverty is linked to Buddhist monasticism from its very beginnings. Shākyamuni and his disciples lived out the poverty of the mendicant monk whose only possessions were a robe and an alms bowl. The question arose whether this poverty, as it was practiced in ancient India, was right for other countries as well. Apparently this question was often put to Dōgen. Once, as so often, he inculcated the necessity of poverty in his monks: "Students of the Way must not worry about clothing or food. They must merely follow the Buddhist rules and not concern themselves with with worldly things." Thereupon a disciple said: ". . . This was the custom in India. In the temples of China the monks share utensils and belongings in common so that they have no need to worry about them. In the temples of Japan there are no such belongings, and the custom of begging for food has, for the most part, not been transmitted. . . ."16

The disciple goes on to depict the various hardships of the situation, and suggests that some patron or some believer who belongs to the temple community be found to provide security for the necessities of life. Then the monks could practice the Buddha way in a quiet place with peace of mind. But Dōgen will hear nothing of this suggestion. This was not the style of the Buddhas and the patriarchs, or of any genuine disciple of the Way in the three countries. He repeats: "Just don't let your mind cling to worldly affairs but study the Way with single-mindedness. The Buddha has said: 'Possess nothing except your robes and bowl and give to starving people the leftovers from what you have begged.' If not a scrap is to be saved from what you receive, how much more so should one avoid rushing about searching for things."17

In order to allay the worries of his monks, Dōgen occasionally points out the generosity of their fellow believers in Japan, which in his experience far surpasses that of Chinese Buddhists.18 In this connection he frequently cites other ideas found in the Chinese world view, as in the following example: "During this brief life span of ours, even if we do not consider accumulating things, we will find that they are supplied naturally [literally, from heaven—*tennen*]. Each one receives his alloted share [in life: *shōbun*], bestowed by heaven and earth [*tenchi*]."19

Dōgen is equally optimistic about the welfare of the parents whose son enters the Zen monastery. He concludes one long conversation on this point with the aphorism: "It is said that if one son leaves his home to become a monk, seven generations of parents will gain the Way."20

Dōgen's requisite of detachment from all things allows no exemptions; it comprises one's possessions, family, and even one's own thinking. The obedience to the master demanded of the disciple implies a kind of blind faith. If up to then the disciple has been accustomed to picture the Buddha as radiant, he must believe it when the master tells him the Buddha is a toad or an earthworm. "If you follow the words of the Zen master . . . you will accord naturally with the Buddha-Way."21

Nevertheless, it would be wrong to think that the Zen disciple was being educated to a merely passive state of mind. When Dōgen states, "Just practice zazen. . . . Sit . . . like a person deaf and dumb,"[22] this means that the Zen disciple is not to take note of the slanders of others or speak of their shortcomings.[23] Rather, paying no attention to others' criticisms, he should conform to the principles of the sacred teachings.[24] "You should," so Dōgen instructs his monks, "secretly do good when no one is watching, and, if you do wrong, you should confess and repent."[25] Like all Zen masters, he rejects discriminatory thinking and does not want the practitioner of Zen to concern himself with discriminating between good and evil. But at the same time, he recommends repentance *(sange)* and constantly doing good. The way to Buddhahood, which he portrays in the chapter on "life and death" *(shōji),* begins with the words, "do nothing evil."

Dōgen teaches a spirituality of inner freedom. What is decisive is to let go of all egoistic clinging. Only a radical renunciation can lead to the experience of realization. In comparison with this, the observation of rules and regulations is of secondary importance. That does not mean, however, that all precepts should be discarded. Dōgen values liberty above all, but monastic obligations also have their worth, as he sees it. In the following text he places these two poles in the proper relationship: "Although the precepts and eating regulations should be maintained, you must not make the mistake of establishing them as of primary importance, and of basing your practice on them; nor should they be considered as a means to enlightenment. Since they suit the conduct of the Zen monk and the style of the true disciple, they are observed. To say that they are good, however, does not make them the most essential teaching. This does not mean that you should break the precepts and become dissolute, but, if you attach to them, your view is wrong and you depart from the Way. The precepts and eating regulations are maintained because they follow Buddhist ritual and represent a monastery style."[26]

Dōgen evinces the same delicate attitude toward Buddhist piety. The usual devotional practices are not what is ultimate and essential, but an understanding reverence toward the Buddhist tradition is proper for the Zen disciple. Dōgen brings these two poles together after relating an anecdote passed down in the Zen tradition. The chronicle tells of a monk who carried around a box containing a golden image of the Buddha and other relics. The monk burned incense and made offerings before the image with great reverence. The Zen master warned him that his worship was of no use and commanded him to throw the box away. When the monk was about to unwillingly leave the monastery, the master called after him: "Open your box and look inside." In it the monk found a poisonous snake. Of this Dōgen remarks: "As I see it, Buddha images and relics should be reverenced, since they represent the Tathāgata's image and his remaining bones. It is wrong, however, to expect enlightenment just by worshipping them. This is an error that delivers you into the hands of demons and poisonous snakes. . . . If you revere and make offerings to the World of the Three Treasures [i.e., the Buddha, the Dharma and the Sangha], you eradicate your crimes and gain merit. . . ."[27]

Dōgen is also familiar with the story of the Chinese Zen master Tan-hsia T'ien-jun, who burned an image of the Buddha in front of his disciples' very eyes. This singular action, Dōgen explains, served to clearly demonstrate complete freedom from any attachment to exterior things. In other respects Tan-hsia was an exemplary monk, as the records of his life show, no different from "all the other enlightened Masters and Patriarchs who . . . observed the precepts and the regulations. . . ."[28] Not only virtuous monks, but all Buddhist monks deserve respect without any difference, Dōgen says on another occasion. The same holds true for artistically valueless images of the Buddha and badly written scrolls.[29] The attitude of reverence coupled with inner freedom is grounded in faith; discriminatory thinking is alien to it.

Dōgen's spirituality would not be Buddhistic if it did not culminate in compassion. Zen practice and enlightenment are immersed in compassion. The Buddha is the paradigm. "It is impossible," Dōgen says, "to put into words the depth of the Tathāgata's compassion. Everything he did was for the sake of all sentient beings."[30] Another time he cites the example of a Chinese emperor who renounced a new palace out of consideration for his people. Dōgen reflects: "When even a layman feels this way about the people, he has transcended his own body. How much more compassionate should be the disciples of the Buddha, who follow in the style of the Tathāgata, be! Their compassion for all people should be like that towards an only son."[31]

At this point, Dōgen gets practical. One should not be hard on his subservients and should treat his fellow students and the older monks with respect. The Buddha was gentle and full of compassion. Dōgen so often exhorts his disciples to be gentle that one might suspect something was amiss in this regard in the medieval monasteries. "Even though you may have charge of an assembly as an abbot or senior priest, you must not use scolding words when you admonish your disciples and correct their errors."[32] Gentleness, he believed, was thoroughly consistent with strict discipline.

Compassion issues into unselfish and self-sacrificing giving. Dōgen relates several anecdotes from the life of Eisai, the founder of Japanese Zen, when he practiced boundless charity as the abbot of the Kennin-ji monastery. To a poor neighbor, who with wife and three children had not had anything to eat for days, he gave a piece of copper meant for the halo of a statue of Buddha, since the monastery had no food, clothing, or money to give them, while the copper could be exchanged for what the man's family needed. When the monks reprimanded Eisai for his action, he told them that it was the will of the Buddha. The Buddha would have sacrificed his entire body to save starving people.[33]

In the passages we have quoted above, the expression "how much more" (Japanese: *iwanya*) occurs several times. This expression is typical of Dōgen, who also employs examples from the secular and non-Buddhist realms and points out good deeds to encourage his own monks. The expression is used, then, particularly in reference to lay people and to non-Buddhists. In both cases Dōgen recognizes the good done by others in a gracious and tolerant manner and refers to it to motivate his Zen disciples.

Dōgen's spirituality is in principle the spirituality of a monk. From Shākyamuni and the original group of disciples he borrows the ancient Buddhist ideal of world renunciation and monastic life in a community. Zen disciples likewise have become homeless, as the Buddhist saying goes, and have opted for the advantages of monastic life. By renouncing worldly possessions, it has become easier for them to let go of all egoistic clinging. But in Dōgen's view, the way of Zen is also open to lay people. He counted quite a few lay Buddhists among his disciples, and also permitted women to practice. One chapter of the *Shōbōgenzō*, entitled "Worship and Realization" *(Raihai tokuzui)*, was meant especially for the female Zen disciples. In this text, itself a rich source for understanding the Buddhist stance toward women, Dōgen urges that a spiritually strong woman who gives herself entirely to her practice can surpass many a male practitioner and thus deserves a leading role in the Zen monastery.

Non-Buddhists as well, as Dōgen recognizes, have good examples to offer. His quotations from non-Buddhist writings are notable in this respect. He accepts all the wisdom contained in the old Chinese (predominantly Confucian) sayings and, with the comparative "how much more," applies it to the Buddhist Zen way. As was common among the better educated of his time, Dōgen had acquired a grounding in Chinese literature as a young boy, but radically abandoned this knowledge when he entered the monastic life; on Mount Hiei, he studied the holy scriptures of Buddhism exclusively. Nevertheless, it seems that much old and new Chinese wisdom came alive for him during his sojourn in China, where he came into actual contact with Chinese mentality. He approves of the good actions of non-Buddhists, just as he does those of the laity, always with the intention of impressing upon the Zen disciples their responsibility to realize "that much more."

Our brief survey shows Dōgen, the master of zazen, to be a master of Buddhist spirituality as well. Zazen becomes the focus of a spiritual way of life in Dōgen more than in any other Zen master. Dōgen finds all of Buddhism brought together in the spiritual way that combines practice and enlightenment. And, as in the following, he often put this view of the way into words: "From ancient times in these countries [India, China, and Japan] the true practicer of Buddhism has been poor, endured physical hardships, and wasted nothing. He has been motivated by compassion and the Way."[34]

TEN

Dōgen's Religious Metaphysics:
The Doctrine of Buddha-Nature

DŌGEN CAN BE CONSIDERED the greatest original thinker that Japan produced until modern times, when an independent Japanese philosophy arose for the first time in the so-called Kyoto school. In recent decades an increasing amount of attention has been paid to him, and he has become the subject of scholarly studies in Japan, Germany, and the United States. The philosophic ventures of Zen are nowhere more apparent than in the works of Dōgen. Religious practice combines with speculative thinking to make for the stature of his character as well as the charm of his written works. The ninety-five chapters or books of his *Shōbōgenzō* were composed for the most part as instructional lectures; they do not give a systematic presentation of his teachings. Proceeding from various points of departure, Dōgen's thought presses forward again and again to the same central focus. This center is his teaching on Buddha-nature (Sanskrit: *buddhatā;* Japanese: *busshō*), summarized in an important chapter bearing that name in the *Shōbōgenzō*.

Buddha-Nature as a Religio-Metaphysical Concept Mahāyāna philosophy contains a great number of expressions for the universal unity of reality; these denote the meaning of this idea with various nuances. Expressions such as mind-nature, Dharma-nature, absolute essence, or emptiness and nothingness are primarily philosophical formulations, whereas those combined with Buddha, such as Buddha-nature, Buddha-mind, or the cosmic Dharma-body of the Perfect One, have a more religious connotation. Dōgen prefers the term "Buddha-nature," which obviously best corresponds to his religio-metaphysical thinking. The doctrine of universal Buddha-nature is the central dogma of Mahāyāna Buddhism. One can view this doctrine philosophically as the conceptual formulation of the absolute character of the universal unity of reality. And yet as stated in the sutras, it is saturated with religious feeling and articulated in reference to final salvation. Dōgen grasped the doctrine of the Buddha-nature of all living beings and of all reality with the fervor of a religious person and threw light on it from ever-new angles.

The religious aspect is apparent first of all in Dōgen's lectures, the tone of which expresses his personal conviction. At the opening of the "Buddha-Nature" chapter he concludes a quotation from a sutra with the following potent remarks: "This word, with which our great teacher Shākya set in motion the wheel of the Law as if with the roar of a lion, is the crown of the head and apple of the eye of all Buddhas, patriarchs, and teachers. Already 2,190 years have passed since his enlightenment, and there have been about fifty generations of Dharma heirs in direct succession. In India twenty-eight generations have preserved the Dharma, in the Land of the East [China] twenty-three generations, together with the Buddhas and patriarchs of the ten heavenly regions."[1]

In the course of the book, the same tone of religious proclamation sounds forth over and again, such as one does not find in a purely conceptual philosophy. In pointing here to the essential qualities of Buddha-nature that have an immediate appeal to religious sensitivity, we anticipate some central points. Buddha-nature is not only eternal and ubiquitous but also pure and immaculate. The man who grasps it as the ground of reality, or reality as Buddha-nature, cannot but help encountering things with religious reverence. The religious aspect of Buddha-nature is especially evident in the teaching on enlightenment.

In speaking of the Buddha-nature, Dōgen combines religious incentive with a propensity for philosophic speculation. In accordance with the consistently held doctrine of universal unity, the relation between reality recognized as the Buddha-nature and the content of other Mahayanist expressions can ultimately be only that of identity. But each of the various terms used by Dōgen evokes a particular idea, especially apparent in such expressions as "mind" or "mind-nature" and "emptiness" or "nothingness." The terms "Buddha-nature" and "the Absolute essence" are frequently gathered into one concept. The following text can serve as an example of how the various expressions are connected: "The Great Way of the Buddha-Law is: in a grain of dust are all the scrolls of the sutras in the universe; in a grain of dust are all the infinite Buddhas. Body and mind are together with a blade of grass and a tree. Because all Dharmas [things] are unborn, the One Mind also is unborn. Because all things are in their true form, so also is a grain of dust in its true form. Therefore the One Mind is all things; all things are the One Mind, are the complete body."[2]

The movement of Dōgen's thought proceeds from unity and aims at unity; the idea of Buddha-nature is its center, where the probes from the religious and the philosophic spheres converge. The same passion for unity motivates Dōgen's religious practice and fuels his thinking. Thinking does not abrogate his enlightened wisdom, for it is inseparably bound to his religious experience of unity.

Buddha-Nature and Reality In the "Buddha-Nature" chapter Dōgen takes as his starting point a saying of Shākyamuni that has been handed down in the *Mahāparinirvāṇa Sūtra*. In literal translation from the Chinese it reads:

> All living beings have the Buddha-nature;
> The Perfected One is permanent, without any change.

This passage contains the quintessence of the Buddhist doctrine of salvation and is understood in the Mahayanist tradition approximately as follows: All living beings that exist in the round of birth and death have Buddha-nature in themselves like a seed. For this reason, at a given time—i.e., when all obscurities are overcome and the Buddha-fruit is ripe—they attain Buddhahood. The one, unchanging Buddha-nature exists in all living beings; it is the eternal mind-nature of the Tathāgata, the Perfect One. As its essence is mind, it is unsullied by the material world.

Dōgen interprets this sutra's passage on the Buddha-nature of all sentient beings in a wider sense, one that deviates from that usually given. First of all, he does not confine the notion of "all sentient beings" to plant or animal life, but includes the inanimate world as well. He goes on to say that not merely living beings but all of reality itself—everything that exists—is meant: "For all beings are Buddha-nature. We call a part of all beings 'sentient beings.' "

Extending Buddha-nature to the inanimate world is not an invention of Dōgen's. Scholars of the Tendai school had already discussed the possibility of the Buddhahood of grass and earth. What is novel is the interpretation Dōgen gives the passage by retaining the central concepts in translating the Chinese ideograms into Japanese, but changing the syntax for his own purposes to read: "All living beings are Buddha-nature." This grammatically unjustifiable translation obviously gives a new and different sense to the quotation. In the traditional reading, the predicate "Buddha-nature" includes but transcends the subject "all living beings." All living beings possess, but do not exhaust, Buddha-nature. Many other even more essential statements could be made concerning Buddha-nature. Contrary to this reading, Dōgen's interpretation claims the perfect convertibility of subject and predicate. The two concepts can only be brought together in a statement of identity. There is no difference in content whether one says "all living beings" or "the Buddha-nature."

Dōgen later comes back to the passage on the Buddha-nature of all living beings in another section of his "Buddha-Nature." There he puts the words into the mouth of the Chinese Zen master Sai-an, a disciple of the famous Ma-tsu. His explanation of the passage again places the comprehensiveness and absolute unity of Buddha-nature in the foreground. Even if the retribution accorded the sentient beings born in the six realms varies according to their karma, still all are one and the same in the identity of the Buddha-nature. And this unity includes the inanimate world as well. "All this, which is mind, is living being; all living beings have the being of Buddha-nature. Grass, trees, and earth—these are mind; being mind, they are living beings; as living beings, they are the being of Buddha-nature. Sun, moon, and stars—these are mind; being mind, they are living beings; as living beings, they are the being of Buddha-nature."

The things of the phenomenal world here identified with Buddha-nature are inanimate beings. Yet they, just as much as beings endowed with life, are mind—namely the cosmic Buddha-mind or or Buddha-nature. They are mind in the here and now of their manifestness, as Dōgen expresses by adding the word "these." Grass, trees, and earth, sun, moon and stars are "these." And "these" are, just as they are, the Buddha-nature.

In the language of Zen the word "this" or "these" has a special usage. Questions like "What is this. . . ?" as used in koans always imply that it is a question of essence. At their very first meeting the Sixth Chinese Zen Patriarch, Hui-neng, asked his disciple Nan-yüeh Huai-juang: "What is this that thus comes?" As a koan this question aims at the essence of reality, at Buddha-nature. For this reason Dōgen can set Hui-neng's question directly beside the words of Shākyamuni. At the opening of "Buddha-Nature," Dōgen questions: "What is the essence of the World-Honored One's words: 'All living beings are Buddha-nature'?" He answers by pointing to the koan-like question of the Six Patriarch: "This is like the turning of the wheel of the Law: 'What is this that thus comes?'" The patriarch Hui-neng's question, like the words of the Buddha Shākyamuni, expresses the essence of reality. Both passages set the Dharma-wheel of truth in motion. Hui-neng's "this," like every "this," is Buddha-nature.

For Dōgen, no other relation can obtain between the reality of all things and Buddha-nature than that of identity. He shuns the frequent tendency of monistic philosophy to find in the One the ground of the many. Although Mahayanist metaphysics denies that the Absolute is an efficient cause, it attempts to derive the multiplicity of phenomena from the One primal ground. One such attempt can be seen in a passage on Buddha-nature by the famous Indian Mahāyāna teacher Aśvagoṣa that Dōgen cites from a dubious Chinese Zen chronicle: "The twelfth patriarch, Aśvagoṣa, when explaining the ocean of Buddha-nature to the thirteenth patriarch, said: 'Mountains, rivers, and the great earth have all come to be through it. Meditation and the six miraculous powers come to be manifest through it.'"

The repeated "through" in this text (indicated in the Chinese by two synonymous ideograms) implies a causal relationship between Buddha-nature and existing reality. Such an interpretation is unacceptable to Dōgen. For him the word "through" cannot signify anything that would weaken the only relation that can obtain between reality and Buddha-nature, namely that of perfect identity. Unconcerned about the original meaning of the passage, Dōgen explains Aśvagoṣa's words as follows: "For this reason these mountains, rivers, and the great earth are all the ocean of Buddha-nature. 'All have come to be through it [i.e., the Buddha-nature]' means: in the moment in which they come to be, these are mountains, rivers, and the great earth. With respect to the phrase 'All have come to be through it,' one has to know that the form of the ocean of Buddha-nature is such. One must not cling to an inside, an outside, or a middle. For this reason, when one sees mountains and rivers, he sees Buddha-nature; when one sees Buddha-nature, he sees the cheeks of the donkey and the mouth of the horse. 'All have come to be through it' means: dependent on all and all in dependence. This must be grasped and not grasped."

This last admonition means that it is not a question of rational knowledge or a logical conclusion. The knowledge of the universal unity and identity of reality derives from enlightenment. It is perhaps best explained as a seeing, as is done in the text quoted above: when one sees mountains and rivers or whatever exists, he sees Buddha-nature. And when one sees Buddha-nature, he sees everything, every "this" in its concrete existence. As examples of concretely existing things, mountains, rivers, and the great earth are named first; that is to say, material things. But mental states such as absorption (samādhi) and miraculous powers *(siddhi)* also rest upon Buddha-nature and are identical with it. The world of matter and of mind prove equally to be Buddha-nature.

All things exist from moment to moment. Hence one can say that in the moment in which they come to be, they are these things. This is another way of putting the favorite expression, "All things are as they are." Buddha-nature must not be taken as the reason for all that exists. Whatever exists in a causal relationship has no need of a reason, for it is Buddha-nature. The reality of beings is simply there in its manifestness. All beings are Buddha-nature.

In the "Bendōwa," the chapter on "Negotiating the Way," Dōgen had already brought every duality into a unity. "You should know that the Buddha Dharma from the first preaches that body and mind are not two, that substance and form are not two."[3] There is no separation between body and mind; no substance lies behind or beyond the phenomenal world. Phenomena and essence are the same; all things are Buddha-nature.

Metaphysical Realism   In contrast to the idealistic trend in Mahāyāna philosophy, Dōgen advocates a radical realism. The mind and things are real in the same sense; they are Buddha-nature, and as such are one. Like Buddha-nature, the three worlds, the ten thousand Dharmas, body, and mind are as they are pure reality, for nothing is different from Buddha-nature.

In a chapter entitled "The Three Worlds Are Only Mind" *(Sangai yuishin)*, Dōgen elucidates the famous passage in the *Avataṃsaka Sūtra* that is a classic expression of the basic idealistic-monist teaching of Mahāyāna philosophy:

> The three worlds are One mind.
> Nothing exists outside the mind.

> Mind, Buddha, and all living beings—
> There is no difference between these three.

The three worlds—the world of desire, the world of form, and the world of formlessness—signify the universe, the totality of physical and mental reality. According to the passage from the sutra, this reality is no different from the one mind to which man breaks through in the experience of enlightenment. In Dōgen's view there is no need to investigate the relations between mind, Buddha, and living beings, since perfect identity obtains between the three. Mind, Buddha, and living beings are one. All things are the one mind; the one mind is all things.

Reality lies beyond affirmation and negation, but not in the sense of some transcendent absolute. It is not temporally or spacially determined, but is present in all times and spaces. Dōgen refuses to subsume phenomena under the mind in any manner whatsoever, be it ontologically or epistemologically. Absolutely nothing is to added to the simple statement of the identity of all reality.

Another favorite axiom of the Zen masters taken from Mahāyāna idealism reads: "The mind is identical with Buddha." Dōgen interprets this statement as well in the sense of a metaphysical realism: "The mind is trees and rivers, and the great earth is sun, moon, and the stars. Going beyond this statement brings dissatisfaction; going behind it renders it false. The mind of mountains, rivers, and the great earth is nothing else than mountains, rivers, and the great earth. Here there are neither waves nor billows, neither wind nor smoke. The mind of sun, moon, and the stars is nothing else than sun, moon, and the stars. Here there is no fog, here there is no mist. The mind of birth and death, coming and going, is nothing else than birth and death, coming and going. Here there is no delusion, here there is no enlightenment. The mind of walls and gravel is nothing else than walls and gravel. Here there is no mud, here there is no water. The mind of the four great elements and five skandhas is nothing else than the four elements and the five skandhas. Here there is no horse, here there is no monkey. The mind of stools and fans is nothing else than stools and fans. Here there is no bamboo, here there is no tree. Because this is so we read 'The mind is identical with Buddha,' that is, the unsullied pure mind is identical with Buddha. All Buddhas are unsullied pure Buddhas. For this reason, 'The mind is identical with Buddha,' means all Buddhas of the mind's awakening, of practice, of enlightenment and nirvana. Where there is not yet the awakening of the mind, practice, enlightenment, and nirvana, 'the mind is identical with Buddha' does not hold."[4]

At the conclusion of this text the unity of mind (or of Buddha-nature) with all things—i.e., the total reality of the cosmos—is related to the awakening of the mind in enlightenment. This becomes perfectly transparent in the moment of enlightenment, when the nonsubstantiality of reality is manifest at the same time as the identity of Buddha-nature with all things. The experience of the enlightened one is: "Buddha-nature is all things."

The concept of the Dharma-nature *(dharmatā)* plays an important role in Mahāyāna philosophy. Like the notions of Buddha-nature and of absolute essence *(bhūtatathatā)*, it signifies true reality or the ground of reality. Besides a literal translation (Sino-Japanese: *hosshō)*, the Chinese canon contains another combination of two ideograms *(jissō)* meaning "real" and "form" respectively. In a philosophically significant section of the *Lotus Sutra* that Dōgen comments on, the concept "real form" is connected to the expression "all Dharmas" (Japanese: *shohō)*—that is, all of reality: "The real form of all Dharmas is this form of all Dharmas, this nature, this body [or, this substance], these powers, these functions, these causes, these conditions, these fruits, these rewards, this inseparable connection of beginning and end [i.e., of form and reward]."[5]

The ten members of this series are taken to represent the ten qualities characterizing all things. Understood in this way, the passage from the sutra explains the true form of reality by listing analytically the ten qualities that characterize all things. Dōgen sees this text differently. In his view, the ten qualities do not characterize reality; rather reality is the ten qualities. At the beginning of his "Chapter on the True Form of All Dharmas" *(Shohō jissō)*, he gives a free variation of the passage from the *Lotus Sutra,* which he reveres as the "king of all sutras": "All Dharmas are this form, this nature, this body, this mind, this world, these clouds and rain, these [bodily activities of] going, staying, sitting and lying, these [emotional states of] sorrow and joy, activity and rest, this staff and fan, this [transmission of the mind by way of] holding up the flower and the face breaking into a smile, this rendering and receiving of the Dharma, this inquiry and practice, this evergreen pine and this faultless bamboo."

Dōgen rejects the idealistic philosophy of consciousness, because for him it does not do justice to the reality and identity of all existence. As long as one distinguishes between consciousness and objects, mind and things, there is room for duality. Moreover, in the idealistic-monistic philosophy of evolution, an admixture of potentiality weakens the reality of beings. In the teaching of the Yogācārya school, the storehouse of consciousness *(ālaya-vijñāna)* contains the seeds *(bīja)* of reality and releases all things from their seminal potentiality into manifest being, according to the law of causality. Dōgen expressly rejects any interpretation that identifies Buddha-nature with the storehouse or the seeds of consciousness. For him, the advocates of this view are unenlightened people, because they misunderstand the true form of Buddhanature. Dōgen writes: "There are people who think Buddha-nature is like the seed of grasses and trees. When continually nourished by the moisture of the Dharma rain, there grow buds and stems, branches and leaves, and blossoms and fruit abound. The fruit produces more seeds. This is the view of the unenlightened man who sees things this way. Even when one pays homage to such a view, still one must regard seeds, blossoms, and fruit together and individually as the pure mind. Within the fruit is the seed, the seed is not visible, but root and stem grow; a great tree with branches and leaves comes to be without assistance. There is no need to discuss whether [the seed] is outside or inside; thus it is unchanged then and now. Even when one once gives in to the opinion of unenlightened people, still root and stem, branches and leaves—which arise together and pass away together—must be the Buddha-nature of all beings."

Buddha-nature is no more like a seed in the universe from which all forms of reality evolve than it is the ground of the world. All phases of becoming that are manifest at the same time are, together and individually, Buddha-nature. The notion of a process of evolution that includes potentiality is alien to Dōgen. In place of such a process we find "manifestation in causal connection," which is pure reality, the same as the Buddha-nature. Dōgen cites the following passage from the *Mahāparinirvāṇa Sūtra:* "Whoever would know the meaning of Buddha-nature must completely apprehend the causal connection of points of time. When the point of time arrives, the Buddha-nature shines forth."

It is apparent that an evolutionary notion of time underlies this passage. At the termination of a process of evolution, the absolute Buddha-nature, potentially containing all time from the very beginning, will shine forth perfectly. Dōgen's explanation, however, proceeds from a different concept of time: "With respect to the phrase 'when the point of time arrives,' people of the past and the present have commonly thought that the point of time when Buddha-nature would be manifest would come later. During one's practice, the point of time when Buddha-nature is manifest would be encountered of itself. Lacking the point of time, one could practice zazen and koans but [Buddha-nature] would not be manifest."

No statement in the future tense can be made about Buddha-nature. One must not expect its manifestation in the future. Buddha-nature is always there—pure reality and constant presence. Applied to Buddha-nature, both the future and the past tenses signify the present. Hence Dōgen writes: " 'When the point of time arrives' means the point of time has already arrived. How could there be any doubt about it?" A few lines later he repeats clearly and emphatically: " 'When the point of time arrives' is synonymous with the point of time has already arrived. Buddha-nature does not first arrive when the point of time arrives. Therefore the point of time already having arrived is the same as the manifestation of Buddha-nature. The reason for this is evident: all points of time will not arrive, and all points of time have not been there. Buddha-nature will not shine forth, Buddha-nature has not been there."

The manifestation of Buddha-nature does not take place in a continuous temporal series of past, present, and future. No potentiality of becoming lessens the reality of beings. Buddha-nature comprises all physical and mental reality. No kind of being is potentially more real than any other kind. All beings are Buddha-nature to the same extent. The one Buddha-nature is completely there in every moment.

The Being of Buddha-Nature From a philosophical viewpoint, Dōgen's doctrine of Buddha-nature can be regarded as a metaphysical realism. However, the being of Buddha-nature is not the same as the empirical existence that man grasps in rational knowledge. Dōgen warns against shortcut solutions and deviant clarifications. The being of Buddha-nature is ". . . not being in opposition to non-being, . . . not an original being or primal being, not miraculous being or anything of the like. Even less does it mean the being that arises in causation or the being in delusion. It bears no relation to subject or object, nature or form or the like. Therefore the foundation for the being of all living things is not the maturation of karma, not delusory causation, not an accidental force of nature, nor a miraculous power or enlightenment acquired through ascetic efforts."

Thus by way of negations various interpretations of Mahayanist philosophy are excluded. The most thorough of Dōgen's confrontations is with the idealistic philosophy of emanation held by the Yogācārya school. The spirituality of Buddha-nature must not be advocated at the cost of the reality of the material universe. We have seen how carefully Dōgen avoids any semblance of duality. Buddha-nature is not the grounds for changing phenomena in the manner of some substantial Absolute. Nor can Buddha-nature be defined in any way in terms of man, neither in terms of the activity of knowing or of ascetic practice. Dōgen rejects all these possible solutions, as shown by the text cited above.

A positive statement arises from the series of negations. It becomes evident that the being of Buddha-nature is real, all-embracing being. It is the three worlds and the One Mind, it is trees, rivers, and the great earth, it is perception, representation, and thinking to the point of enlightenment, it is the openly manifest world and subjectivity, it is all sides of reality taken individually and together at every moment. Reality is not a plurality of parts, but a whole; and the whole of reality is not a static unity like an iron rod, but the infinite multiplicity of things. One can add nothing to Buddha-nature. Every being is Buddha-nature. "Buddha-nature is necessarily all being, because all being is Buddha-nature. All being is not a hundred fragments of something; all being is not [like] an iron rod, is not large or small. . . ."

The being of Buddha-nature is openly manifest and at the same time concealed. One cannot see Buddha-nature with his eyes, or hear it with his ears, or know it with his mind. Just as one cannot see his eyes with his eyes, so too does Buddha-nature, precisely because of its manifestness, evade the grip of knowledge. How then can the being of Buddha-nature manifest itself; how can it be recognized? At the climax of his chapter on Buddha-nature, Dōgen comments on the subtle story handed down in a Chinese Zen chronicle telling how the Indian patriarch Nāgārjuna revealed the perfect form of the body. We present the story here in summary.[6]

Once, the chronicle relates, the most venerable Nāgārjuna was traveling in southern India and preaching the doctrine of the Buddha-nature to the people there. From the beginning he encountered only complete lack of understanding. "Who can see Buddha-nature?" he was asked. "Is it large or small?" Nāgārjuna commanded the people to first lay aside their self-delusion and explained to them: "Buddha-nature is neither large nor small, neither broad nor narrow, neither happiness nor retribution; it does not die and is not born." Thereupon the most venerable one revealed his figure in the form of the full moon. Those gathered around him heard him preaching, but did not perceive the master. Nāgārjuna's enlightened disciple Kānadeva was present among the people and explained to them: "The most venerable one manifests the form of Buddha-nature and shows it to us. Buddha-nature is open and vast, empty and lucid."

In his commentary, Dōgen throws much light on the "immeasurable sermon" of the most venerable Nāgārjuna, as he calls it. The people to whom the venerable one brings the supreme doctrine possess no advanced insight. Tied completely to the sensual world, they demand to see Buddha-nature with their physical eyes. The patriarch commands them to rid themselves of their self-delusion and all the dark passions that hinder enlightenment. The people are willing to do this, but desire some idea of the form of Buddha-nature—whether it is large or small. They are told rather that Buddha-nature is formless and cannot be enclosed in any shape. Nāgārjuna shows this in the full-moon form of his body, which he reveals to those gathered around him. This full-moon form is not a transfigured body; rather it signifies the revelation of the true form of the body transcending all forms, although all forms are rooted in it.

Two paradoxical but essential features are expressed in the manifestation of the full-moon figure—its universality and its individuality. The full-moon form is Nāgārjuna's body in all its concreteness. It is not an illusory appearance, but rather the transcendent perfection of Buddha-nature that it reveals at the same time. Dōgen goes on to explain: "One must fully understand that at this time there is only the venerable one upon the high seat. The posture of his manifested body is the same as the sitting of all here. This body, just as it is, is the manifestation of the round figure of the moon. The manifestation of the body is neither square nor round, neither being nor non-being, neither hidden nor evident; it does not have the 84,000 means of salvations [for the 84,000 passions], but is simply the manifestation of the body."

The full-moon form is a mysterious reality; its meaning is not exhausted by the symbolism of this figure, which is relatively simple. The roundness portrays all-around perfection. The moon, as a waxing and waning shape, symbolizes for Dōgen the manifestness and hiddenness of Buddha-nature. Yet the true meaning of the event does not lie in a symbolism perceptible by the senses. In the wonderous vision of the full-moon form, a spiritual reality is disclosed to the eye of enlightenment. Of all those gathered around, only the enlightened disciple Kānadeva recognized Buddha-reality as manifested by his master Nāgārjuna. It was his task to explain the meaning of the wondrous event to the people. In formless samādhi, the manifestation of the body in the full-moon form is known to be the Buddha-nature. This formless samādhi is not adequately clarified in the text, but is in any case removed from the realm of the senses. Dōgen remarks that the manifestation of the body bears no sensually perceivable qualities. It is "not of a sensible form, not like the skandhas, bases or worlds. . . . It is form-less." Further, "Although all those gathered saw and venerated the full-moon form of formless samādhi; they did not see it [Buddha-nature] with their eyes."

We are told no more about this formless samādhi, but Kānadeva does make a ponderable remark about the appearance of the body—i.e., Buddha-nature as manifested in the full-moon form. He says: "The essence of Buddha-nature is open and vast, empty and lucid." Dōgen does not go much beyond this straightforward statement in his ex-planation: "The essence of the Buddha-nature is open and vast, empty and lucid. If this is such, then the appearance of the body is the open-ness and vastness, emptiness and lucidity of Buddha-nature."

Hence the appearance of the body in the full-moon form is not mere symbolism. And it would also be foolish to take what is perceivable in the phenomenon for reality. Dōgen cites many instances of attempts to capture the full-moon form in a picture. But all such portrayals have as little value and reality as "a picture of a rice cake." Buddha-nature cannot be pictured.

Buddha-nature transcends all human statement, be it by way of word or picture. Hence one will have to make efforts to come as close as possible to reality. This is best achieved by stating the "openness and vastness, emptiness and lucidity of Buddha-nature." This saying comes very close to Buddha-reality, but reality cannot be spoken entirely. When one is sufficiently aware of this, he may again take delight in portrayals of the appearance of the full-moon form. And since all pictures fail in the end, one may even "paint a picture of a rice cake, in jest." Here Dōgen's commentary empties into the psy-chology of the koan. Because all words and signs are inadequate, one can employ any arbitrary phrase, even—and preferably—any para-doxical, nonsensical phrase. True reality is above all words and signs. The enlightened one is aware of it.

The Way of Negation   Everything speaks for the fact that Buddhism's preference for negation derives from the founder of the Buddhist religion, Shākyamuni himself. In Mahāyāna, the father of negativism is Nāgārjuna. Religiously and philosophically, Dōgen follows in the tradition of this man, the greatest Buddhist thinker India produced. Nāgārjuna employed all the keenness of his dialectical thinking to demolish the very last claim to reality the phenomenal world could make. Dōgen accepts his basic thesis. He too denies the substantiality and autonomy of the phenomenal world, to embrace with religious fervor the goal of the doctrine of the Middle Way (mādhyamika), which is the essential sameness of the phenomenal world (saṃsāra) and supreme truth (nirvana). Nāgārjuna arrived at this conclusion by way of dialectical negation. Just as he almost exclusively stresses the negative qualities of supreme truth—its ungraspability, indeterminateness, and emptiness—he demonstrates the same negative essential traits in the phenomenal world and finally equates the two worlds in a complete non-duality. Dōgen appropriates Nāgārjuna's basic metaphysical ideas and develops them in part independently, expressing them in his own particular language. He too belongs to the lineage of Buddhist thinkers well advanced on the *via negationis*.

Four sections of the "Buddha-Nature" chapter treat of the "nothingness of Buddha-nature [*mu-busshō*]," which Dōgen opposes to the "being of Buddha-nature [*u-busshō*]." It is hardly possible to convey the full import of the expression *mu-busshō* in another language. The word *mu* can be translated as "not," "nothing," "not being," or "nonbeing"; but the Chinese ideogram for *mu* has various syntactical roles. Sometimes it is so closely connected to the ideograms for "Buddha-nature" that the translation into one concept as "Not-Buddha-nature" would suffice. Other times it must be taken as negating the verb in the sentence. In the following we attempt to capture its rich and incisive content by translating the term as "the nothingness of Buddha-nature" wherever possible.

Dōgen develops the doctrine of the "nothingness of Buddha-nature" quite straightforwardly in his commentary on the words of the Chinese Zen master Wei-shan: "All living beings are not Buddha-nature."[7] As they stand, these words negate Master Sai-an's previously cited statement: "All sentient beings are Buddha-nature." Wei-shan's statement of negation contradicts in form the Buddha's and Sai-an's statements of affirmation. For Dōgen there arises the necessity of probing the full range and mutual relation of the two statements. Naturally they cannot really contradict one another. Rather, the statement of negation excludes the possibility of mistaking entity—that is, the particular being of things—for the being of Buddha-nature. Because of its delimitation and determination, the statement of affirmation has a certain deficiency that must be overcome by way of negation.

It would be wrong to hear a reproof of Sai-an in Dōgen's words. The statement of affirmation concerning Buddha-nature has its right, but does not exhaust reality. Hence it must be transcended in negation. Since the statements of affirmation and negation are dialectically related to one another, one cannot inquire which of the two has priority.

The phrase "the nothingness of Buddha-nature" combines two significant currents of Mahayanist thought: the doctrine of universal Buddha-nature in the *Mahāpariṇirvāna Sūtra* and the speculation about śūnya in the Mādhyamika school. Dōgen attributes the synthesis achieved and decisive for Zen metaphysics to the fourth Chinese Zen patriarch, Tao-hsin. According to the (historically dubious) chronicle, Tao-hsin was the first to proclaim the "nothingness of Buddha-nature" —during a koan-like exchange of words with his successor, Hung-jen— and hence the first to introduce the *via negativa* to Zen. Dōgen names the following stages in the spreading of the way of negation: "The word of the nothingness of Buddha-nature sounds far beyond the room of the fourth patriarch, is heard in Huang-mei, spreads to Chao-chou, is uttered upon Mount Ta-wei."

Huang-mei is the name of the monastic seat of the fourth and fifth Chinese Zen patriarchs, who exerted considerable influence in implanting Zen in China. One of the most original Zen masters of the T'ang period was named after the locality Chao-chou. He was made famous by the question whether a dog has the Buddha-nature, the first case in the *Mumonkan* and to this day the most widely practiced koan. Chao-chou's answer was "mu" (Chinese: "wu"). Chao-chou's dog is the classic koan of the nothingness of Buddha-nature. Finally, Ta-wei, which Dōgen mentions last, is the mountain where Master Wei-shan, the author of the statement of negation, was active.

Before explaining the nothingness of Buddha-nature, Dōgen relates the legend of the fifth patriarch's calling, which peaks in a koan-like exchange on name and Buddha-nature. The fifth-patriarch-to-be was already an old man, living as an ascetic in the forest, when he first encountered the fourth patriarch, Tao-hsin. Tao-hsin immediately recognized the ascetic's excellent aptitude for the Dharma and wished to make him his successor. He regretted that this was not possible because of the advanced age of the man standing before him. Thereupon the ascetic entered the womb of a maiden and was reborn. In his seventh year, he again met the fourth patriarch; at this time the following exchange took place:

> When the patriarch saw him [the boy], he inquired of him: "What is your name?"
> He answered: "I have a name, but this is no ordinary name."
> The patriarch said: "What name is this?"
> He answered: "This [name] is Buddha-nature."
> The patriarch said: "You have not Buddha-nature!"
> He answered: "Because Buddha-nature is empty, you say 'not'."

This exchange of words puns on a Chinese ideogram that is read the same way but can mean "name" or "nature." The inquiry after the name, which fits a first meeting so well, turns into a question of essence. Such questions are commonly found in the mondō of the Zen masters. Whereas one's ordinary name—i.e., what one is called by others—is deprived of being, reality underlies the essential name. It is no ordinary name, but rather Buddha-nature. A bit of profound speculation on "this" and "what" clarifies the matter here. "This" (Japanese: *ze*) stands for the openly manifest phenomenal world; "what" (Sino-Japanese: *ga*) signifies the world of emptiness. "This" is definite, concretely delimited existence; "what" is indefinite, the realm of the metaphysical ground of reality. According to Mahayanist metaphysics, both worlds are completely identical.

The ground of the nothingness of Buddha-nature is emptiness. In his extensive comments, Dōgen makes it clear that "nothingness" is not simply the negation of being on the same level with it. The statement of negation implies no absurdity or tautology. Rather, it opens the way to the other dimension of transcendence, frequently indicated by a repetition of the same word in Dōgen's writings. The nothingness of transcendence has a double weight; emptiness is "emptiness as emptiness." "Absolute emptiness is wholly emptiness. Because of this, the fourth and fifth patriarchs could make the statements in their conversation about the nothingness of Buddha-nature, the emptiness of Buddha-nature, and the being of Buddha-nature."

According to the philosophy of the Mādhyamika school, to which Dōgen adheres, the phenomenal world and absolute emptiness are identical. But the operation of thought that uncovers the non-substantiality of phenomena, demolishes false appearance, and shows the phenomenal world to be empty is insufficient in its exclusively negative formulation. Absolute emptiness is known in the enlightened intuition of reality. In this supreme view of wisdom, the being of Buddha-nature and the emptiness of Buddha-nature are perfectly one.

The enlightened view of reality is inexpressible. The being of Buddha-nature and the nothingness of Buddha-nature are only accessible to immediate experience. Rational statements cannot be made about either. "For this reason Pai-chang says: 'Whoever teaches that living beings are Buddha-nature slanders the Buddha, the Dharma, and the Sangha. Whoever teaches that living beings are not Buddha-nature, he too slanders the Buddha, the Dharma, and the Sangha.'"8 To this Dōgen remarks: "Hence both the statement on the being of Buddha-nature and the statement on the nothingness of Buddha-nature turn into slander. Even if it turns into slander, one must still make statements."

The slander of the three jewels of the Buddha, the Dharma, and the Sangha, like the expression "kill the Buddha," belongs to the paradox of the koan. It is not a question of reprimand here, but solely of the inexpressibility of reality.

Dōgen also comments upon an exchange of words between the fifth and sixth patriarchs, in which the statement on the nothingness of Buddha-nature is subtly tied in with "becoming Buddha." In Mahā-yāna thought, becoming Buddha usually means realizing the Buddha-nature intrinsic and potential in all living beings. Dōgen, as we have already pointed out, does not recognize any potentiality in Buddha-reality. In his view there is no ontological difference between Buddha-nature and becoming Buddha.

The fifth patriarch puts the usual question to the newcomer:

"Where have you come from?"
The Sixth Patriarch said: "I am a man from Ling-nan."
The fifth patriarch said: "[Now that you have] come, what do you want?"
The Sixth Patriarch said: "I want to become a Buddha."
The fifth patriarch said: "People from Ling-nan have no Buddha-nature; how can you expect to become a Buddha?"9

In his commentary, Dōgen first of all maintains a transcendental sense in the negation of Buddha-nature: "This [phrase] 'People from Ling-nan have no Buddha-nature' does not mean that people from Ling-nan are not Buddha-nature, nor does it mean that people from Ling-nan are Buddha-nature. Rather it means the nothingness of Buddha-nature of the people from Ling-nan."

The nothingness of Buddha-nature is understood in the sense of the transcendental reality of Buddha-nature. With respect to becoming Buddha it is said that "the sense of Buddha-nature is not that Buddha-nature is not possessed before becoming Buddha; rather that after becoming Buddha it is in possession. Buddha-nature and becoming Buddha necessarily go together."

The identity of Buddha-nature and becoming Buddha is not affected by the experience of enlightenment. "People attain Buddhahood, but there is no becoming Buddha in Buddha-nature."

The phrase about the nothingness of Buddha-nature leads to a fathomless abyss, upon which rest all statements of reality. The phrase is like a crutch from the past for generations to come. Receiving this aid, "the Buddhas Kāśyapa and Shākyamuni and all Buddhas upon attaining Buddhahood and proclaiming the Dharma were able to make statements on the Buddha-nature of all beings. The being in 'all beings' inherits the sense of nothingness in absolute nothingness [*mu-mu*]. . . ."

The nothingness of Buddha-nature is the foundation, because in essence Buddha-nature is empty. The phrase about nothingness, in its reach to transcend the being of things, grasps emptiness. One who clings to no particular being gains the unobstructed view of vast emptiness. In his speculations on nothingness, Dōgen often brings phrases from the Chinese koan literature into play, but in his case it is not a game of paradoxes, but rather a passionate thrust to transcendence. Dōgen is among those Eastern thinkers for whom the *theologia negativa* was the most commensurate way to the most profound essence. In his words one hears echoes of the *neti, neti* (not so, not so) of the great sage of the Upanishads. His way of negation reveals the profoundly religious character of his metaphysics.

Buddha-Nature and Becoming By way of negation, Dōgen reaches the primal ground of reality that is formless and non-substantial, transcending affirmation and negation. The primal ground cannot be named. If it is called being, then reality is delimited; if it is called nothingness, then there is danger of falling into a nihilism. Indian philosophy was not always able to escape nihilism, and Chinese Zen occasionally took enlightenment to be a static condition.

In order to curtail this danger, Dōgen constantly keeps the changing world of phenomena in mind. In the pregnant opening of the chapter called "Genjō kōan," the way of transcending negation leading through being and nothingness ends with the changing phenomena of everyday life. Dōgen writes: "When all dharmas are the Buddha Dharma, there is illusion and enlightenment, practice, birth, death, buddhas, and sentient beings. When myriad dharmas are without self, there is no illusion or enlightenment, no buddhas or sentient beings, no generation or extinction. The Buddha Way is originally beyond fulness [affirmation] and lack [negation], and for this reason there is generation and extinction, illusion and enlightenment, sentient beings and buddhas. In spite of this, flowers fall always amid our grudging, and weeds flourish in our chagrin."[10]

However high an enlightenment one may experience, however deep an emptiness he may discern, when wilted flowers fall it seems sad, when weeds flourish rampantly there is dislike. Everyday, changing phenomena remain most real.

The entire world of becoming is Buddha-nature, both the changing, natural phenomena of the universe and the altering states of consciousness of the psychic world. From the identity of Buddha-nature and the phenomenal world, Dōgen draws several consequences for the way of enlightenment. The attempt to completely eliminate the stream of consciousness is futile in his view, for enlightenment does not simply consist of the annihilation of consciousness. Ta-hui Tsung-kao, one of the leading exponents of the koan Zen of the Rinzai sect in the Sung period, distinguished two things in the mind-nature: the mind—i.e., conscious mental functions such as sensation, representation, willing, thinking, etc.—and the nature, its motionless foundation. He advocated a radical pacification of the mind by eliminating all conscious activities and held that enlightenment was experienced in the sudden breakthrough from conscious layers to the nature. Dōgen rejects any distinction between "mind" and "nature." In his translation, the dynamic functions of consciousness prove to be no less Buddha-nature than the changing physical universe. Motion and change are not contradictory to enlightenment.

In several places in the *Shōbōgenzō*, Dōgen is critical of Ta-hui's views. Although the latter affirmed the unity of mind and nature, under the influence of Neo-Confucianist philosophy he distinguished in nature between the changing phenomena of the conscious activity of the mind, on the one hand, and its motionless foundation, on the other. In the understanding of the Chinese Zen master, the mind *(shin)* is nature *(shō)* in motion, modified by the activity of consciousness. The point for him is to intercept the activity of consciousness and uproot it entirely. The nature-foundation shines forth only when the mind is completely stilled. In contrast to this view, Dōgen recognizes the dynamics of the functions of consciousness that naturally unfold, for example, whenever there is contact with external things. He draws no distinction between a mind affected by the conscious activities of representing, sensing, thinking, and understanding, and a motionless Buddha-nature. The activities of consciousness are also Buddha-nature. All of reality is the one Buddha-nature, it is movement and pure clarity. The enlightened one understands the becoming of generation and extinction as Buddha-nature, and Buddha-nature as becoming; he does not seek to arrive at an unmoved nature at the basis of becoming.

It is true that stilling the consciousness by means of mental concentration plays an important role in practice, but in essence enlightenment is understood cosmologically and universally, not psychologically. Psychic activities, even if they do indicate illusion and hindrance, are ontologically Buddha-nature. But Buddha-nature is not confined to conscious life. "It is the non-believers who steadfastly maintain that Buddha-nature is there or not there depending on movement or nonmovement, that it is active or not active depending on consciousness or nonconsciousness, that it is nature or not nature depending on knowledge or non-knowledge. For a long time unknowing ones have taken the activity of consciousness for Buddha-nature and the original face—those are people who deserve to be laughed at."

Dōgen's identification of Buddha-nature proceeds in a dialectical ascent. In the being of Buddha-nature there unfolds universal Buddha-reality: all reality, as Buddha-nature, is one. The way of negation requires the constant step beyond into the formless, the indeterminate. All limitation is overcome in a transcending by way of negation. But nothingness is not a point of rest attained. Only by realizing the dynamism of reality in becoming is Buddha-nature fully unfolded. For this stage, Dōgen makes use of the expression "the impermanence of Buddha-nature" *(mujō-busshō)*. Impermanence (Sanskrit: *anitya*) is a theme in all forms of Buddhist teaching, and Dōgen himself was deeply shaken by an experience of the transiency of all earthly things when only a child. In his adult life he developed a metaphysic of becoming that found its strongest expression in the brief but significant chapter "Genjō kōan." Proceeding from subjectivity, this chapter tries to clarify the essence of "becoming manifest" *(genjō)*. Its contents can be summarized in one sentence: this impermanent world of phenomena is, just as it is, true and openly manifest reality. Although the term "Buddha-nature" does not appear in the "Genjō kōan," true reality is the same as the cosmic Buddha or Buddha-nature.

The sixth paragraph of the Buddha-nature chapter treats of the "impermanence of the Buddha-nature," beginning with a quotation of the Chinese Zen patriarch Hui-neng: "The Sixth Patriarch taught his disciple Hsing-ch'ang: 'The impermanent is the Buddha-nature, the permanent is the mind discriminating good and evil and all Dharmas.' "11

The words of the patriarch purposely deviate from the usual form of Buddhist teaching, according to which Buddha-nature is permanent, whereas the world of phenomena (including the changing activities of human consciousness) is impermanent. Hui-neng is able to transpose these easily, since nirvana and saṃsāra are completely the same, and hence interchangeable, in the Mahayanist metaphysics of identity. The words of the Chinese Zen Patriarch evoke some profound remarks from Dōgen on the element of becoming in all reality: "When the impermanent itself undertakes to clarify, practice, or grasp the impermanent, then all is impermanent. . . . For this reason the Sixth Patriarch said: 'The impermanent is Buddha-nature.' The permanent does not change. Not changing means: even when the subject changes and the object changes, still no trace of coming or going arises. Thus [Buddha-nature] is permanent. If this is true, then the impermanence of grass, tree, and forest is Buddha-nature; the impermanence of men and things, body and mind, is Buddha-nature; the impermanence of land and earth, mountain and river is Buddha-nature. Supreme enlightenment [*anuttara-samyak-saṃbodhi*], because it is Buddha-nature, is impermanent; great nirvana, because it is impermanent, is Buddha-nature."

Buddha-nature is the permanent and the impermanent. In permanence it is impermanent; in impermanence it is permanent. Reality is a dynamic process of becoming so much that generation and extinction leave no trace behind. The absolute states of enlightenment and nirvana, transcending the cycles of saṃsāra and hence regarded as permanent, are, like Buddha-nature, nothing other than the impermanent. For there is permanence only in becoming.

The being of Buddha-nature is time.[12] The twelve hours of the day, during which the enlightened one clings to no thing, are Buddha-nature. Every moment of illusion and every moment of enlightenment contains all of reality. For illusion and enlightenment are Buddha-nature in the same way. Hence Dōgen can conclude a passage on the twelve hours of the day in the "Buddha-Nature" chapter with the words: "In one illusion is the entire time of the twelve hours. Clinging and not clinging are [one] like the tendril and the supporting tree, as also are heaven and earth and the universe."

In its core, Dōgen's philosophy is just as much a philosophy of being as of becoming. Buddha-nature is reality in becoming. This philosophy rests upon a genuine experience of nature. As his nature poems reflect, Dōgen was deeply touched by the change of natural phenomena of the four seasons: "Life is a stage of time, and death is a stage of time, like, for example, winter and spring."[13]

The example of the seasons of the year gives a naturalistic hue to the philosophic statement. But any naturalism in Dōgen's world view is surmounted by the notion of pure, holy Buddha-nature. In the chapter called "Life and Death" *(Shōji)*, he writes: "This life and this death are the sublime life [on-inochi] of the Buddha. Whoever would aspire to discard this out of dislike would lose the sublime life of the Buddha."

Such a thought, of which there are many in Dōgen's writings, clearly betrays his religious sentiment, sometimes concealed by his dialectical philosophizing.

Dōgen's writings do not show his thinking to be a closed philosophical system. Various thoughts are grouped around a central focus, approached now from this side, now from another. We have deliberately limited our presentation here to give a more or less clear, well-rounded picture. Our guideline was the notion of Buddha-nature; other themes and motifs were pursued only to the extent that they helped clarify this central thought. We had to content ourselves with opening a door to Dōgen's metaphysical thinking. The chapters of the *Shōbōgenzō* offer a wealth of philosophical thought waiting to be disclosed.

We let Dōgen himself be our guide, read passages from his works, and attempted to clarify them and fit them together. Such a method may be commendable in the case of a thinker whose thinking is so different from our own. While reading the texts, we felt perhaps the proximity of some of the great thinkers in the history of Western philosophy. It must be left to further inquiry to throw light upon the relationship of Dōgen's thought with Western analogies. Modern Japanese philosophers, especially of the Nishida school, have already contributed to this work. The religious character of Dōgen's metaphysics seems rather clear.

ELEVEN

The Zen Experience
in Contemporary Accounts

THE ZEN WAY OF ENLIGHTENMENT, which originated in Buddhism and was passed down from generation to generation, has been kept alive to the present. Today this way is being investigated by modern science, particularly psychology, with its exact methods to study the psychosomatic changes and therapeutic effects resulting from the practice of Zen. Although contemporary accounts of the experience by Zen disciples do not satisfy the strict requirements of scientific experimentation, they do give us a good picture of what happens to the practitioner during the course of his endeavors. At the same time such reports cast light on early historical sources. In the following we shall have a look at a group of modern accounts, all of which derive from the same Zen school and present a unified picture.

The numerous schools and lines that originated in Zen Buddhism, although united in their fundamental tenets, differ in the interpretation of the experience of enlightenment, in their manner of practice, and in the evaluation of the relation between the two. Rinzai Zen was the first to become known in the West, through the work of D. T. Suzuki. In present-day Japan, the Sōtō school is at least of equal importance. Besides this main division there are intermediate forms that have evolved from the originality of individual Zen masters.

In present-day Japanese Zen monasteries three typical forms of practice are clearly discernible. What comes nearest to the classical Chinese Zen of the T'ang and Sung periods is the systematic koan exercise practiced in the monasteries of the Rinzai school, especially in Kyoto and Kamakura. Through extensive effort that may take years, the koans are penetrated by the mind and finally experienced. To master all 1,700 or more koans in one lifetime is, of course, impossible. But one can work through and appropriate a large number of the "examples of the Elders" contained in the paradoxical deeds and sayings of the masters and the verbal exchanges with their disciples. An essential part of this kind of koan practice is the guidance given by the master in dokusan, for only the master has the authority to propose the problem, supervise one's progress, and ascertain one's successful solution. In some Rinzai masters, a more speculative direction is observable, in others, a more practical bent, according to individual preference and predisposition.

The fundamental dogma of Sōtō Zen teaches that practice and enlightenment are basically the same. The practitioner is already in possession of everything in his practice and should not seek enlightenment outside practice. However, this does not exclude the sudden experience of enlightenment. Dōgen gained enlightenment through a powerful, psychic jolt, and to this day his experience is regarded in Sōtō Zen as the highest expression of enlightened Buddhahood. However, in the temples of the Sōtō sect the experience of enlightenment is not methodically sought after. Even during the sesshin, it is not considered desirable to aim at a sudden experience. Whether such experiences occur or not, in the round of practice from moment to moment each instant is equally related to the absolute center. Following his individual inclination, a Sōtō monk may also devote himself to the koan exercise, but he need not do so. Simple meditation in the lotus posture is sufficient. This one practice of zazen includes everything; neither the koan nor the private guidance of the master in dokusan is necessary. This form of Zen practice is also called Dōgen-Zen, after its originator and ideal master.

In recent times, a third form of Zen practice, combining elements from the two principal forms of Rinzai and Sōtō, arose through the achievement of the Zen master Sogaku Harada (1871–1961). Master Harada's method is aimed directly at the experience of enlightenment. From Rinzai it adopts the koan exercise and dokusan, but the koans are systematized to a certain extent and used for practical realization. Its unmistakable propensity for emotional asceticism most likely derives from Sōtō Zen. Master Harada was extremely cautious when it came to recognizing the genuineness of his disciples' experiences of enlightenment. Yet many Buddhist monks and lay people were able to attain the full experience under his guidance. His school is continued today by his disciples. Whereas Master Harada exhorted his followers to observe discreet silence regarding their experiences, in recent years several collections of accounts have been published by men and women of the third generation that in no small way enrich our knowledge of the psychology of Zen practice and the experience of enlightenment.

The following report is based, first of all, on two volumes of accounts by disciples from the school of the Zen master Ryōkō Yasutani (d. 1973), who traveled throughout Japan for many years giving Zen courses, while a small temple in a suburb of Tokyo sufficed as his dwelling place. At a mature age he attained enlightenment under Sogaku Harada, whom he revered as a "great and true master of Zen practice and of the seal of enlightenment." The two volumes contain thirty accounts, some rather extensive. Most are from Buddhist laymen and laywomen who reached the goal of enlightenment under Master Yasutani's direction.[1]

Another volume of sixty accounts from the school of Abbess Sozen Nagasawa, a disciple of Master Harada, makes very interesting reading. The disciples of this important woman are of both sexes, but the majority of these accounts derive from Buddhist nuns who gained enlightenment under her direction. The accounts depict life in the Zen hall as well as the stimulating guidance of the abbess.[2]

All the accounts quoted in the following stem from Japanese Buddhists. It is important to emphasize this because the line of Zen characteristic of masters Harada and Yasutani has been made known and spread in the West by such leading exponents as the American Buddhist Philip Kapleau and the German Jesuit H. M. Enomiya-Lassalle. An account of the changes that this line of Zen has undergone in the West does not lie within the confines of the present book, which seeks rather to bring out the typical Buddhist aspects of Zen practice.[3]

Meditation, like all genuine expressions of spiritual culture, is given the task of establishing harmony between the inner and the outer, balance between content and form, exterior habit and interior spontaneity. In Zen practice, exterior technique is strongly pronounced, but personal asceticism and devotion are not lacking, as the contemporary, accounts show. Almost all the Zen disciples whose testimony we shall follow took part in a practice period, or sesshin, where the Zen technique is consistently carried out. Yet these disciples also speak of their ascetic practices and devotional attitude in very frank terms.

The Course of Practice in the Exterior   Practice sessions usually last five or seven full days, regulated by a strict timetable in which the hours set aside for zazen predominate and can be increased as individual zeal may prompt. In the stricter instances, a day may begin at three o'clock in the morning and not end till nine at night. Except for the time taken up by the recitation of sutras, house and garden work, and partaking of three meals, one sits uninterrupted for periods of almost an hour. Larger monasteries have a separate meditation hall with the statue of Mañjuśrī, the Bodhisattva of wisdom, in the center. Straw mats along the walls serve as seats for zazen. In smaller monasteries, the meditation hall is often combined with the Buddha Hall, which contains an image of Shākyamuni as the principal object of worship. The traditional pattern of "life on one mat"—namely, meditating, eating, and sleeping on the same straw mat—cannot be followed strictly in monasteries without a separate meditation hall; one eats and sleeps in different rooms, but all comfort is lacking. Nourishment consists simply of a thin rice gruel with a few pickled vegetables. The impression this program makes on a new arrival may be gauged from the notes a laywoman took after listening to the instructions of the abbess on the eve of the practice session: "Become serious; persevere at all costs. Absolute silence. Simple meals. . . . Since the nuns in charge are busy, everyone must help. I am expected to sweep the halls and garden in the mornings and evenings. When work is over, return forthwith to *zazen*. . . ."[4]

A daily lecture (teishō) by the Zen master animates the meditation. In a brief, half-hour talk usually based on a passage from a sutra or an old master, or on a koan story, the master knows how to give sufficient stimulation for the long day of practice. The master's personal guidance during dokusan is felt to be even more effective. There he is at his best to join strictness with gentleness and give each his due serving. The accounts contain astonishing examples of sage moderation and unrelenting severity.

In the Harada school, the practice of meditation proceeds more or less along the following course. After some brief instruction concerning bodily posture, one begins by counting breaths *(sūsokkan)*. Sitting in the lotus posture *(padmāsana;* Japanese: *kekka-fuza)* with his eyes open and fixed on a point a few feet ahead, one counts his inhalations and exhalations from one to ten over and over again, until breathing becomes perfectly rhythmical. It may take days, indeed a whole session, until this effect is achieved, but the period of practice is not in vain, since regulated breathing calms the entire body. In this way the disciple also gets used to the lotus posture, which even Japanese, accustomed as they are to the formal way of Japanese sitting *(seiza)*, can find quite painful at first.

Counting the breath is a preparatory exercise meant to calm the body and the mind. Actual practice begins with the next stage, when the practitioner is given a koan. In the Harada school this is always the mu (nothingness) koan, adopted from the first case of the *Mumonkan*. The aim, however, is not to arrive by ratiocination at the hidden sense or paradoxical nonsense of the koan, but rather to reduce it to its quintessence: in other words, all sensory and mental capacities are concentrated on the word "nothingness." It is doubtful whether the practitioner is aware of the meaning of the word, that is, the significance of "nothing" or "nothingness." Concentration is intensified further by shouting the syllable *mu*.

The psychic changes brought about by the koan exercise pass through stages that vary with the individual. The first reaction is almost always one of pain, which can become quite intense. Discouragement sets in to the point of wanting to give up the practice. This may be followed by a noticeable feeling of alleviation, and the disciple may believe he has already achieved the goal. But the end is not yet; the beguiling visions and hallucinations experienced next are regarded as so many deceptions that hail from the makyō. The master and his assistants will not permit the enjoyment of such false pleasures, but mercilessly restore the disciple's psychic balance.

Previous Experience and Preparation   All the writers of the accounts are Buddhist devotees of various backgrounds and education, young and old alike. Some arrive at inner calm and insight after leading an active life. Young nuns prepare themselves for the practice zealously and with a boundless willingness to sacrifice. The typical features of Japanese religiosity are evident everywhere: above all an alert and very sensitive appreciation of nature that savors stillness and moves one to higher aspirations. It is in stillness that the Japanese experiences the loneliness and dread of his existence, blended into nature and subject to nature's impermanence. Turning inward leads to the discovery of deeper layers of the self. As an Oriental, it is obvious to him that ultimate truth is not an object of theoretical knowledge but something to be grasped through practice.

Most practitioners of Zen are first motivated to seek truth through their struggle with the problem of existence. The problem enters their experience as loneliness and dread, as the senselessness of everyday life, some plight brought about by fate or their own fault, as inner unrest or outer threat, or as man's subjection to impermanence and death. The chaos following World War II also elicited a personal crisis in some cases. "Since the war ended, a righteous man sees nothing but folly. The world has become topsy-turvy. Nothing can satisfy one anymore. Man's life is miserably short. Stick it out! To laugh and to weep, that is to live."[5] The writer of these lines had succumbed to the flurries of pleasure in his previous life, until the painful antagonism between sensuality and conscience brought him to reflect on the meaning of human life. This problem was intensified in the riddle of life and death, and the possibility of overcoming death.

The encounter with death is where humans most strongly feel religious experience of the impermanence of all earthly things. Orientals close to nature also experience it at the same elementary level in the changing seasons. One devout Buddhist woman, who was already middle-aged when she turned to the practice of Zen, relates a childhood incident that imparted a religious tone to her entire life. When she was nine or ten, she saw a picture of Buddhist nuns, at work in the autumn landscape, gazing pensively at the falling red leaves of a maple tree. This image of impermanence and renunciation never left her. In retrospect, her life seemed like so many autumn seasons that had flowed past as swiftly as water—until the picture of the nuns finally became a reality for her.[6] Another disciple recalls noticing the impermanence of nature and being struck by a feeling of "inexpressible loneliness and dread" in his childhood.[7]

Psychic anomalies in previous life are rare in the accounts under review here. Of more than one hundred practitioners, only two are identifiable as neurotic: a physician who for decades had been an alcoholic and a morphine addict,[8] and a hypersensitive lady who, after several nervous breakdowns and a stay in a mental asylum, had tried various religious sects and finally found her way to Zen Buddhism and enlightenment.[9] Apart from these exceptions, the accounts show the participants to be normal, mentally healthy people. Nor do they reveal that morbid urge to escape from the self and the environment that Aldous Huxley considers as one of the basic aspirations of the soul and the principal stimulus to extraordinary states of consciousness.[10] For striving to solve the riddle of existence is the most normal of human yearnings and inspires sound religious activity in man. It provides the personal motivation for most of the Zen practitioners and remains effectual during practice itself.

The Austerities of Practice   Upon embarking on the way of enlightenment or beginning the practice session, the Zen disciple is strongly determined to undergo all the austerities involved. Many are stimulated above and beyond this by the idea that this, here and now, is the great opportunity of their life. And Zen masters encourage this mood: "If only you want resolutely to attain enlightenment, you can attain it."[11] Or: "This is the opportunity that will not come again a second or third time. Heaven and earth be thanked! . . . Practice with determination."[12]

The reaction to pain is never exactly the same in any two people; this holds true for the austerities of Zen practice as well. The practitioners may deal with pain in various ways, but no one is spared the exertion. Though accentuating different points, the accounts of actual pain are the same throughout. First of all, there is the complaint of aching feet. Even though they are accustomed to the posture to some degree or other, almost everyone reports of pain in the feet and knee joints, setting in on the first day, reaching a climax on the second or third day, and then gradually diminishing. In some cases the beginner's entire practice session can be spent getting used to the lotus posture. Bodily fatigue arises and increases as a result of short hours of sleep. Some even complain of a sore throat at the end of a day of hard practice, after shouting mu at the top of their lungs for hours.

It is well known from the anecdotes of numerous Chinese Zen masters that the disciple is occasionally whacked with a stick *(kyōsaku)* during practice. Western writers tend to take this custom lightly, interpreting it symbolically or as the occasional remnant of the rough brutes of old. But in the Harada school, at least, striking the practitioner with a stick by no means has a merely symbolical meaning: it produces actual pain. Zen masters emphasize primarily two purposes. The first is to stir up one's fervor. Sitting in the lotus posture for long periods of time can cause the disciple to doze off. This in turn hampers his meditation, for the ideal state of meditation is one of alertness amidst interior and exterior quiet. One or more brisk whacks, which the disciple may himself request, awaken him when he is half asleep; hence they are welcomed by disciples who are fighting off sleepiness.

The stick also serves to arouse one from erring further into the "devil's realm." The second effect desired by the master is repentance (sange), which we shall treat in a later section.

Many accounts vividly portray the painful side of practice. Dōgen, in his early treatise entitled *Universal Promotion of the Principles of Zazen*, once said: "Zazen is the Dharma-gate of great repose and joy." Alluding to this celebrated dictum, a student writes, not without irony, of his first experiences in the lotus posture: "I felt as if entering hell. As soon as I sat and began to count my breaths, I experienced an onslaught of all manner of confusing ideas. At the same time a stinging pain penetrated my legs to the marrow and mounted grindingly to my head. . . . I came to only after unfolding my legs and rubbing my aching feet."[13]

In general, young people are spurred by pain to greater fervor. One student who, plagued by the problem of existence, resolved to participate in a practice session, was at first unable to summon the ardor needed. On the third day, he writes: "I began to struggle with all my force. The straining energy filled my belly with vigor. I concentrated on the ideogram mu visualized in space. Perspiration ran down my back in torrents, breathing became difficult, my eyes were swimming, but grimly I held on with locked teeth. Thus continued the painful phase of zazen. . . . "[14] This phase must not, of course, be taken in isolation. The same student recounts that after a while the body recovers its balance, breathing becomes easy, and then the beneficial character of the practice is felt.

The salutary effect of the stick is particularly conspicuous in awakening the disciple from the intrigues of the "devil's realm." One high-ranking civil servant who devoted his entire self to the practice of Zen with the noblest of motives, soon fell into this state. Pleasurable visions began to transport him so that his eyes filled with tears of joy. The ache in his legs was as if blown away. A watchful fellow-devotee, who had himself undergone similar experiences, immediately recognized his state of mind. "He rose, and down came the stick on my shoulders, blow after blow. 'Persevere and do not cry,' he said as he continued dealing me powerful blows. Slowly I returned to a normal state of calm."[15] After he successfully completed the practice session, his wife and children congratulated him on having attained enlightenment.

Women are no less courageous in undergoing the austerities. Some are well prepared for the severity of the practice from their own renunciations or endurance of hardships. One well-educated young

Buddhist woman had the ideal requisites for the spiritual ascent. She had been in the habit of rising an hour before her parents in order to perform zazen at home. When her heart's desire to enter the convent of Abbess Nagasawa was at last fulfilled, she was overjoyed at the unpretentious yet strenuous way of convent life. The abbess had found the right words to spur her on to an unconditional fervor: "Anybody not resolved to grasp the truth should rather leave forthwith." This was precisely the total commitment she had been yearning for, and she devoted herself to the cloistered life with all her strength. But at the very first practice session her good will was to be sorely tried. How she had wished to sit solidly, but now her legs ached and no solution to the koan was apparent. The pain increased with each new day. She writes: "The severity of practice penetrates, as it were, every pore of my body. What is 'nothingness'? Besides the anguish of finding no solution, the whole exercise is painful. On the third day the abbess began to whack me horribly and I had never been struck in my life. I cried out loud. Afterwards the thought occurred to me: truly, here one practices like the illustrious masters of old did; one is struck with full force—it is terrible, but precisely that is gratifying."[16]

The austerities drive the disciple on until tension reaches a climax when, in spite of self-sacrificing efforts, the desired goal remains absent. At this phase, temptations arise that put courage, perseverance, and patience to the supreme test. Why all this pain if I just can't do it, if I am too weak, too pitiful, if I am not among the chosen because of entanglements in bad karma? Such temptations can irritate the practitioner or else lead him into deep despair over the senselessness of his efforts. In either case, the prevention of psychic collapse depends upon the skill of the master.

The accounts reported here are, with a single exception, by people who attained the goal of enlightenment. It is understandable that they speak with a certain smugness of the exertions they have endured. Still, while depicting their painful efforts to gain the way in strong colors, they stress again and again that their own strength would have been insufficient without outside help.

Devotion Buddhist schools have been classified into groups according to whether salvation is attained through "one's own power" *(jiriki)* or through "power from outside" *(tariki)*. The Amida schools are considered the prime examples of salvation through external assistance, whereas the Zen schools are seen as the typical way of salvation by means of one's own endeavors. A look at the literature of Zen Buddhism can strengthen this impression, especially when one reads the Chinese Zen masters, who admonished their disciples to seek the Buddha not outside but in their own heart. However, this does not contradict the fact that the atmosphere of many a Zen monastery is hardly less devotional in mood than that of the Amida temples. Master Harada was familiar with the polarity jiriki-tariki and devised the practical exercises in a way that did not suppress either pole. His disciples unite trusting devotion and ascetic endeavor.

The disciples' personal devotion is expressed in an unproblematical, religious atmosphere. Turning to Zen is often combined with a resolve to perform certain devotional exercises. Thus the first resolution of one educated layman is to recite the *Kannon Sutra* every morning.[17] A girl worships before the Buddha image morning and evening by reciting a sutra, all this by way of diligently preparing for zazen.[18] Another fervent Buddhist woman, before the practice session begins, puts her yearnings into a prayer that implores: "All you Buddhas of the three ages and all you patriarchs, have mercy on me and deign to make me worthy of the true Dharma!"[19] Upon departing for an important practice session, a nun takes leave of her home temple and prays before the main Buddha image: "I am not capable with my own power; I am in absolute need of the power of the Buddha. Pray, grant me your power!"[20]

During the practice session, the devotional attitude passes through many phases of expression and intensity. One student considers it quite natural "to worship the main image *(honzon)* of the Buddha" before meditation.[21] The following account gives a vivid picture of an extensive devotional exercise: "Each time I started out to do zazen I visualized the honzon of the Buddha and prayed, 'Please let me attain enlightenment!' Then I worshiped Kannon, the sixteen Arhats, the Bodhisattva Jizō [Sanskrit: Kṣitigarbha], and the two Patriarchs,[22] and when I prayed for the intercession of my parents, who died when I was still a child, my feelings welled up in me. Thus I experienced for the first time in my life the meaning of trusting surrender to the Buddhas and patriarchs."[23]

The devotional attitude becomes embedded in the certain conviction: the Buddha protects me. Whatever I may encounter on the hard way of Zen practice, I am born in the Buddha's keeping. "However hard one's efforts become, the Buddhas and Patriarchs protect him—there is no need to worry."[24] Such words from the master's mouth comfort the aspirant in dark hours. An elderly man is ready to quit the session after the first sleepless night and try again another time. Persuaded by the master to persevere, he then resolves to sit during the night as well. "The Buddha protects me. Even insomnia, which was my worst enemy up to now, has become my ally."[25]

Popular piety has endowed Kannon, the Bodhisattva of mercy, with feminine, indeed maternal traits. Devotion to this figure plays an important role, as the previous citations already indicate. If there exists a personal surrender and trust anywhere in Buddhist piety, it is in the worship of Kannon. One text, a prayer to Kannon, is remarkable for its psychology; it aims at the experience of universal unity apparently by disposing the devotee to this goal by a kind of auto-suggestion. The pious woman at prayer in this case distinguishes between her empirical self, the basis of all dualistic concepts and ideas, and an absolute self corresponding to Kannon. "Kannon, you are always with me and protect me. Kannon, give strength to my absolute self that brings you no disgrace and kill this ugly and loathsome dualistic ago. A cleft is still open!"[26]

Obviously attracted to this manner of prayer, she continues in the same vein on the next day: "Kannon, please, never avert your eyes from me! I show myself to you sincere and simple, according to your heart—you who with absolute power are sure of victory. Not 'being' and 'non-being,' but only 'non-being' is. . . ."[27]

Such a prayer seems to destroy the personal intent of the devotee. All her mind's efforts are directed to bringing her self into contact with nothingness. But nothingness is the absolute.

These descriptions throw light on a problem that cannot be solved in its entirety: how the devotional attitude fits in with the basically monistic metaphysics of Zen Buddhism despite the logical contradiction. To be sure, the history of religions offers ample evidence of personal attitudes in nontheistic religious systems. The truth of divine immanence in the universe and of the original sanctity of creation is apparently able to evoke religious responses. Zen Buddhism, furthermore, recognizes a relative transcendence beyond the world of perceptible phenomena and the empirical self. On this basis, the transcendence achieved by the committed Zen disciple can be experienced religiously. One female Zen student, reflecting intensely on the essence of enlightenment, came across the words "self-nature," "nonnature," and "emptiness" while reading a book by her master. "Ah, transcendence," she exclaimed, "if it is transcendence then I can well understand it."[28]

The word "transcendence" awakened an immediate echo in the heart of this yearning woman, whose account shows her to be a thoroughly religious Kannon devotee.

Repentance and Purification Repentance (the Japanese word *sange* is hardly translatable otherwise) plays a surprisingly important role in the practice of Zen. Several accounts make mention of repentance, and quite a few aspirants tell of profoundly emotional experiences of repentance. This aspect seems even less compatible with Zen metaphysics than that of devotion, considered, as it is, a most remarkable special case. The personal character of repentance is, of course, ultimately rescinded in Zen Buddhism, since all personal acts in the last analysis empty into universal unity.

A treatise called *Shushōgi,* compiled from the writings of Dōgen, gives valuable information on the significance of repentance in Zen.[29] The *Shushōgi* distinguishes between two sorts of repentance: superficial or factual repentance and radical or essential repentance. Factual repentance has to do with all the sinful deeds that produce bad karma, be they committed in this life or in a previous existence. In radical or essential repentance, sin is grasped in its relation to Buddha-nature. In this view, sin is equivalent to that ignorance without beginning that gives rise to all the desires, defilements, and passions obscuring man's Buddha-nature.

Both motivations underlying the distinction in the *Shushōgi* are given expression, separately or combined, in the accounts of the devotees' experiences. The sense of repentance, like that of devotion, tends to be personal and frequently reaches a high degree of intensity. The confession of sins usually remains quite general, although actual sins committed in one's previous life are also mentioned.

One elderly woman had a very personal experience of repentance during sutra recitation: "My eyes well up, tears flow, the letters of the sutra become blurred. 'The inexhaustible defilements—I vow to cut through them.'[30] That pertains to me. The sutra admonishes me. If I were to die tonight, it would not be an early death. Sixty years have already passed. But can I die thus, so full of errors and defilements? . . . Tears flow, tears of repentance, tears of sympathy. O Kannon, Bodhisattva of great kindness and great mercy, take away my passions and defilements!"[31] Pious Buddhists, reciting the passage of the "inexhaustible defilements" from the vow of the Bodhisattva daily and often habitually, thus evoke repentance. To cleanse oneself from the dust of the defilements means to realize one's Buddha-nature. The woman in the above example took the goal of the Mahayanist way and made it her personal concern, offering it to Kannon in the form of a prayer.

The sense of repentance in pious Buddhists is usually sparked by a passage from the sutras or an admonition from the master. But at times it arises spontaneously, as in the case of a student who, in a state of inner need, paid a visit to a quiet rural temple. Sitting in his room late in the evening, he heard the monks chanting the sutras in the temple, when all at once "the history of a powerless life appeared before my eyes. Unnoticed tears of repentance wet my cheeks. . . ."[32] He felt guilty for his failures, especially for wasting the precious power of life.

"For the unenlightened, zazen and dokusan are the two indispensable means to combat the defilements"—thus writes a young man who long avoided the interview with the master out of timidity.[33] The master provokes a zeal leading to more intensive meditation, which in turn augments the sense of repentance. Another timid practitioner, who had abandoned his first practice session on the third day, finally overcame his pusillanimity and confessed: "Ah, I was bad. . . . Even while I recited the sutras with hands folded, it was only external ceremony: my thoughts were far removed. Then suddenly I experienced an inner transformation. Tears welled up—I have been wicked. I pray you, O Buddha, protect me! Awakening repentance in this manner, I turned to practice again with renewed resolve."[34]

A nun who had passed many years of her life in negligence of her duties experienced a fundamental change of attitude. At her very first interview with the abbess, she made her confession in sorrow, expecting to be severely reprimanded. But all she encountered was the gentle voice of the master, whose penetrating face seemed to disclose the thirty-three majestic Kannons: "You need not ask me for forgiveness. If you have been indolent, it is for this reason that you meet the true Dharma so late. The Buddhas and patriarchs weep." These words pierced her like a nail, and she became willing to undergo all the pains of practice.[35]

The accounts cited here clearly display something personal in the acts of repentance. Indeed, personal attitudes are evident throughout Buddhism to a considerable degree. On the other hand, Zen Buddhists, adhering to the Mahayanist doctrine of the nonduality, steer away from the Western notion of person, which in their view necessarily introduces a duality to the one and only reality. But it is not our purpose here to pursue the philosophical and theological questions that arise in this context.[36]

One can hear many different motives in the accounts of experiences of present-day Zen disciples, and yet their basic tone is the same. At its center is the inner tension between techniques of meditation and personal motivation—at least as long as the accounts depict the efforts made in preparation for the liberating experience. This aspect of Zen should not be overlooked, although emphasizing it to the exclusion of other factors would give a one-sided picture. As D. T. Suzuki amply showed throughout the various phases of his long life, Zen spans an enormous area. The names of Hui-neng, Ma-tsu, and Lin-ch'i, or Sesshū, Ikkyū, and Bashō, or Dōgen, Hakuin, and Nishida open doors to many different worlds. All these names and more, and especially the multitude of the nameless, must be taken into account in treating Zen in its entirety.

TWELVE

Satori: Zen Enlightenment

BUDDHISTS SEE THE PROTOTYPE of enlightenment in the great experience of Shākyamuni that made this homeless seeker the Enlightened One, the Buddha. According to Zen tradition, there followed the Indian and Chinese Zen patriarchs, all of them enlightened men in full possession of the experience—a life of transmission continuing through the centuries. Transmitting the seal of enlightenment is not a physical event; rather in the meeting of minds the light is sparked ever anew.

Zen history relates of many enlightened people, but only hesitatingly does it give any information about what the experience of enlightenment is. It was not customary among the early Chinese Zen masters to speak of their own experiences. The chronicles and collections of koan are exceedingly terse as soon as experience is the subject matter; usually they merely indicate the fact of enlightenment in a short word or two. Master Wu-men, the famed compiler and commentator of the koan collection named after him, reprimands Zen masters who in his opinion talk too much. But it is only natural that experiences of enlightenment occur in a human context and permit certain essential traits to be discovered upon deep study.[1]

Japanese Zen history gave more expression to the experience of enlightenment. The Japanese Zen masters show themselves from the start to be more loquacious than their Chinese predecessors. Not only do they frequently express themselves in explicating the terse and puzzling words of the Chinese; their discourses and sermons on the Zen way contain admonitions and instructions that occasionally relate directly to experience. We have the Japanese Zen masters to thank for the first pieces of testimony permitting an actual description of the experience. Unexcelled to this day are the great Zen master Hakuin's depictions of his experience.² Another valuable document is the account by Master Kōsen Imakita from the Meiji era.³ These and a few other classical texts on Zen enlightenment have received attention in our day and invite further psychological assessment.

Psychological interest was activated among Japanese when they came into contact with the West. The Masters learned to answer the hitherto unheard-of questions of their Western disciples without losing any of their dignity. And Zen disciples in the West told or wrote about what they learned from their masters. In this way a new source of information was made available whose value can be judged in part by the insight, psychological understanding, and individual destiny of the writer.⁴

Like all mystical experience, Zen enlightenment is ineffable. It is, however, worthwhile to make efforts toward some knowledge of this significant phenomenon, even if such efforts are inadequate. Two ways suggest themselves: describing the phenomenon psychologically and attempting a philosophical understanding of the essence. But the latter approach cannot produce strictly valid results in the case of an experience that absolutely transcends any human categories of thought. The way of description is more in line with the present introductory work. For this reason, we turn to the accounts given by contemporary Zen disciples of their experience, again referring primarily to the aforementioned reports from the Harada school.⁵ These reports are of particular interest for the very fact that this school directly and effectively aims at the experience of enlightenment. It cannot always be taken for granted that the practitioner of Zen directly aspires to enlightenment in his meditation. To this day Zen circles seriously discuss whether and to what extent the disciple should seek and aim for a satori experience. The accounts of experience from the Harada school permit us to follow the course of the Zen experience from its preliminary stages to its culmination.

Psychic Changes During Practice In the Harada school, the practice of Zen, aimed directly at the satori experience, is geared to psychic changes from the beginning. One Zen disciple, instructed about the dynamic and purposeful character of the practice, returned to a vigorous practice after several initial failures. He reports: "The only aim is enlightenment. There are only two more days of the sesshin left. Telling myself this, I returned to the meditation hall. To my surprise I noticed what a difference in energy consumption there is between meditation aimed toward a goal and merely sitting. After that I was able to go on full of vigorous energy."[6]

Such zazen charged with power is a dynamic exercise, the outward tranquility of sitting in the lotus posture being animated from within. Zen masters continually awaken and strengthen the conviction that one can accomplish the goal, and this stimulus sets the psychic process toward enlightenment in motion. Some masters even instruct their disciples on their state of mind, especially near the end of the practice session, to spur them on to their best efforts.

The monotony of practice evokes diverse and constantly changing impressions in the mind of the students, varying with their personality and temperament. Both swells of emotion and sensitivity to pain go through changes. In the course of practice, the mind experiences various "disturbances" *(mōsō)*. Such disturbances, thoughts, and images that excite and divide one's attention come and go in rapid succession. From about the third day on, as practice becomes more intensive, they become more vehement and painful. "My body was glowing with heat," one particularly sensitive student reports.[7] As practice progresses further, the disturbances diminish and the student is able to concentrate solely on his koan. At this point he thinks he has it made. But the devil's realm awaits, and many must go through it before attaining enlightenment.

What in Zen language is called makyō covers a large number of diverse phenomena, some distressing, others delightful, a few purely psychic, but most accompanied by somatic changes. All of them hinder progress and divert one from the goal of enlightenment. Zen masters warn against the fascinations of the "devil's realm," which are all the more dangerous the less the student recognizes them for what they are. Confusing them with enlightenment can lead one far astray. Thanks to the vigilance of the master, the adventures of makyō usually end with the student restored to a healthy, sober state. But sometimes these experiences cast even the zealous Zen disciple into utter dispair, causing him to break off his practice. This was the case with one student practicing the famous koan of Hakuin concerning the sound of one hand. During one cold winter night, he felt a glowing heat in his body. He relates the following experience: "The figure of the Zen master Hakuin appeared to me with a ghostly white face. Suddenly the one hand turned into a jewel that began to circle around wildly in my body and shattered after some ten minutes of high-speed circulation. Then, like the refreshing feeling after a rain shower in summer, a strange joy, an unutterable joy, overcame me. . . ."[8]

His disillusionment was bitter when, the next morning, after a sleepless night, he was told by the master that all this was only manifestations from the devil's realm. The student hastily concluded that Zen was not for him, and it was a good while before he again took up the practice.

A woman who, full of great expectations, was participating in a sesshin for the second time was, on the other hand, not shaken by the most severe tests. She recounts the following: "One after the other, apparitions from the devil's realm arose and oppressed my eyes and ears. My hands, feet, and face trembled constantly, sometimes one part after the other, sometimes my whole body. In bad moments I felt a piercing pain, like being stuck with needles or drawn up by glowing points of iron. A man condemned to death by electrocution must feel like this."[9] Another disciple, a Zen monk who felt a burning, piercing sensation up and down his spine, wants to reexperience the strange pain because he confuses it with enlightenment.[10]

Visions and hallucinations are frequent manifestations from the devil's realm and evoke particularly strong impressions on account of increased sensitivity during practice. The following report is typical of this sort of makyō: "During zazen all kinds of apparitions from the devil's realm oppressed me. The paper windows appeared to me like a horse's head or bull's face, or like a Buddha or a monk. A whack from the stick soon set me straight as I continued meditating."[11]

Heavenly beings from the Mahayanist pantheon frequently appear as manifestations from the devil's realm, setting in especially when the body begins to become fatigued because of intensive effort. One woman's report reminds us of Theresa of Avila, who prescribed a hearty breakfast to her fellow nuns visited with all sorts of visions. As the woman herself recognized, "probably the apparitions were brought about because I stopped taking nourishment. I was admonished, and resolved to eat three meals a day from then on to strengthen my body and mind, and to devote myself seriously to meditation."[12]

The very refined feeling for nature characteristic of the Japanese is related to their highly developed sensitivity to sense impressions. During Zen practice, light reflections, colors, and sounds are perceived sharply and felt deeply. The sensitivity of those meditating increases from day to day and apparently reaches a climax before the liberating experience comes. After conquering restlessness and nervous fatigue, the disciple enters a state of mental clarity and physical tranquility. It can even happen that he becomes insensitive to pain and is unable to determine whether the stick of the vigilant monk has struck him or his neighbor. Lights and sounds delight or frighten him in the middle of the day or—more frequently—during the night. One student catches a glimpse out of the corner of his eye of "the wonderful, majestic figure of an old mistletoe tree, floating quietly in the dark light—an indescribable vision."[13]

A nun who had inclinations toward ecstasy and who literally practiced her koan day and night was inflicted with the strangest psychic and physical conditions. Suddenly one night she was awakened by a loud noise, and her feet began to stretch and dance under the covers by themselves. An indescribably intense feeling of pleasure rippled through her body. Later the other side of the experience showed itself in sharp pains. Parapsychological phenomena like levitation and cessation of breathing followed her all the way to enlightenment.[14]

The few accounts we have chosen to cite here seem to justify the conclusion that it is absolutely necessary that one entrust himself to a reliable and experienced guide in the practice of Zen. This becomes all the more necessary the further along the student progresses. One should be strongly warned against venturing on his own.

Symptoms and Preliminary Stages In many cases, the liberating experience is foretold by symptoms that the experienced master recognizes but does not confuse with enlightenment. The student himself may easily mistake the very high stages of concentration for enlightenment. One disciple, for example, straining with all his might, suddenly experienced a breakthrough. "I forgot myself and cried aloud for a few seconds. Oh! The iron wall shattered."[15] However, this powerful surge of emotion was not yet enlightenment. Told this by the master, he continued to practice and soon reached the goal. A similar experience occurred in a woman to whom all sounds seemed to converge into one single mu. She, too, had to make another final effort.[16] In such cases the abbess encourages the practitioners by assuring them that only a paper-thin distance separates them from Oneness, and only a little push is needed to break open the shell.

The liberating experience is different from the feelings of exultation and sudden luminous insights that occur along the way of practice, particularly in the final phases. One disciple already had an "experience like satori" before coming to the practice session: "Once, on a day late in March when I was sweeping the garden, a feeling suddenly overcame me: am I myself and the world not together one? Can there be anything like a solitary ego at all?" He let himself be absorbed by this feeling and reflected: "I am now sweeping the garden with the bamboo broom. The broom moves, making a sound and turning its eyes to the ground, as it were. This ground is nothing other than a part of the whole earth. Then I myself am united to the whole earth. The sound of the broom could not arise if I myself and the broom and the whole earth did not exist here. They are inseparably connected together." However, the joy that these thoughts at first awakened in him soon faded away, and he realized that mental reflections are not enlightenment.[17]

For a teacher who, in spite of some endeavor, had no success in attaining the goal, the light first dawned in the midst of his professional work. After a nightlong vigil with examination papers, day began to break at about four o'clock, and the heading of the nineteenth koan of the *Mumonkan* suddenly came to his mind: "Everyday life is the way." He reflected: "Yes, this is it—to live the moment, the now. If there is any eternity, it is in this moment. Whoever lives the moment well lives eternity. Is not truth in the very moment that embraces eternity—in the eternal now?"[18] But, like most luminous insights, this light, too, fast loses its illuminating power: the initial good effects fade away, and a considerable time elapses before the teacher again turns to Zen practice. Then, while taking part in a sesshin, the lecture by the master evokes another profound insight upon subsequent reflection. Taking a walk through the temple cemetery and the adjoining school garden, he feels immersed in the indestructible life of the universe and relishes the two words *nyo* (equality) and *soku* (identity), which had been central to the exposition that morning. His joy is profound, but again is quickly lost.[19] In Zen language, joy is called Dharma-rapture *(hōetsu)*; it is no more to be confused with enlightenment than are illuminating insights. It is likely that this enraptured joy is closely connected to the liberating experience; yet the two are kept distinct. Hence the Zen master Yasutani says: "If the enlightenment is profound, the joy too is great. But joy and enlightenment are two different things."[20]

Cosmic Consciousness and Nothingness   The accounts show Zen enlightenment to be a cosmic experience. In the sudden breakthrough of the mind, the universal unity of reality that includes or expands the self is experienced, and this in an indescribable—and hence nonarticulated—way. Experiences of so-called cosmic consciousness perhaps come closest to the Zen experience, but in the case of Zen enlightenment, the basic Mahayanist doctrine of universal Buddha-nature in all living beings gives this term a more precise sense: that of the holiness and original pureness of all reality, which is one.[21]

The liberating experience in Zen is given a special coloring by the mu koan, by means of which many Zen disciples attain enlightenment. Most likely it is rare indeed that a practitioner understands this koan in its full bearing. But even the unassuming student is somehow drawn by the constant practice of negating all determinations and relations into the metaphysical atmosphere, where it is a question of being and nonbeing. From the will of negation is born, in dialectical process, the thrust of reaching for the absolute.

The liberating experience erupts when the process of maturation is completed. This process is facilitated by the intensive koan exercise in which all faculties of the body and mind are directed toward nothingness. The body is tightly erect in the lotus posture, and mental endeavor is joined to bodily exertion. At the moment of greatest tension, as it were, the shell bursts and the cosmic dimension opens up. Often there remains in the experience some vestige of one's initial state or prevalent preconceptions. Thus an engineer at home in the sciences and technology was struck by the egocentricity of modern man. In the liberating experience he realized the nullity of the ego. He depicts how the experience developed from the koan concentration as follows: ''The paper door in front of me is nothing; consciousness too is nothing; yesterday's thought of having become one with the Great Being is nothing. There is nothing but 'nothingness.' Is it a moment? Is it eternity? I was astonished that unnoticeably the Zen hall and I myself were radiant in an absolute light.'' All this time he experienced an unspeakable feeling of happiness. ''It is all good.'' In the next moment he reflects back to the beginning of his practice: ''The self to which I had fastened myself was originally nowhere. But the words [of the sutra] are unchangeable: 'In heaven and under heaven I alone am the Perfected One.' Are not the sliding doors of the Zen hall the Perfected One? Do not the straw mats dance under the feet of the Perfected One? Do not the red maple leaves gleam in the light of the Perfected One? The universe is enveloped by the Perfected One; the Perfected One lives in the universe.''[22]

The merging of all things into nothingness; the identity of nothingness, the universe, and the Buddha—these aspects recur in many accounts of the liberating experience.

During dokusan a nun complains of her failure to the abbess: "No matter how I look at them, the paper windows only look like paper windows." The answer: "Well, paper windows *are* paper windows." At this moment the spontaneous outcry of enlightenment overtakes her. "Whether I look at the Buddha, or the abbess, or the sitting cushion, all have become 'nothingness.' Unbounded nothingness expands infinitely and is everywhere the same."[23]

A Naturalistic Hue　Until rather recently the Japanese lived in close contact with nature and in this way are somewhat conditioned for the cosmic experience. In some accounts of the liberating experience a vivid feeling for nature is expressed. A woman suddenly grasps enlightenment: "As the sound of the bell rouses me, my self that is practicing is Buddha. Like a waterfall, tears gush out of my eyes in this moment. . . . I sit on in ever more profound tranquility, in ever more pure clarity. While I gaze at 'nothingness,' I perceive the sound of raindrops and the wind rustling through the trees, and steps in the night. From afar the clear voice of a bird is heard. Already it is dawn and in the morning sun the dew sparkles on the tips of leaves. It is as if the whole sun came pouring down drop by drop. Oh, what glory! Oh this splendor, this vastness is nothingness; like the great ocean, all is nothingness. From the depths of my body tears gush forth in solitude."[24]

Contemporary Zen disciples emulate the masters of old in expressing their experiences of nature in poetic language. From the vision of enlightenment, Dōgen composed this poem:

> The color of the mountain side and
> 　the rushing of the valley streams;
> All is my voice and my figure, Shākyamuni.[25]

A woman practicing Zen grasped the meaning of Dōgen's words in her experience: "Yes, my voice and my figure. I am Shākyamuni. The glorious sky, paradise, and the Pure Land, the voices of birds and frogs, the fresh foliage of the mountainside, the dancing butterflies—all is nothingness, only nothingness."[26]

After a weak experience of a "light beginning like a grain of sand in the vast sea," another disciple is exhorted to practice more intensely. The more fervently she immerses herself in meditation, the vaster the flood of light extends, the deeper it seizes her. She then composes the following verse:

> Soundless and without scent, heaven and earth
> Are incessantly repeating unwritten sutras.[27]

Sudden Release   The liberating experience occurs suddenly, but usually after certain indications have announced its approach. Often it is elicited by a visual or an auditory sensation. We read of enlightenment flashing forth at the sound of the evening bell, the strokes of a clock, or rain pattering outside.[28] In the case of a sudden whack by the stick, it is less the pain—which is hardly felt any more at this stage—than the sound that acts as the catalyst.

The liberating experience not infrequently occurs during the interview with the master. Here, there is literally a seeing of eye to eye between master and disciple. The master fixes an incisive gaze on the student to detect the narrow cleft in his consciousness that opens into his interior. This situation has been compared with the pecking of a hen on the eggshell, while from the inside the chick hammers its way out to freedom. The reports of the abbess's disciples, both men and women, contain a wealth of impressive descriptions that testify to the extraordinary skill of this master. On the seventh day of the sesshin, she asks one student during dokusan: "How is it with nothingness?" "I don't know," replies the young man, who had been able to endure the severity of the practice only with a great deal of effort. "How is it with nothingness?" the abbess asks a second time and deals him a sharp blow on the knee. At this instant an exclamation of enlightenment comes out of the disciple's mouth: "Suddenly I feel that it has become bright. Oh, it is nothingness, this is nothingness, and that is nothingness."[29] On other occasions the abbess touches the tip of a disciple's nose with her stick, or points with the stick to the blackboard hanging behind the student; both times the unusual gesture suddenly elicits the liberating experience, which is expressed in cosmic terms. "I became one with the immense universe," one woman disciple relates. "Whether I turned my gaze upward or to the side, it expanded infinitely far, far. Finally I toppled over to the floor."[30]

The practice session is without a doubt particularly suited to reaching the high degrees of concentration necessary for the liberating experience. However, it can also occur outside the sesshin. One of the most stimulating reports is that of a highly placed bureaucrat who experienced enlightenment at home. In his youth he had been inspired by the old Japanese Zen masters. In his student days he had for a time succumbed to the appeal of Marxism. After taking up an occupation, however, he studied intensively the philosophy of Kitarō Nishida and the Kyoto school, drew closer to Zen Buddhism, and immersed himself in the sources of Zen literature. For the sake of practice, he joined a group of lay Buddhists who meditated regularly. Thus he came into contact with Master Yasutani and his circle of disciples. He was given the koan of "one's original face." From then on he made it a rule to meditate daily for thirty minutes each morning and evening, extending this time on some days.

He recounts his experience as follows: "One night I practiced more than an hour; the next day more than two hours. The next day, May 3, I was supposed to pick my wife up at the hospital by three o'clock. I practiced for an hour in the morning, sat again at 12:15, intending to meditate about thirty minutes. . . . With body and mind I struggled with the koan. After about half an hour, I noticed that my breath was becoming heavy and it was growing dark around me. This is it, I thought, and sat on, straining my whole body. But suddenly my whole body began to tremble, around me it was pitch black, and nothing was visible any longer; my thinking was cut off, past and future obliterated. Only my tears flowed steadily. I cried out unconsciously and wept. . . . When the trembling stopped, I felt completely absent-minded. I stirred and looked to see that it was exactly one o'clock. The 'original face' that until then rose up before me like a silver mountain or a wall of iron had disappeared. In the depths of my mind I only felt: 'It was not there at all . . . just as it now is, it is all right.' In an instant everything had changed without having to rack my brain at all. I felt completely cleansed. 'What is this? Could it be enlightenment?' "[31] The master, who at the time of these happenings was away, later subjected this disciple to a searching examination, and concluded that his experience was genuine.

Accompanying Traits The feeling of exaltation that, according to the accounts under review, commonly accompanies the liberating experience is generally expressed as a release of ecstatic joy and rapture oblivious of self. Only in rare cases is joy altogether absent. Yet "Dharma-rapture" is not the same as enlightenment. Even less is it possible to consider other strong emotions that occasionally erupt as essential traits of the experience. To some who attained enlightenment, the world seemed to be flooded with transsensual light and, as it were, transfigured. Often there is a feeling of levitation, a hovering lightness, and transparent brightness of the body. Zen disciples themselves pay little attention to such phenomena, for their awareness is absorbed in cosmic nothingness. In this respect the following account of a nun is typical: "I had forgotten myself. Oh, this is it, this is it. It is nothingness, it is nothingness. Heaven and earth become bright in an instant; my body has suddenly become light. I feel as if I could fly to the ends of heaven. All is nothingness; with hands folded I revere nothingness."[32]

Such phenomena accompanying the liberating experience are clearly distinguished from the phantoms of the so-called devil's realm. In contrast to those phantoms, these phenomena are highly esteemed by Zen masters on account of their proximity to enlightenment. "Oh, here is the entrance to reality as it really is!" one disciple exclaims, for to his astonishment the monastery garden presented an indescribable spectacle of resplendence. After the full release of enlightenment, he sees "all things in living motion and as if inviting my gaze. All things are in their place or they dwell securely in their place and appear to breathe. I was able to discover the existence of a world not entered by knowledge. The color of a flower on the altar of the Bodhisattva Mañjuśrī was incomparably resplendent."[33]

The Root of Nothingness After the disciple has attained his first, relatively weak experience, Zen masters insist on further practice and exhort him to intensify the liberating experience. Master Yasutani distinguishes between grasping nothingness and grasping the "root of nothingness," and he encourages his disciples to penetrate deeper until they have reached the root itself. To one student whose experience he recognizes as genuine he thus admonishes: "You have already grasped nothingness; now look at the root of nothingness!"[34] The root of nothingness is the source of unbounded vitality, in contrast to a conceptual and "lifeless nothingness" devoid of any value.[35] When experienced, nothingness is not lifeless, but its whole dynamism is not apparent until the root is grasped.

The various degrees of intensity of the liberating experience were realized by a post-office official from northern Japan. First, he envisioned the ideogram for nothingness and felt so much joy that he believed he had already grasped enlightenment. During the very first day of the following practice session, he again had the vision, this time even more clearly. Soon everything became nothingness for him. The master was convinced of the authenticity of this experience and exhorted the student to "see the root of nothingness!" He continued to practice with great zeal, and new experiences occurred, but none were recognized by the master as having grasped the root of nothingness. Then suddenly he was overwhelmed: "At once I gripped the root. It was as if a ball of fire had exploded." Thereupon ensued the following dialogue between him and the master. It reminds one of the classical exchanges between master and disciple in the history of Chinese Zen:

"Have you come here with the root?" the master asks.
"Yes."
"Then show it to me!"

The disciple still hesitates, so the master yells "Katsu!" The disciple's report continues: "At that moment my abdomen became hardened like a diamond, glowing as if on fire. When the master further urged: 'Show it!' I beat my body with my fist so that it reverberated loudly, and cried out: 'That's it! . . .' I surely had seen the root of nothingness; after three years of practice I saw my original face."[36]

The "original face" reveals the Zen disciple's true self, toward which he had been moving since his first departure. In many cosmic experiences, grasping the self is explicitly called an essential part of the realization. This aspect of the experience shows up very clearly in the account of one pious Buddhist woman for whom the question of the essence of things congealed in the question of the true form of Kannon. At the moment of enlightenment, she comprehended nothingness and, at the same time, "the true form of Kannon and the true form of the self, indeed the true form of all things. All is one. Whatever one may say, there can be no denying it. What I attained was seeing through to the original self."[37]

The more powerful the experience is, the more the person is caught in a current, both inwardly in the direction of the fundamental root and outwardly in eruptive ecstasies. With respect to the power of the realization, one Zen disciple's account of his second enlightenment experience reminds one of the ecstasies of the famed Zen master Hakuin. This particular disciple, a Buddhist layman, had already become acquainted with Hakuin's writings as a young student. His first enlightenment experience took place at Engaku-ji, a Rinzai temple in Kamakura, under the direction of Abbot Asahina. Later he came into contact with the Harada school and felt a need for further systematic practice. The second great experience took him by surprise one day in the express train between Tokyo and Kamakura. He was reading on Zen and came across the words of Dōgen: "Clearly I know, the mind is mountains, rivers, and the great earth; sun, moon, and stars." He had known this passage for a long time, but on this occasion it gripped him strongly. Streams of tears fell from his eyes, and he tried to conceal them with his handkerchief. The experience continued in all its intensity while he walked home along a side alley from Kamakura Station. After supper and a bath, he retired to sleep, but soon woke up again. It was then that the tumultuous experience erupted fully. Again the words of Dōgen pierced him, but this time "like a bolt of lightning going through my entire body. Heaven and earth dissolved. Like the roaring surf, great joy burst forth." He uttered a cry and burst out laughing. "There is no sophistry here!" he cried, again laughing loudly. He had gotten up and was tearing at the blankets and thumping the bed with both knees when his wife and child appeared at the door in utter consternation. His wife tried to hold his mouth shut with both her hands, and the child was sure Daddy had gone mad. "I have grasped enlightenment; the Buddha and the patriarchs do not deceive," he exclaimed after a while. But the whole event, though seeming to him to last a considerable time, took only three or four minutes, according to his wife. After he calmed down somewhat, he offered incense in thanksgiving before the image of Kannon. But his body trembled with excitement for days.[38]

What reminds one of Hakuin in this experience is not only its unusual vehemence but also the ecstatic condition of being beside oneself. The experience overpowers the disciple and is repeated in strong surges. As with Hakuin, after the great ecstasy described in detail, there follow many experiences of lesser intensity that enhance his joy and awareness of unity with the Buddha. He spontaneously recalls comparisons and expressions from the writings of the old masters. "The Buddha is set into motion." "All things flow freely, as the fish swims in the water." He experiences what the master of old called the "casting off of body and mind," and what he feels to be a part of the current of Zen tradition.

In examining the many accounts of the liberating experience, a difficult but important question arises. Are all satori experiences in Zen essentially the same? In particular, are the experiences of recent times identical with those realizations related in the chronicles and the sayings of the ancient masters? It appears that Zen masters, both today and in earlier days, recognize different degrees of intensity in the enlightenment experience, but nowhere do they discuss whether or not qualitative differences are possible, or how they might be characterized. Moreover, in the practice of contemporary Zen masters there is no agreement on the minimum requirements for recognizing a genuine satori. Neither do the accounts disclose how the masters determine the authenticity and degree of the particular enlightenment experience during dokusan. Master Yasutani justified keeping the method of ascertainment secret with the remark that indicating the procedure could mislead following generations to unauthentic answers. Indeed there probably are no external, objectively certain criteria for the authenticity of the experience. It appears that Zen masters recognize the genuineness in an immediate contact between master and disciple, or mind and mind. The question remains to what extent the Buddhist world view and Mahayanist philosophy play a role in this procedure.

At this point the phenomenological-psychological viewpoint that has guided our perusal of the accounts leads us back to the question of essence that so far has been bracketed. Of course, aspects of the experience colored by a world view were repeatedly brought to light by psychological investigation—as, for example, when a similarity shows up between Zen enlightenment and cosmic consciousness, or when the master urges the disciple to seek out the ''root of nothingness'' with all his might. In the Buddhist understanding, satori is a cosmic experience of universal unity opening the way to nothingness. Accordingly, in the epilogue to the first volume of accounts by his disciples, Master Yasutani explains the essence of Zen enlightenment as follows: ''Enlightenment means seeing through to your own essential nature, and this at the same time means seeing through to the essential nature of the cosmos and of all things. For seeing through to essential nature is the wisdom of enlightenment. One may call essential nature truth if one wants to. In Buddhism, from ancient times it has been called suchness or Buddha-nature or the one Mind. In Zen it has also been called nothingness, the one hand, or one's original face. The designations may be different, but the content is completely the same.''[39] This, then, is the Buddhist interpretation of the experience given by a Zen master.

The ''Christian interpretation'' of the same experience (or is it different?), in the words of H. N. Enomiya-Lassalle, is as follows: ''Satori or enlightenment is a transrational and immediate perception of self in connection with the nondifferentiated view of all created being—giving the impression of perfect unity, grasping the authentic self of one's personality upon dissolution of the empirical ego, and coming into contact with the absolute insofar as it is the source of created being. It is an experience that allows for many variations in intensity and constitution, according to the disposition of the individual; but which is invariably accompanied with joy, peace, certainty, and liberation from fear and doubt."[40]

These two interpretations of the essence of an ineffable experience indicate differences that recall the possibility of alternate ways of Zen hinted at in the opening chapter. One can find convincing reasons for assuming a plurality of Zen ways in the contemporary situation of worldwide meditation movements. But the question of the identity of Zen and the criteria of genuine enlightenment will not be silenced. Whatever the case may be for the plurality of Zen ways, the basic phenomenon remains "the Zen Buddhist way of enlightenment." A complete and correct understanding of Zen must take this original phenomenon into account.

The Ten Oxherding Pictures

ONCE WHEN I WAS STAYING in a rural city in Japan, a friend took me to an aged Zen master who directed a small monastery in a nearby rural village. He was held in great esteem for his enlightenment and during his long life had intensively studied the literature of his school. I was introduced to the master as a student of Zen, but had difficulty in engaging him in a conversation. What I told him of my readings in Zen literature was obviously of little interest to him. He gave my questions monosyllabic answers and clearly indicated that he considered talking about Zen to be basically useless. Zen is practice, experience, life—not explaining, interpreting, investigating, quibbling. All talk, as the Chinese masters of old say, is at best a finger pointing to the moon. The finger is not the moon and cannot pull the moon down.

The contemporary Japanese Zen master Ohtsu interprets the Ten Oxherding Pictures with these words: "What magic! Something that is actually nothing gets divided here into ten stages and explained in many words. . . . Foolish nonsense! The effort is completely wasted! It is work for nothing, and for nothing again."[1]

In writing a book about Zen, one has the same feeling. And yet it is necessary to write about Zen, and countless more books will be written about Zen. The last word can never be said, but Zen must be spoken about.

What further entices one to write about Zen is its inexhaustible wealth of interconnections with every area of human life. The experience of enlightenment is the highest peak and deepest core of Zen, but at the same time Zen encompasses many dimensions of human life. It possesses a profound metaphysics; it inspires numerous branches of art; and, for psychology (especially in its therapeutic function), it opens unexplored vistas and sets novel tasks. These aspects have often fascinated Western people so much that they have forgotten that first and foremost Zen is the most important school of meditation in Mahāyāna Buddhism. In this brief introductory and summary study we took the place of the Zen school in Buddhism as our point of departure, and always kept this basic character in mind—even when we endeavored to take as many aspects of Zen as possible into account.

In classical Chinese Zen Buddhism there developed a story that contains the quintessence of Zen and, when seen and practiced, may well lead to the experience of enlightenment. It is the tale of the ox and the oxherd. It has often been told and interpreted, and in China and Japan it came to be portrayed in pictures. But the story was always the same: the ox and the oxherd, two at the start, become united in the course of the way, for the ox symbolizes the true, profound Self, and the oxherd stands for nothing less than the human being.

The oxherd has lost his ox and stands alone on the vast pasture (first picture); but can the human being lose his Self? He searches and catches sight of the tracks of the ox (second picture); there is a mediatory assistance, in which religious things like sutras and monasteries can also play a part. Following the tracks, he finds the ox (third picture); but this is still a distant, intellectual knowledge or intuition of the ox. With fervent effort he tames the beast (fourth picture) and sets it out to pasture under careful surveillance (fifth picture). These two stages comprise practice in the Zen hall, the severe and painful practice until enlightenment is grasped, and the irrevocable practice of the enlightened one. The practitioner finds complete certainty; already the oxherd straddles the back of the ox and rides home triumphantly, playing the flute (sixth picture); the joy of the oxherd and the head of the ox, no longer bent in craving for grass, intimate the perfect freedom attained. Now the two have become one; the oxherd in his freedom no longer has need for the "ox" and forgets it, just as the trap and the net become useless after the hare and the fish are caught in the famous parable of Chuang-tzu. The oxherd stands alone with the ox (seventh picture). Now both oxherd and ox have disappeared in the securing, embracing nothingness of a circle (eighth picture). When the oxherd reappears, everything around him is just as it is (ninth picture)—the everyday life of the enlightened one. And the oxherd enters the town and the marketplace and bestows goodness to all about him (tenth picture). The enlightened one lives with his fellow human beings and lives like them, but the benevolence he radiates has its source in his enlightenment.

The origin of the values surrounding the Zen way become evident in the Ten Oxherding Pictures. Plenitude comes from nothingness, for nothingness is indistinguishably at one with perfect being.

Many ways lead to perfect being. Therefore, in conclusion, we are permitted to remark that no one is bound to Zen. One can accept Zen for himself and practice it, or one can choose another way of practice. One way is not for everybody, but all true ways converge in the way open for man's salvation.

Chinese-Japanese Equivalents

Chao-chou—Jōshū

Ch'ing-yüan Hsing-ssu—Seigen Gyō-shi

Fa-yen—Hōgen

Fen-yang Shan-chao—Funnyō Zen-shō

Hsüeh-tou Ch'ung-hsien: Setchō Fū-ken

Huang-po Hsi-yun—Ōbaku Kiun

Hui-k'o—Eka

Hui-neng—Enō

Hung-chih Cheng-chüeh—Wanshi Shōkaku

Hung-jen—Gun'in

Ju-ching—Nyojō

Kao-an Ta-yü—Kōan Daigu

Lin-chi—Rinzai

Lung-t'an—Ryōtan

Ma-tsu Tao-i—Baso Dōitsu

Nan-ch'üan P'u-yüan—Nansen Fugan

Nan-yüan Hui-yüng—Nan'in Egyō

Nan-yüeh Huai-jang—Nangaku Ejō

Pai-chang (*also* Po-chang) Huai-hai—Hyakujō Ekai

Seng-chao—Sōjō

Shen-hsiu—Jinshū

Shen-hui—Jinne

Shih-t'ou Hsi-ch'ien—Sekitō Kisen

Ta-hui Tsung-kao—Daie Sōko

Tai-i Tao-hsin—Dai-i Dōshin

Tao-hsüan—Dōsen

Tan-hsia T'ien-jun—Tanka Tennen

Te-shan—Tokusan

Ts'ao-tung—Sōtō

Wei-yang—Ikyō

Wu-men Hui-k'ai—Mumon Ekai

Yang-Ch'i—Yōgi

Yang-shan Hui-chi—Kyōzan Ejaku

Yüan-wu K'o-ch'in—Engo Kokugon

Yün-men Wen-yen—Ummon Bun'en

Notes

Full reference information is given in the Bibliography. If an author has two or more works listed there, these are distinguished in the Notes by abbreviated titles as well as the author's name.

Chapter 1

[1]The Japanese edition of Suzuki's works in thirty volumes is published by Iwanami Shoten, Tokyo, 1968–79. A selection of eleven volumes is published by Shunjūsha in Tokyo.

[2]Cf. Suzuki, *Mysticism*. This book includes a comparison of Eckhart and Zen mysticism, and some notes on Amida devotion.

[3]Otto, p. 242.

[4]*Ibid.*

[5]Dumoulin, *History*, p. 281.

[6]See Hirai.

[7]The Japanese Jesuit Kakichi Kadowaki, for example, attempts a synthesis of "the Ignatian Exercises and Zen" in a program for American Jesuits.

Chapter 2

[1]Oldenberg, p. 418.

[2]Majjhima Nikāya 26.

[3]Compare with the quotation in Chapter 12, p. 145.

[4]This and the following English translations of the *Mumonkan* are based upon the author's German translation of the original Chinese.

[5]Yamada, p. 200.

[6]Cf. Eliade.

[7]Suzuki, *An Introduction*, p. 5.

[8]*Ibid.*, p. 101.

[9]*Ibid.*, p. 16.

[10]Abe and Waddell, "Shōbōgenzō Genjōkōan," p. 134 ff.

[11]Merton, p. 23.

Chapter 3

[1]Dumoulin, *History*, pp. 32–51.

[2]Case no. 21

[3]Suzuki subtitles his *Studies in the Lankavatara Sutra* "one of the most important texts of Mahayana Buddhism, in which almost all its principal tenets are presented, including the teachings of Zen."

[4]This and the following quotations from the *Tao-te ching* are based upon the translations of de Bary, *Sources,* and Lau, *Lao Tzu,* I. The roman

numeral indicates the chapter number of the original.

[5]*Ibid.*, XXV
[6]*Ibid.*, XL
[7]*Ibid.*, XXI
[8]*Ibid.*, XXXIV
[9]*Ibid.*, XVI
[10]XII. Chan, *Source Book*, p. 202.
[11]XXV. Translation by James Legge; cf. Müller.
[12]XXII. Chan, *Source Book*, p. 203.
[13]Translation by Arthur Waley in Conze, *Buddhist Texts*, p. 295.
[14]Translation by Blofeld, *The Zen Teaching of Huang Po*, p. 55. This discourse addresses the Zen disciples as "disciples of the Tao" throughout.
[15]Chan, *Source Book*, p. 201.
[16]Miyuki writes about this in his *Kreisen des Lichtes*, pp. 39–62.
[17]Cf. the section on Tao-sheng in Dumoulin, *History*, pp. 61–66.
[18]Miyuki dates this text in the 12–13th centuries in his *Kreisen des Lichtes*, p. 176.
[19]*Ibid.*, pp. 48 ff.
[20]*Ibid.*, p. 53.
[21]*Ibid.*, p. 130.

Chapter 4

[1]See the articles by Liebenthal listed in the Bibliography.
[2]See the author's historical study on Bodhidharma, "Bodhidharma und die Anfänge." Of importance for further research is a recent work by Yanagida.
[3]Case no. 37.
[4]Quotation from the text entitled *Two Entrances and Four Acts*, long considered to be the only authentic writing of Bodhidharma until modern research proved otherwise
[5]*Keitoku Dentōroku* (Chinese: *Ching-te ch'uan-teng lu*), vol. 3. This chronicle was written down in thirty volumes by the Zen monk Tao-yüan and first

published in 1004 or 1011. In spite of the fact that it is historically unreliable, it offers a wealth of material on the history of Chinese Zen.
[6]*Ibid.*

Chapter 5

[1]Several English translations of the *Sutra of the Sixth Patriarch* have been published; see Chan, *Platform* and Yampolsky, *Platform*, two recent ones. Here the translation of the verses is based upon this material, but also takes the original Chinese text into account.
[2]Case no. 23.
[3]Case no. 29.
[4]Chuang-tzu, chapter 7. Cf. Chan, *Source Book*, p. 207. Lao-tzu also compares the mind with a mirror in chapter 10 of the *Tao-te ching*. The symbol of the mirror plays an important role in Chinese philosophy and religion; cf. Démieville, pp. 112–37.
[5]Suzuki, *Zen Doctrine*, p. 43.
[6]Yampolsky, *Platform*, p. 136.
[7]*Ibid.*, p. 163.
[8]Suzuki, *Zen Doctrine*, p. 57.
[9]Yampolsky, *Platform*, pp. 137 ff.
[10]Merton, p. 25.
[11]*Ibid.*, p. 27.
[12]*Ibid.*
[13]*Ibid.*
[14]Suzuki, *Zen Doctrine*, p. 45.
[15]D. T. Suzuki calls him "the father of Chinese Zen" (*ibid.*, p. 26) and "the first great native expounder of Zen" (*ibid.*, p. 14).

Chapter 6

[1]*Keitoku Dentōroku*, vol. 6.
[2]Suzuki, *Zen Doctrine*, p. 45.
[3]See Dumoulin, *Development*, p. 3.
[4]*Keitoku Dentōroku*, vol. 5.
[5]*Mumonkan*, case no. 28.

[6]*Ibid.*
[7]Gundert, vol. I, p. 439.
[8]*Keitoku Dentōroku,* vol. 6.
[9]Quoted in Dumoulin, *Development,* p. 11.
[10]English translation based upon Gundert's German translation of the original. (Vol. II, p. 152.)
[11]*Keitoku Dentōroku,* vol. 6.
[12]*Rinzairoku* (Chinese: *Lin-chi lu*), chronicle of the Zen master Lin-chi, translated and discussed in Suzuki, *Zen Buddhism and Psychoanalysis,* pp. 33–43; quotation from p. 32.
[13]Dürckheim, p. 368.
[14]From the *Rinzairoku.*

Chapter 7

[1]Miura and Sasaki, *Zen Koan,* p. xi ff.
[2]Miura and Sasaki, *Zen Dust,* p. 163.
[3]Gundert, vol. I, p. 37 ff.
[4]*Ibid.,* p. 44.
[5]*Ibid.,* p. 55.
[6]*Ibid.,* p. 59.
[7]*Mumonkan,* case no. 7.
[8]Buber, p. 995.
[9]*Ibid.,* p. 982.
[10]*Ibid.,* p. 886.
[11]*Ibid.,* p. 888.
[12]Scholem, p. 205 ff.
[13]Buber, p. 884 ff.
[14]Johnston, *Christian Zen,* p. 61 ff.

Chapter 8

[1]Translation (slightly modified) by Sadler, p. 22.
[2]Miura and Sasaki, *Zen Koan,* p. 7.
[3]Cf. "The Zen Mysticism of Hakuin" in the author's *History,* pp. 242–68. Miura and Sasaki's *Zen Koan* also pays Hakuin his due respect. See also Yampolsky's monograph on Hakuin.
[4]Keene, p. 355.

[5]*Ibid.,* p. 369.
[6]Buber, p. 982.

Chapter 9

[1]Watanabe, p. 15 and p. 18 ff. Watanabe quotes Dōgen's answer to the question whether the Zen disciple must observe the precepts. The observation of precepts, Dōgen explains in the "Bendōwa" chapter of the *Shōbōgenzō,* is the rule of the Zen school and part of the tradition of the Buddhas and the patriarchs.
[2]Abe and Waddell, "Dōgen's Fukanzazengi," p. 122. Dōgen also clarifies the practice of Zen in his *Shōbōgenzō.* A very detailed account of the technique of zazen is given by Keizan (1268–1325), the fourth successor to Dōgen and the founder of the Sōtō monastery Sōji-ji; see his *Zazen yōjinki* (Notebook of the Practice of Zazen), translated by the author in his *Östliche,* pp. 291–307.
[3]Abe and Waddell, "Dōgen's Fukanzazengi," p. 122.
[4]Masunaga, *A Primer,* p. 16. The six books of the *Zuimonki* were compiled after Dōgen's death by his main disciple and successor, Ejō (1198–1280). They include episodes from Dōgen's life that cast a good deal of light on the master's personality.
[5]*Ibid.,* p. 16.
[6]Abe and Waddell, "Dōgen's Bendōwa," p. 137.
[7]Masunaga, *A Primer,* p. 7 ff.
[8]*Ibid.*
[9]*Ibid.,* p. 39.
[10]*Ibid.,* p. 62.
[11]*Ibid.,* p. 92.
[12]Cf. *ibid.,* p. 44.
[13]*Ibid.,* p. 63.
[14]Abe and Waddell, "Dōgen's Bendōwa," p. 144.
[15]Masunaga, *A Primer,* p. 7 ff.
[16]*Ibid.,* p. 17.

[17]*Ibid.*, p. 17 ff.
[18]Cf. *ibid.*
[19]Cf. *ibid.*, p. 57 ff.
[20]*Ibid.*, p. 60.
[21]*Ibid.*, p. 15.
[22]*Ibid.*, p. 84 ff.
[23]Cf. *ibid.*, p. 91.
[24]Cf. *ibid.*, p. 58.
[25]*Ibid.*, p. 20.
[26]*Ibid.*, p. 6.
[27]*Ibid.*, p. 5.
[28]*Ibid.*, p. 56.
[29]Cf. *ibid.*, p. 55.
[30]*Ibid.*, p. 54.
[31]*Ibid.*, p. 53.
[32]*Ibid.*, p. 27 ff.
[33]*Ibid.*
[34]*Ibid.*

Chapter 10

[1]All quotations in this chapter are, unless otherwise indicated, from the "Bussho" chapter of the *Shōbōgenzō*. The English translations are based upon the author's German translation of the original. Since this manuscript was prepared, an English translation of the "Bussho" by Abe Masao and Norman Waddell has appeared in *The Eastern Buddhist*, vol. VIII, no. 2 (1975), pp. 94–112 and vol. IX, no. 1 (1976), pp. 87–105, no. 2, pp. 71–87. Here Dōgen counts twenty-eight patriarchs in India since the Buddha's great enlightenment and twenty-three in China up to and including his own master, Ju-ching.

[2]From the *Shōbōgenzō*, "Hotsumu-jōshin" chapter.

[3]Abe and Waddell, "Dōgen's Ben-dōwa," p. 146 ff.

[4]From the *Shōbōgenzō*, "Sokushin-zebutsu" chapter.

[5]Dōgen quotes the Chinese version of the *Lotus Sutra* in his *Shōbōgenzō*, "Shohōjissō" chapter.

[6]Dōgen takes the story from the Chinese Zen chronicle *Keitoku Dentō-roku*, vol. 3.

[7]Wei-shan Ling-yu (771–853) was a disciple of Pai-chang Huai-hai (720–814) in the lineage of Ma-tsu (709–98) during the peak of Chinese Zen in the T'ang period.

[8]Dōgen quotes Pai-chang's words from the collection of sayings called *Kosonshuku goroku* (Chinese: Ku-tsun-su yü-lu), vol. I.

[9]Quoted from the *Keitoku Dentōroku*, vol. 3.

[10]Abe and Waddell, "Shōbōgenzō Genjōkōan," p. 133.

[11]Quoted from the *Keitoku Dentōro-ku*, vol. 5.

[12]Compare the *Shōbōgenzō*, "Uji," on being and time; English translation by Kapleau, pp. 295–99.

[13]Abe and Waddell, "Shōbōgenzō Genjōkōan," p. 136.

Chapter 11

[1]See Yasutani in the Bibliography. All references to Yasutani below are to either the first or the second series of this work.

[2]See Iizuka in the Bibliography.

[3]In my essay "Technique and Personal Devotion," I investigated the Japanese accounts of the experience by contrasting exterior technique and personal devotion. In *The Three Pillars of Zen*, Kapleau utilized some of the accounts in his discussion of the teaching and practice of his master, Yasutani Rōshi.

[4]Iizuka, p. 6.

[5]Yasutani, first series, p. 144.

[6]Iizuka, p. 74 ff.

[7]Yasutani, second series, p. 17 ff.

[8]Yasutani, first series, p. 237 ff.

[9]*Ibid.*, p. 1 ff.

[10]*The Doors of Perception* by Aldous Huxley, quoted in Zaehner, p. 15.

[11]Yasutani, first series, p. 199.

[12]Iizuka, p. 16.

[13]Yasutani, first series, p. 197.

[14]Yasutani, second series, p. 4.

[15]*Ibid.*, p. 95 ff.

[16]Iizuka, p. 126.

[17]Yasutani, second series, p. 89.

[18]Iizuka, p. 51.

[19]*Ibid.*, p. 68.

[20]*Ibid.*, p. 255.

[21]Yasutani, second series, p. 5.

[22]The two Patriarchs are Bodhidharma and Dōgen.

[23]Iizuka, p. 190.

[24]*Ibid.*, p. 25.

[25]Yasutani, second series, p. 152.

[26]Iizuka, p. 18.

[27]*Ibid.*

[28]Yasutani, second series, p. 13.

[29]For a German-language translation of this, see Ishimoto and Naberfeld. For an analysis of the *Shushōgi* see Dumoulin, *Östliche,* pp. 257–77.

[30]One of the four vows of a Bodhisattva, this is familiar to every Mahāyāna Buddhist.

[31]Yasutani, first series, p. 178 ff.

[32]*Ibid.*, p. 197.

[33]Yasutani, second series, p. 176.

[34]Iizuka, p. 115.

[35]*Ibid.*, p. 262.

[36]On the problem of the personal dimension, of particular importance for the Buddhist-Christian dialogue of the present, see my *Christianity Meets Buddhism,* pp. 145–93.

Chapter 12

[1]D. T. Suzuki often treated of the essence of enlightenment in his works and cites several essential traits on the basis of early Zen literature; cf. especially his *Essays,* vol. 2, pp. 31–39. See also my *History,* p. 269 ff. and my *Östliche,* pp. 79–97.

[2]Miura and Sasaki, *Zen Koan,* p. 7.

[3]Cited in Dumoulin, *History,* p. 273.

[4]During his meetings with Japanese Zen masters, G. Schüttler asked a number of pointedly psychological questions. See his *Die Erleuchtung,* pp. 39–74.

[5]This chapter again uses Yasutani, first and second series, and Iizuka.

[6]Yasutani, second series, p. 41.

[7]*Ibid.*, p. 203.

[8]Yasutani, first series, p. 198.

[9]Iizuka, p. 52.

[10]Yasutani, first series, p. 167.

[11]Iizuka, p. 28.

[12]*Ibid.*, p. 53.

[13]Yasutani, first series, p. 192.

[14]Iizuka, p. 265. G. Schüttler obtained much useful information from the Zen masters he questioned on such bodily sensations as levitation, extension, falling, etc. See especially his *Die Erleuchtung,* pp. 40–44.

[15]Yasutani, second series, p. 6 ff.

[16]Iizuka, p. 14.

[17]Yasutani, second series, p. 201 ff.

[18]Yasutani, first series, p. 224.

[19]*Ibid.*, p. 232 ff.

[20]Yasutani, second series, p. 14.

[21]The Canadian psychiatrist R. M. Bucke first used the expression "cosmic consciousness" to describe his own experiences. William James, in his *Varieties of Religious Experience,* recognized a relationship between Bucke's cosmic consciousness and Oriental mystical phenomena. R. C. Zaehner is of the opinion that Bucke's cosmic consciousness is the same as Jung's collective unconscious. Furthermore, in the replies of Japanese Zen masters reported by G. Schüttler, there is a definite proximity to cosmic consciousness; cf. his *Die Erleuchtung,* pp. 50, 59, 61, 63.

[22]Yasutani, first series, p. 215.

[23]Iizuka, p. 193.

[24]*Ibid.*, p. 70.

[25]Yasutani, first series, p. 181.

[26]*Ibid.*

[27]Iizuka, p. 11.

[28]R. C. Zaehner has called attention to the remarkable fact that Marcel Proust's novel *A la recherche du temps perdu* is based on extraordinary experiences occasioned, like many Zen experiences, by accidental shocks from external sources (uneven cobblestones, the sound of a spoon, etc.).

[29]Iizuka, p. 115.

[30]*Ibid.*, p. 198.

[31]Yasutani, second series, p. 162 ff.

[32]Iizuka, p. 152.

[33]Yasutani, second series, p. 193 ff.

[34]*Ibid.*, p. 60.

[35]*Ibid.*, p. 205.

[36]Yasutani, first series, p. 151 ff.

[37]Iizuka, p. 245 ff.

[38]Yasutani, second series, p. 212 ff.

Like all accounts in *Kyūdō no tabi,* this one is given anonymously; but today we know it derives from Yamada Kyōzo, the leading lay disciple of Master Yasutani and the man who became the master's successor. Although remaining a lay person, Yamada directs a Zen hall in Kamakura. Today he calls himself Yamada Kōun and is held in great esteem by a large number of disciples.

[39]Yasutani, first series, p. 288 ff.

[40]Enomiya-Lassalle, *Zen-Buddhismus,* p. 398.

Afterword

[1]Tsujimura and Buchner, p. 64. Other versions of the Ten Oxherding Pictures can be found in Suzuki, *Essays,* vol. I, and Kapleau, p. 301 ff.

Bibliography

Abe, Masao. "Dōgen on Buddha Nature," in *The Eastern Buddhist,* vol. IV, no. 1 (May 1971), pp. 28–71.

Abe, Masao and Waddell, Norman, trans. "Busshō," in *The Eastern Buddhist,* vol. VIII, no. 2 (1975), pp. 94–112 and vol. IX, no. 1 (1976), pp. 87–105, no. 2, pp. 71–87.

———, trans. "Dōgen's Bendōwa," in *The Eastern Buddhist,* vol. IV, no. 1 (May 1971), pp. 124–57.

———, trans. " 'One Bright Pearl': Dōgen's Shōbōgenzō Ikka Myōju," in *The Eastern Buddhist,* vol. IV, no. 2 (Oct. 1971), pp. 107–18.

———, trans. "Shōbōgenzō Genjōkōan," in *The Eastern Buddhist,* vol. V, no. 2 (Oct. 1972), pp. 129–40.

———, trans. "Dōgen's Fukanzazengi," in *The Eastern Buddhist,* vol. VI, no. 2, (Oct. 1973), pp. 121–26.

Albrecht, Carl. *Psychologie des mystischen Bewusstseins.* Bremen, 1951.

———. *Das mystische Erkennen.* Bremen, 1968.

Anesaki, Masaharu. *History of Japanese Religion.* London, 1930, and Rutland, Vermont, 1963.

Benoit, H. *The Supreme Doctrine: Psychological Studies in Zen Thought,* with a foreword by Aldous Huxley. New York, 1955.

Benz, Ernst. *Zenbuddhismus und Zensnobismus: Zen in westlicher Sicht.* Weilheim, 1962.

Blofeld, John. *The Zen Teaching of Huang Po on the Transcendence of Mind.* London, 1958.

———. *The Zen Teaching of Hui Hai on Sudden Illumination.* London, 1962.

Buber, Martin. *Schriften zum Chassidismus, Werke,* vol. III. Munich, 1963.

Chan, Wing-tsit trans. *The Platform Scripture.* New York, 1963.

———. *A Source Book in Chinese Philosophy.* Princeton, 1963.

Chang, Chung-yuan. *Creativity and Taoism: A Study of Chinese Philosophy, Art and Poetry.* New York, 1963.

Chang, Garma C. C. *The Buddhist Teaching of Totality: The Philosophy of Hwa Yen Buddhism.* University Park and London, 1971.

————. *The Practice of Zen.* New York, 1959.

Ch'en, K. S. *Buddhism in China: A Historical Survey.* Princeton, 1964.

Conze, Edward. *Buddhism: Its Essence and Development.* Oxford, 1953.

————, et. al., ed. *Buddhist Texts Through the Ages.* Oxford, 1954, and New York, 1964.

de Bary, Wm. Theodore, Wing-tsit Chan, and Burton Watson, eds. *Sources of Chinese Tradition,* vol. I. New York, 1969.

Démieville, P. "Le miroir spirituel," in *Sinologica,* vol. I (1948), pp. 112–37.

Dumoulin, Heinrich. "Bodhidharma und die Anfänge des Ch'an-Buddhismus," in *Monumenta Nipponica,* vol. VII (1951), p. 67–83.

————. *The Development of Chinese Zen After the Sixth Patriarch in the Light of Mumonkan.* New York, 1953.

————. "Die religiöse Metaphysik des japanischen Zen-Meisters Dōgen," in *Saeculum,* vol. XII, no. 3 (1961), pp. 205–36.

————. *A History of Zen Buddhism.* New York, 1963, and Boston, 1969.

————. trans., *Mumonkan: Die Schranke ohne Tor.* Mainz, 1975.

————. *Östliche Meditation und christliche Mystik.* Freiburg-Munich, 1966.

————. "Techniques and Personal Devotion in the Zen Exercise," in J. Roggendorf, ed., *Studies in Japanese Culture.* Tokyo, 1963, pp. 17–40.

————. "The Zen Experience According to Modern Japanese Accounts," in *Studia Missionalia,* vol. XVII (1968), pp. 223–43.

Dürckheim, Karlfried Graf. "Werk der Übung-Geschenk der Gnade," in *Geist und Leben,* vol. 45, no. 5 (Oct. 1972), p. 368.

Eliade, Mircea. *Yoga-Immortality and Freedom.* New York, 1958.

Eliot, Sir Charles. *Japanese Buddhism.* London, 1935.

Enomiya-Lassalle, H. M. *Zen-Buddhismus.* Cologne, 1966.

————. *Zen Meditation for Christians.* LaSalle, Illinois, 1974.

————. *Zen-Way to Enlightenment.* London, 1966.

Fung Yu-lan. *A History of Chinese Philosophy.* Princeton, 1953.

Graham, Aelred. *Zen Catholicism.* New York, 1963.

Gundert, Wilhelm, trans. *Bi-yän-lu: Die Niederschrift von der Smaragdenen Felswand,* 3 vols. Munich, 1964, 1967, 1974.

Hamilton, C. H. *Buddhism: A Religion of Infinite Compassion.* New York, 1952.

Heiler, F. *Die buddhistische Versenkung.* Munich, 1922.

Herrigel, Eugen. *Zen in the Art of Archery.* New York, 1957.

Hirai, T. *The Psychophysiology of Zen.* Tokyo, 1974.

Hisamatsu, Shin'ichi. *Zen and the Fine Arts.* Tokyo, 1974.

Hoffman, Yoel. *The Sound of the One Hand.* New York, 1975.

Humphreys, Christmas. *Zen Buddhism.* London, 1949.

————. *Zen Comes West: The Presence and Future of Zen Buddhism in Great Britain.* London, 1966.

Iizuka, T., ed. *Sanzen taikenshū*. Tokyo, 1956.
Ishimoto, K. and Naberfeld, E. "*Shushōgi:* Prinzipien der Übung und Erleuchtung," *Monumenta Nipponica*, vol. VII (1943), pp. 355–69.
Iyengar, B. K. S. *Light on Yoga*. London, 1966.

James, William. *The Varieties of Religious Experience*. New York and London, 1902.
Johnston, William. *The Stillpoint*. New York, 1970.
———. *Christian Zen*. New York, 1971.
———. *Silent Music: The Science of Meditation*. New York, 1974.

Kaltenmark, Max. *Lao Tzu and Taoism*, Stanford, 1969.
Kapleau, Philip. *The Three Pillars of Zen: Teaching, Practice, Enlightenment*. Tokyo, 1965.
Keene, Donald, ed. *Anthology of Japanese Literature from the Earliest Era to the Mid-Nineteenth Century*. New York, 1955.
Keith, A. B. *Buddhist Philosophy in India and Ceylon*. Oxford, 1923.
Kennett, Jíyu. *Selling Water by the River: A Manual of Zen Training*. New York, 1972.

Lau, D. C., trans. *Lao Tzu: Tao Te Ching*. Penguin Books, 1963.
Leggett, Trevor. *Zen and the Ways*. London, 1978.
Liebenthal, W. *The Book of Cao: A Translation from the Original Chinese with Introduction, Notes and Appendices* (Monumenta Serica Monographs, vol. XIII). Peking, 1948.
———. "A Biography of Chu Tao-sheng," in *Monumenta Nipponica*, vol. XI (1955), pp. 284–316.
———. "The World Conception of Chu Tao-sheng," in *Monumenta Nipponica*, vol. XII (1956), pp. 65–103.
———. "The World Conception of Chu Tao-sheng: Texts," in *Monumenta Nipponica*, vol. XII (1956), pp. 241–68.
Lin, Yutang. *The Wisdom of Laotse*. New York, 1948.
Lu K'uan Yü (Charles Luk). *Ch'an and Zen Teaching*, 3 vols. London, 1962.
———. *Taoist Yoga: Alchemy and Immortality*. London, 1970.

Masunaga, Reihō. *The Sōtō Approach to Zen*. Tokyo, 1958.
———. *A Primer of Sōtō Zen: A Translation of Dōgen's Shōbōgenzō Zuimonki*. Honolulu, 1971.
Merton, Thomas. *Mystics and Zen Masters*. New York, 1967.
Miura, Isshū and Sasaki, Ruth Fuller. *Zen Dust: The History of the Koan Study in Rinzai (Lin-chi) Zen*. New York, 1966.
———. *The Zen Koan*. New York, 1965.
Miyuki, M., trans. *Kreisen des Lichtes: Die Erfahrung der Goldenen Blüte*. Weilheim, 1972.
Müller, Max F., ed. *Sacred Books of the East*. Oxford, 1891.

Nishimura, Eshin, Satō, Giei, and Smith, Bardwell L. *Unsui: A Diary of Zen Monastic Life*. Honolulu, 1973.

Ohasama, S. and Faust, A. *Zen: Der lebendige Buddhismus in Japan mit einem Geleitwort von Rudolf Otto.* Gotha-Stuttgart, 1925.

Okakura, Kakuzo. *The Book of Tea.* New York, 1900. With introduction and notes by Hiroshi Muraoka, Tokyo, 1934; New York, 1968.

Oldenberg, H. *Buddha: Sein Leben, seine Lehre, seine Gemeinde.* Munich, 1963.

Otto, Rudolf. *Das Gefühl des Überweltlichen.* Munich, 1932.

Robinson, Richard H. *Early Mādhamika in India and China.* Madison, Wisconsin, 1967.

Rzepkowski, H. *Das Menschenbild bei Daisetz Teitaro Suzuki.* St. Augustin, 1971.

———. *Leben für Zen: Daisetz Teitaro Suzuki.* St. Augustin, 1973.

Sadler, A. L., trans. *The Ten Foot Square Hut and Tales of the Heike.* Rutland, Vermont, 1972.

Schoel, Irmgard. *The Wisdom of the Zen Masters.* London, 1975.

———. *The Zen Way.* London, 1977.

Scholem, G. *Judaica.* Frankfurt a. M., 1963.

Schüttler, G. *Die Erleuchtung im Zen Buddhismus: Gespräche mit Zen Meistern und psycho-pathologische Analyse.* Freiburg Munich, 1974.

Seckel, D. *The Art of Buddhism.* New York, 1964.

Shibayama Zenkei. *Zen Comments on the Mumonkan.* New York, 1974.

Suzuki, D. T. *Essays in Zen Buddhism,* 3 vols. London, 1970.

———. *An Introduction to Zen Buddhism.* Kyoto, 1934. Revised edition with a foreword by C. G. Jung, London, 1960.

———. "Lectures on Zen Buddhism," in *Zen Buddhism and Psychoanalysis.* New York, 1970.

———. *Manual of Zen Buddhism.* New York, 1960.

———. *Mysticism: Christian and Buddhist.* London, 1957.

———. *Studies in the Lankāvatāra Sutra.* London, 1930.

———. *The Training of the Zen Buddhist Monk.* Kyoto, 1934, New York, 1965.

———. *The Zen Doctrine of No Mind.* London, 1969.

———. *Zen and Japanese Culture.* New York, 1959.

Taimni, I. K. *The Science of Yoga.* Wheaton, Illinois, and London, 1967.

Thomas, E. J. *The Life of Buddha as Legend and History.* London, 1956.

———. *The History of Buddhist Thought.* New York, 1951.

Tsujimura, K., and Buchner, H. *Der Ochs und sein Hirte.* Pfullingen, 1973.

Waley, Arthur. *Zen Buddhism and Its Relation to Art.* London, 1922.

Watanabe, Shoko. *Japanese Buddhism: A Critical Appraisal.* Tokyo, 1970.

Watts, Alan W. *The Way of Zen.* New York, 1957.

Welch, Holmes. *Taoism: The Parting of the Way.* Boston, 1957.

Yamada, Mumon. *Shakuson ni kaere.* Tokyo, 1967.

Yampolsky, P. B., trans. *The Platform Sutra of the Sixth Patriarch.* New York, 1971.

Yampolsky, P. B., trans. *The Zen Master Hakuin: Selected Writings.* New York, 1971.

168 BIBLIOGRAPHY

Yanagida, Seizan. *Shoki zenshūshi sho no kenkyū*. Kyoto, 1967.
Yasutani, Ryōkō, ed. *Kyūdo no tabi: Gendaijin ga kataru Zen no satori no taikendan*.
    First series: Tokyo, 1959. Second series: Tokyo, 1962.
Yogananda, Paramhansa. *Autobiography of a Yogi*. London, 1945.
Yokoi, Yuho. *The First Step to Dōgen's Zen: Shōbōgenzō Zuimonki*. Tokyo, 1972.

Zaehner, R. C. *Mysticism, Sacred and Profane*. Oxford, 1967.

Index

accompanying traits of enlightenment, 148–49
Akṣobhya, 41
ālaya vijñāna, 110
Amida (Amitābha), Amidism, 6, 26, 34, 74, 77, 133
Amidism, *see* Amida
Amitābha, *see* Amida
anitya, 121
anuttara-samyak-saṃbodhi, 122
Asahina, Sōgen, 150
asociality, charge of, 22, 23–24
Aśvagoṣa, 106
Augustine, 22
austerities of practice, 131–33
Avalokiteśvara, 69
Avataṃsaka Sūtra (Garland Sutra, Kegon Sutra), 26, 27, 60, 107–8

Baalschem, 74
Bashō, 82, 83–84, 85, 138
Bau-dschi, 69
Beat Zen, 8
"Bendōwa" chapter of *Shōbōgenzō* (Dōgen), 92, 95, 107
Benz, Ernst, 8
Bible and koans, 76
Blue Cliff Records, The, see *Hekiganroku*
Bodhidharma, 25, 34, 35–41, 69, 70, 71; as legendary figure, 35–37; as a master of meditation, 37–39;
his role in the Zen tradition, 39–41; and Emperor Wu-ti, 40, 69; and Hui–k'o, 40, 41
Bodhisattva, 23
Bodhi tree, 14, 17, 44
breath, breathing, 19, 20, 31, 33, 128–29
Buber, Martin, 74–76, 86
Buddha, *see* Shākyamuni
Buddha-nature, 16, 22, 30, 55, 57, 63, 71, 92, 95, 102–24; and becoming, 119–24; the being of, 111–14; Dōgen on, 102–24; as metaphysical realism, 107–11; and reality, 104–7; as a religio-metaphysical concept, 102–4; way of negation in, 115–19
"Buddha-Nature" chapter of *Shōbōgenzō,* 103, 104, 115
Buddhism: in China, 25–34; as foundation of Zen, 3; in India, 14–24; in Japan, 77–79; *see also* Zen
Buddhistische Versenkung (Buddhist Meditation; Heiler), 7, 19

"casting off of body and mind," 92, 93, 94, 95
ch'an, 38
ch'an-na, 38
Chao-chou, 71, 116
Chassidism and Zen, 74–76, 86

Ching-te ch'uan-teng lu, 46
Ch'ing-yüan Hsing-ssu, 53
Chou I Ts'an T'ung Ch'i, 32
Chuang-tzu, 30, 31–32, 47, 56, 58, 155
Chu-hsi school, 80
Circles of Light, The, 32–33
clue word, 73
Collection of Forty-eight Koans, see *Mumonkan*
communal life in Chinese Zen, 58–60
compassion, 99–100
Confucianism, 29, 60, 80, 81, 101; as element of Zen, 80, 81; *see also* Neo-Confucianism
Confucius, 32
consciousness, 9, 48, 75, 76, 91, 109–10, 120–21; *see also* cosmic consciousness
cosmic consciousness, 15; in enlightenment, 144–47, 152
cosmic teachings of Mahāyāna, 26, 27
cosmotheism, 27

darśana, 19
deva, 15, 40
devil's realm, see *makyō*
devotion, 133–36
Dharma, 16, 22, 49, 50, 54, 57, 63, 77, 91, 92–93, 99, 102, 103, 106, 107, 109, 118, 120, 122, 134, 137
Dharma-nature, 109
Dharma-rapture, 144, 148
dhyāna, 15, 19, 20, 38, 49; *see also* meditation, zazen
Diamond Sutra, 44, 50, 55
discriminating and non-discriminating knowledge, 58, 62
disturbances, see *mōsō*
doctrine of no mind, 50–52
Dōgen, 6, 17, 21, 22, 79, 86, 88–124, 132, 138, 151; on Buddha-nature, 102–24; on enlightenment, 92–95; on zazen, 90–98
dokusan, 73, 126, 128, 137
drugs, 9
Dürckheim, Karlfried Graf, 63–64

Eckhart (Meister Eckhart), 6
ecstasy, 48, 148–52
egocentrism, charge of, 22–23
Eihei-ji, 81, 89
Eisai, 79, 89, 100
Ejō, 93
Eliade, Mircea, 19
emptiness, 26–27, 33, 40, 48, 50, 51, 55, 57, 58, 114, 115, 117–18, 119
Engaku-ji, 150
enlightenment, 5, 15, 16, 38–39, 46–52, 54, 64, 92–95, 109, 126 139–53; accompanying traits of, 148–49, as cosmic experience, 144–46; naturalistic hue of, 146–47; and root of nothingness, 149–52; of Shākyamuni, 15; sudden release in, 147–48; symptoms and preliminary stages of, 143–44; way of sudden, 38, 39, 46–52, 54; zazen and, 92–95
Enomiya-Lassalle, H. M., 11, 12, 76, 127, 152
enstasis, 23
esoterism and Zen, 9
Essays in Zen Buddhism (Suzuki), 5
experience of the numinous, 7–8

Faust, August, 7
Fa-yen, 60; House of, 60
Fen-yang Shan-chao, 66
Five Houses, 60–61
Five Mountains, 79, 80
Five Ranks, 61
formless *samādhi,* 114
full-moon form of Nāgārjuna, 113–14

Garland Sutra, see *Avataṃsaka Sūtra*
Gefühl des Überweltlichen, Das (Otto); 7
Gemmyō, 90
"Genjō kōan" chapter of *Shōbōgenzō,* 120, 122
Gion, 78
gradualness and suddenness, 38, 39, 46–50
"Gradual school," 49

Graham, Aelred, 11
Great Doubt, 82
Gundert, Wilhelm, 54, 69, 70
guru, 20, 41, 73

haiku, 83–84
Hakuin Ekaku, 81–82, 83, 138, 139–40, 141, 150, 151
Harada, Sogaku, and Harada school 126–27, 128–29, 131, 134, 140, 151
Ha Shan, 32
Heike monogatari, 77–78
Heiler, Friedrich, 7, 19
Hekiganroku, 7, 54, 66, 68–70
Hīnayāna (Theravāda) Buddhism, 23, 25–26, 38, 57, 59
ho, see *katsu*
House of Fa-yen, 60
House of Ts'ao-tung, 61
House of Wei-yang, 60
Hsing-ch'ang, 122
Hsüeh-tou Ch'ung-hsien, 66–67, 69 70
Hsü-kao-seng-chuan, 36
Huang-mei, 116
Huang-po, 31, 60, 61–62
Hua-yen school, *see* Kegon school
Hui-k'o, 31, 36, 39, 40, 41, 42; and Bodhidharma, 40, 41
Hui-neng, 23, 42–52, 53, 55, 56, 57, 80, 105–6, 118, 122, 138; on meditation and enlightenment, 49
Hung-chih Cheng-chüeh, 67, 68
Hung-jen, 42, 44, 116
Hu Shih, 5
Huxley, Aldous, 130
hypnosis, 9, 23

iconoclasm, 17, 56
Ikkyū, 85, 86, 138
Imakita, Kōsen, 140
Indian roots of Zen, 14–24
Introduction to Zen Buddhism, An (Suzuki), 5

Jakkō-in, 78
jakugo, see clue word
James, William, 5, 15

Jetavana, 78
jiriki, 133–34
Jizō, 134
John of the Cross, 27, 51
Johnston, William, 11, 76
Ju-ching, 79, 89, 91, 92

kaivalya, 21
kalpa, 58
Kānadeva, 113, 114
kanjō, 48
Kannon, 135, 136–37, 150
Kannon Sutra, 134
Kapleau, Philip, 127
karma, 14, 105, 111, 133, 136
Kāśyapa, 16, 75, 119
katsu, 62, 75, 150
Katsura Rikyū, 85
Kegon school, 53, 63
Kegon Sutra, see *Avataṃsaka Sūtra*
Keitoku Dentōroku, 53
kenshō, 48
Kiyomori (Taira Kiyomori), 78
kleśa, 48, 51
koan, 5, 27, 37, 41, 45, 46, 55, 65–76, 80, 93–94, 125–26, 129; in Chinese Zen, 65–76; collections of, 68–72; defined, 65, 68; Dōgen on, 93–94; *Hekiganroku* collection of, 68–70; and history of religions, 74–76; *Mumonkan* collection of, 68, 70–72; origin of practice of, 65–68; parallels of, in Chassidism, 74–76; parallels of, in Christianity, 76; Sasaki on, 65; significance of, for Zen way, 72–74
Kobori, Enshū, 85
Kobryn, Mosche von, 74–75
Kumārajīva, 39, 47
kyōsaku, 131–32
Kyoto school, 88, 102

Laṅkāvatāra school, 42–43
Laṅkāvatāra Sūtra, 26, 28, 42
Lao-tzu, 29, 32, 33, 56, 58
liberating experience in enlightenment, 143–53
Lieh-tzu, 56, 58

Lin-chi (Lin-chi I-hsüan), 31, 60, 61–64, 138
Lin-chi school, *see* Rinzai school
lotus posture, 20, 49, 55, 80, 81, 91, 128, 131
Lotus Sutra, 109
Lo-yang Ch'ieh-chi, 36
Lung-t'an, 55

mādhyamika, Mādhyamika school, see Middle Way
Mahāparinirvāṇa Sūtra, 104, 110, 116
Mahāyāna Buddhism, 18, 21, 23, 25–28, 34, 38, 57, 59, 63, 102–3, 104, 106, 111–12, 116, 155
makyō, 73, 129, 132, 141–43
Mañjuśrī, 27, 128, 149
Manual of Zen Buddhism (Suzuki), 5
mappō, 77
Ma-tsu (Ma-tsu Tao I), 31, 53, 54, 57, 58, 59, 62, 71, 94, 105, 138
meditation, 15, 19, 20, 31–34, 37–39, 46–49, 67–68, 90–92, 128–29; Bodhidharma as master of, 37–39; Dōgen on, 90–92; silent and dynamic, 67–68; Taoist and Zenist compared, 31–34; two Zen ways of, 46–49; see also *dhyāna,* zazen
Meister Eckhart, *see* Eckhart
Merton, Thomas, 23, 51–52
Middle Way, 50, 115, 116, 118
"mind only," 63
Ming, 45
mirror-mind, 47–48
Miura, Isshū, 65
Miyuki, Mokusen, 32, 33
mondō, 66, 92, 117
mōsō, 141
mu, mu koan, 37, 71, 115, 116, 129, 145
mu-busshō, 115
mujō-busshō, 121
Mumonkan, 7, 16, 27, 37, 45, 46, 55, 68, 70–72, 75, 93, 116, 144
Musō Kokushi, 85
myōkōnin, 6
mysticism, 6, 8, 39, 51, 67, 74, 86, 140

Nāgārjuna, 48, 50, 112–14, 115
Nagasawa, Sozen, 127, 133, 147
Nan-ch'üan P'u-yüan, 58, 71
Nan-yüan Hui-yüng, 65–66
Nan-yüeh Huai-jang, 53, 54, 94, 105
narcissism, charge of, 22–23
nature, see *prakṛti*
negation, way of, 115–19
negativism, *see* negation
nembutsu, 74
Neo-Confucianism, 66, 80, 121; *see also* Confucianism
Nichiren, 77
nirvana, 16, 19, 57, 78, 115, 122
Nirvāṇa Sūtra, 46
Nishida, Kitarō, 88, 124, 138, 148
Nishimura, Eshin, 63
no mind, doctrine of, 50–52
Northern school of Chinese Zen, 23, 43, 47, 54, 67–68
nothingness, 50, 129, 145–46, 155; root of, 149–52
nothingness in enlightenment, 149–53; see also *mu*
nothingness of Buddha-nature, *see* negation
numinous, experience of the, 7–8

Obaku sect, 80
Ōhasama, Shūei, 7
Ohtsu, R., 154
Oldenberg, Hermann, 15
original face, 91, 121, 150
Otto, Rudolf, 7–8
Oxherding Pictures, 154–56

padmāsana, see lotus posture
Pai-chang, 59–60, 62, 118
Pāli canon, 7, 19
parāvṛtti, 28
Pascal, 63
Patañjali, 19, 21
phenomenal world, see *saṃsāra*
piety, 98–99
pi-kuan, 38
poverty as an ideal, 96–97
practice, 125–33
practice session, see *sesshin*

prajñā, 47, 48, 49, 51, 57
Prajñāparamitā Sūtra, see *Sutras of Perfect Wisdom*
prakṛti, 21
prāṇāyāma, see breath
pṛthagjana, 38
psychic changes during practice, 129, 140–43
psychotherapy and Zen, 8–9
purification, *see* repentance and purification
puruṣa, 21, 22; *see also* self

quietism, 34, 48, 67, 68, 92

Ramakrishna, 19
realism, reality, as viewed by Dōgen, 104–11
repentance and purification 98, 136–38
Return to the Honored Shaka (Yamada), 17
Rinzai, *see* Lin-chi
Rinzai-roku, 62, 63
Rinzai school, 5, 6, 10, 61, 62–64, 66, 79, 80–82, 86, 120, 125–26
root of nothingness, 149–52
rōshi, 20, 41, 73

Sai-an, 105, 115–16
Salinger, J. D., 8
samādhi, 19, 21, 79, 107, 114
Sāmkhya, 19, 21
saṃsāra, 57, 78, 115, 122
sange, see repentance
Sangha, 99, 118
Sasaki, Ruth Fuller, 65, 72, 80–81
satori, *see* enlightenment
Scholem, Gershom, 75
secularization of Zen, 84–86
self, self nature, 15, 21–22, 33, 38, 50, 52, 57, 63, 93, 129, 135, 145, 150, 152, 155
Seng-chao, 35, 47
Sense of the Transworldly, The (Otto), 7
sesshin, 73, 127, 128–29
Sesshū, 27, 82, 83, 85, 138

Shaku Sōen, 4
Shākyamuni, 14–18, 99, 118, 119; enlightenment of, 15; as one of the Three Treasures, 99, 118; veneration of, 16–17
Shen-hsiu, 23, 42, 43, 44–45, 46, 47, 54
Shen-hui, 43, 53, 57
Shih-t'ou (Shih-t'ou Hsi-ch'ien), 53
shikan taza, see "sitting only"
Shin school, 6
Shōbōgenzō (Dōgen), 90, 92–93, 102, 120, 123
Shramana Bodhidharma, 36
Shushōgi (Dōgen), 136
"sitting only," 95
Sixth Patriarch, *see* Hui-neng
skandhas, 41, 108, 114
Sōen, *see* Shaku Sōen
Sōtō school, 6, 10, 67, 79, 80, 81, 86, 88, 89, 125, 126
Southern school of Chinese Zen, 23, 43, 47, 54, 67–68
spirituality, 95–101
Sri Aurobindo, 19
suddenness and gradualness, 38, 39, 46–50
sudden release in enlightenment, 147–48
"Sudden school," 49
sumie, 83
śūnya, 26, 57, 116; *see also* emptiness
śūnyatā, 26, 48; *see also* emptiness
Sutras of Perfect Wisdom (Prajñāparamitā Sūtra), 26, 48, 50
Sutra of the Sixth Patriarch, 43–44, 46, 47, 48, 49, 50, 57
Suzuki, D. T., 4–7, 9, 20, 28, 48, 50, 51–52, 54, 72, 74, 125; books by, 5; on doctrine of no mind, 50, 51–52; on dust-wiping meditation, 48; and *Laṅkāvatāra Sūtra,* 28; and Rinzai Zen, 4, 125; on Zen masters, 54; on Zen and Yoga, 20
Suzuki, Shōsan, 81
"Suzuki Zen," 7
symptoms and preliminary stages of enlightenment, 143–44

Ta-hui Tsung-kao, 66, 67, 120
taigi, see Great Doubt
Tale of the Heike, The, see Heike monogatari
Tan-hsia (Tan-hsia T'ien-jun), 99
Tao, *see* Taoism and Zen
Tao-fu, 41
Tao-hsin, 59, 116, 117
Tao-hsüan, 36, 40
Taoism and Zen, 28–34, 38, 49, 58, 64, 71, 84
Tao-sheng, 32, 35, 39, 47
Tao-te ching, 29, 32
Tao-yü, 41
tariki, 133–34
Tathāgata, 99, 104
Ta-yü, 61
tea ceremony, 84
teishō, 73, 128
temple schools, see *tera-koya*
Tendai sect, 89, 104
Ten Oxherding Pictures, 154–56
tera-koya, 80
Te-shan, 55–56, 62
theologia negativa, 7, 17, 27, 119
Theravāda (Hīnayana) Buddhism, 9, 21, 23
Theresa of Avila, 142
Three Treasures, 99, 118
total isolation, see *kaivalya*
Toynbee, Arnold, 3
Training of the Zen Buddhist Monk, The (Suzuki), 5
trance, 23; see also *samādhi*
transcendence, 27, 48, 51, 63, 64, 75, 117, 119, 135–36
transcendental wisdom, see *prajñā*
transmission of mind, 16–17
tree of enlightenment, *see* Bodhi tree
Ts'ao-tung, 61; House of, 61
Ts'ao-tung school, 67
Tsung-chih, 41

u-busshō, 115
Universal Promotion of the Principles of Zazen, The (Dōgen), 132
universe, 21, 57, 108, 123, 145, 147
Upanishads, 119

Varieties of Religious Experience, The (James), 5
Vimalikīrti, 27
Vimalikīrti Sūtra, 26, 27
Vinaya, 59, 61

wall-gazing, see *pi-kuan*
Watanabe, Shōkō, 90
way of negation, 115–19
ways and arts, 82–84
Wei Po-yang, 32
Wei-shan, 60, 115
Wei-yang, House of, 60
wisdom, see *prajñā*
Wisdom Sutras, see Sutras of Perfect Wisdom
women and Zen, 100, 132–33
Wu-men (Wu-men Hui-k'ai), 16, 46, 70, 71, 75, 139
Wu-ti, 36, 39, 40, 69; and Bodhidharma, 40, 69

Yamada, Mumon, 17
Yanagida, Seizan, 62
Yang-ch'i, 66, 70
Yang-shan, 60
Yasutani, Ryōkō, 127, 144, 148, 149, 152
Yen Hui, 32
Yin and Yang, 33
Yin-tsung, 46
Yoga, 8, 18–22; and Zen, 18–22
Yogācārya school, 57, 110, 112
Yoga Sūtra, 19
Yüan-wu K'o-ch'in, 66–67, 69
Yün-men, 60, 67

zazen, 10, 80, 88, 90–101, 126, 132, 137; and enlightenment, 92–93; as focus of Buddhist spirituality, 95–101; promotion of, by Dōgen, 90–92; see also *dhyāna,* meditation
Zen: and arts, 82–84; as Beat Zen, 8; and Chassidism, 74–76; in China, 25–63; and Christianity, 11–12; Confucian element in, 80, 81, 101; doctrinal aspects of, in China, 56–60; and esoterism, 9;

five phases in Western introduction of, 3–4; Indian roots of, 14–24; in Japan, 77–87; and nature, 83–84; neither narcissistic nor asocial, 22–23; Rudolf Otto and, 7–8; and pluralism, 9–11; and psychotherapy, 8–9; secularization of, 11, 84–87; D. T Suzuki and, 4–7, 9, 20, 28, 48, 50, 51–52, 54, 74, 125; and Taoism, 28–34; Western view of, 3–13; and Yoga, 18–22

Zen Doctrine of No Mind, The (Suzuki), 50, 52
"Zen forest," 62
Zen Koan, The (Sasaki and Miura), 65
Zen: der Lebendige Buddhismus in Japan, 7
Zen: Living Buddhism in Japan, 7
Zen monastery, 21
"Zen snobbism," 8
Zuimonki, 93, 96

The "weathermark" identifies this book as a production of John Weatherhill, Inc., publishers of fine books on Asia and the Pacific. Editorial supervision: James T. Conte. Book design and typography: Meredith Weatherby and James T. Conte. Production supervision: Mitsuo Okado. Composition, printing, and binding: Samhwa, Seoul. The typeface used is Monotype Baskerville.